Doing Business with China

For Mairi, my infinitely patient, tolerant and long-suffering wife of 43 years with much love. – SH

This book is dedicated to my dear parents, Jiaqi Wu and Qunfang Zhang, who have unconditionally supported, indulged and tolerated me having a "breakaway" from a conventional career path, trying out and pursuing something not so "serious," such as writing a book. It is also dedicated to Jinsong, Jia and all my friends (you know who you are) whom I have bored during the "tedious" process of writing a book. – Jinxuan

Doing Business with China

Avoiding the Pitfalls

Stewart Hamilton
*Emeritus Professor of Accounting
and Finance, IMD, Switzerland*

&

Jinxuan (Ann) Zhang

palgrave
macmillan

First published 2012 by
PALGRAVE MACMILLAN

Palgrave Macmillan in the UK is an imprint of Macmillan Publishers Limited, registered in England, company number 785998, of Houndmills, Basingstoke, Hampshire RG21 6XS.

Palgrave Macmillan in the US is a division of St Martin's Press LLC, 175 Fifth Avenue, New York, NY 10010.

Palgrave Macmillan is the global academic imprint of the above companies and has companies and representatives throughout the world.

Palgrave® and Macmillan® are registered trademarks in the United States, the United Kingdom, Europe and other countries.

ISBN 978–0–230–22265–6

This book is printed on paper suitable for recycling and made from fully managed and sustained forest sources. Logging, pulping and manufacturing processes are expected to conform to the environmental regulations of the country of origin.

A catalogue record for this book is available from the British Library.

A catalog record for this book is available from the Library of Congress.

10 9 8 7 6 5 4 3 2 1
21 20 19 18 17 16 15 14 13 12

Printed and bound in Great Britain by
MPG Group, Bodmin and King's Lynn

Contents

List of Exhibits

List of Abbreviations

AOT	Approved Oil Trader
BP	British Petroleum
BSN	Boussois Souchon Neuvesel
CAAC	Civil Aviation Authority of China
CAD	Commercial Affairs Department (of Singapore Police Force)
CAO	China Aviation Oil
CAOHC	China Aviation Oil Holding Company
CAOSC	China Aviation Oil Supply Corporation
CAOT	A wholly owned subsidiary of CAO, set up to carry on its jet fuel procurement business on an agency basis.
CICC	China International Capital Corporation Limited
CITIC	China International Trust and Investment Corporation
CLH	Compania Logistica de Hidrocarburos
CLIC	China Life Insurance Company Limited
CNEF	China National Enterprise Federation
CNOOC	China National Offshore Oil Corporation
CSRC	China Securities Regulatory Commission
DBS	Development Bank of Singapore
GTP	Global Trader Program
HCFF	Hangzhou Canned Food Factory
MAS	Monetary Authority of Singapore
MERM	Mitsui Energy Risk Management
PwC	PricewaterhouseCoopers
SAIC	State Administration for Industry & Commerce of the People's Republic of China (i.e., the administrative authority for industry and commerce in China)
SASAC	State-owned Asset and Supervision Administration Commission
SBL	Standard Bank Limited
SFA	Securities and Futures Act
SGX	Singapore Exchange Limited
SIAS	Securities Investors Association (Singapore)
SMBC	Sumitomo Mitsui Banking Corporation
SOE	State-owned enterprise
SPC	Singapore Petroleum Company Limited
STB	State Trademark Bureau

TVE	Town and village enterprises
WFC	Hangzhou Wahaha Food City
WFCL	Hangzhou Wahaha Food Company Limited
WNFF	Wahaha Nutritional Food Factory

Preface

The idea for this book was sparked by a comment from a Hong-Kong-based senior investment banker with more than twenty years' experience in the region. At a major open enrolment program for senior executives at IMD,* the authors were presenting one of the cases described in this book when he remarked that he had never known of a Chinese–foreign joint venture that had been successful over the long term.

Intrigued, we decided to do some further research to see if we could identify any reasons why this should have been the case. This book is the result of our efforts.

We have selected a number of examples of high-profile joint ventures which have turned out to be less fruitful than initially hoped, and of Chinese companies who have encountered difficulties in foreign ventures. Some of them have been recorded in published IMD cases which can be obtained through the European Case Clearing House.†

All are different but contain similarities. We believe that the lessons to be drawn will be of value to both those foreign companies wishing to take part in the great Chinese story, and those Chinese companies determined to establish successful overseas operations.

Our basic thesis is that pitfalls can be avoided by careful research and planning, and that those who can learn faster and better are more likely to succeed.

We hope that the lessons contained herein will be useful to executives and boards from both Chinese and foreign companies.

---

* A leading international business school based in Lausanne, Switzerland.
† http://www.ecch.com/educators/ (accessed August 12, 2011).

Acknowledgements

All books are inevitably the outcome of collaborative effort and outside assistance. This is no exception, and we would wish to publicly acknowledge the debts of gratitude that we owe.

First and foremost to all those who gave freely of their time to allow us to interview them and provide us with details of the cases we have described. Some are mentioned in the text but most are not. For this we ask their forgiveness.

We are indebted to Dr Dominique Turpin, President of IMD (and his predecessor, Dr John Wells) for their encouragement and support in allowing us to make use of IMD resources which has been invaluable.

We would like to thank our colleague, Professor Bill Fischer, an old China hand, for his insistence that we persist with the project at a time when we were beginning to flag.

We are also grateful to Lindsay McTeague, IMD's senior editor, and her team for their help with the manuscript at various stages.

Our copy editor at Palgrave Macmillan, Alec McAulay, has been most helpful and efficient.

While many have contributed, the ultimate responsibility for any errors or omissions lies with us, which we readily accept.

Stewart Hamilton
Edinburgh/Lausanne

Jinxuan (Ann) Zhang
Shanghai

Prologue

For foreign corporations and executives, doing business in and with China can be either incredibly inspirational or horribly frustrating, or both. The experience depends on you—not China! Likewise, Chinese corporations and executives coming onto the world stage need to understand that things are different outside China, and they must remain open-minded and willing to adapt to the outside world.

In either case, we believe that the better and faster learner wins.

The real question is when and how to go to China

It is perhaps redundant to ask whether companies that aspire to have a global reach should go to China. The Chinese market is simply too rich to ignore. As noted by Orville Schell, a China scholar and dean of the Graduate School of Journalism at the University of California, Berkeley, "As businesses contemplate entering the China market and begin their processes of due-diligence, most of them have actually already made up their minds: They cannot but be in China."[1] As China emerges, or re-emerges as some scholars say, on the world stage, it is showing up on the corporate agendas of most companies, whether as a well-thought-out business decision or simply a result of herd mentality.

Understanding China

Joerg Wuttke, president of the European Union Chamber of Commerce in China, with almost two decades of experience in the country, describes China as "vast by any measure" and "a challenge to the imagination."[2] Wuttke was humbled after witnessing China's rapid transformation. However, he has voiced a concern that many foreign executives underestimate the country's ability to make the changes necessary to transform itself, perhaps because public opinion about China has often been shaped by Western media, which has tended to be either "anti-China" or "pro-China." Others have taken a different stance. James McGregor, for example, a former *Wall Street Journal* China bureau chief turned corporate executive, and author of *One Billion Customers: Lessons from the Front Lines of Doing Business in China*,[3] surprised the media during one of his book tours when he claimed that he was the "let's-try-to-understand-China"⁴ type.

Although the country and its corporations have made amazing progress in a very short period of time, many foreign executives continue to experience deep frustration when they attempt to do business in and with China because "political developments and regulatory restrictions have converged to create … [an environment] that, for many companies, smacks of protectionism." The market sentiment has become so "bleak" and "pessimistic" that many foreign businesses feel as though "they have run up against an unexpected and impregnable blockade," and they are contemplating leaving China altogether or routing part of their future investment away from China.⁵ And this despite the "have to be in China" mantra.

Since foreign investors began setting their sights on China, we have seen a variety of results, from some remarkable achievements to some momentous failures, with others still trying to find their way. No matter what the result is, everyone who goes to China has a story to tell.

No simple solutions

This book is not intended to be a manual on how to go about doing business in and with China. China is one of the most dynamic markets in the world in which change is the only constant. It would seem arrogant to claim to have a customized toolkit for every situation or eventuality. There is too much turbulence in the world. Furthermore, many events have significantly altered the global economic environment (e.g. the 9/11 terrorist attacks on the World Trade Centre in New York, the Indian Ocean tsunami of 2004, the Sichuan earthquake of 2008, the global financial crisis of 2008 and its aftermath, the Greece debt crisis, Iceland's volcanic ash disruption and the Irish economic crisis of 2010 and, most recently, the earthquake and tsunami in Japan).

In order to learn from the mistakes of others, we examine a number of cases of high-profile corporate scandals or *causes célèbres*, both inside and outside China, which we hope will serve as a guide for foreign companies reviewing their China strategy and interacting with Chinese corporations coming abroad. Similarly, we hope that Chinese companies now expanding overseas will find some of our comments and suggestions helpful as they enter into a very different environment from their domestic one. Through exclusive interviews with many of the key players, we have uncovered some of the root causes of what went wrong, and have identified a number of lessons that can be put into practice. By sharing these lessons, we hope that we can help companies anticipate, avoid and manage some of the pitfalls of doing business in or with China, and conversely for Chinese companies better understand the norms of doing business with the West.

Understanding the "Chinese way"

There are often complaints about the Chinese way of doing things. Most foreign companies would concede that China is different. Few have managed to fully understand the differences. Instead, they tend to assume that their way is the one and only way.

"*Veni, vidi, vici* (I came, I saw, I conquered),"* was perhaps the thinking of those who expected that a quick win was in store for them when they went to China. They assumed that China could (or should) work the same way as they did. Few have tried to understand how the Chinese way actually works (or they have tried and failed) or how important it is to comprehend the underlying Chinese logic. As a result, the Chinese way, or the Chinese culture, is often blamed when things go wrong. We ask: Is culture a cause or an excuse?

The following excerpt is from an open letter written in 2007 by Zong Qinghou, chairman and managing director of the Danone–Wahaha joint venture and of the Wahaha Group in the midst of a public dispute between the two partners. It gives the reasons for his resignation as chairman of the decade-long joint venture in China.

> It was very hard to work with people who do not understand the Chinese market and culture. They only want to take the profits and benefits instead of taking on risks and carrying out their responsibilities. Therefore, I decided to resign from the joint venture companies.[6]

Things are moving fast in China. The rate of growth and the speed of change have reached explosive levels. So tremendous are the opportunities that foreign investors are desperate for a slice of the action. However, they often overlook some of the key risk factors because they do not understand the Chinese way of doing things. Often, they simply do not have the patience or they have not invested the necessary resources in trying to understand their Chinese counterparts.

There is a delicate balance between the appetite for growth and the ability to manage the risks associated with it. This is easier said than done, however, because in reality, investors' pursuit of short-term growth opportunities may encourage them to ignore factors that might cause problems in the long run.

Going a step too far

Unfortunately, some foreign companies have gone a step too far in grasping old customs. For example, spurred by the hunger for China's huge market

---

* Julius Caesar.

(the 1.3 billion question) and the vast potential for profits, they may have shifted from following the "hidden rules" to actively pursuing more corrupt behaviors such as commercial bribery, in order to gain, or not to lose, "competitive advantage."

According to the Xinhua News Agency, 64 percent of the 500,000 corruption cases investigated in China in the past decade have involved international trade and foreign businesses.[7] Included among the 320,000 cases were major multinational corporations with well-known names such as McKinsey, Alcatel-Lucent, IBM, Walmart, Diagnostic Products Corporation, Carrefour, and Siemens. The list has far more big-name multinationals than many would have expected.

On August 12, 2009, Chinese prosecutors formally charged Stern Hu, an Australian citizen of Chinese origin, and three of his Chinese colleagues with bribery and violation of commercial secrets. Hu was Rio Tinto's chief negotiator for the iron ore business, and is facing up to a seven-year jail term, along with heavy fines.

> To succeed in China, multinational corporations must turn the aphorism "think global, but act local" on its head. Although they have to master the art of local operation, their behavior must match their global standards, as expected by the Chinese.[8]

It is critical that company has a clear set of company values—acceptable on a global scale, including in China—that will guide employee decisions and actions. When in doubt, apply the Golden Rule: Do unto others as you would have them do unto you, or, as Confucius says, "Do not impose on others what you do not wish for yourself."

Getting on the ground

Every time the typical chief executive officer (CEO) of a multinational company goes on a trip to China, he or she collects the notes and numbers compiled by the best brains in the company. The CEO does not really know if they will be of any use, but at least feels prepared. But, it's a quick trip and there will hardly be time to recover from jet lag, and yet there is a hugely ambitious agenda. It is little wonder that, oftentimes, not much is achieved.

Genuine sincerity goes a long way in China, but few people realize it. It takes time to build up trust and quick visits are not the answer. Hank Paulson, former United States Treasury secretary, made some 70 trips to China during his days as the chairman and CEO of Goldman Sachs. As a result, he is well regarded in China and well informed. Jim Rogers, a perceptive investor and travel adventurer, escaped from the confines of Wall Street and toured China three times—twice by motorcycle and once in his customized Mercedes. The outcome? He has made a great deal of money over the years and his two daughters speak Mandarin fluently—his best investment ever. In his book *A Bull in China—Investing Profitably in the World's Greatest Market*, Rogers suggests that:

> Now is the time to engage China and all things Chinese. Go there if you can, or if you've already climbed the Great Wall, go back again to see the great changes.[9]

Understanding China properly requires not only passion and initiative, but also commitment, time, resources and action.

1　In Search of a Perfect Answer

Figuring out how to deal with China has been a difficult exercise for Google.

Elliot Schrage, vice president, global communications
and public affairs, Google Inc.[1]

Perhaps the clearest, or most extreme, example of the problems for foreign companies entering China is the case of Google. Certainly, it is the one that has generated most press coverage and heated debate. Business and politics clashed head on.

Google owns me. Sad, but true. Not just web searches—googling—but everything. My e-mail is Googlemail. My calendar is Google Calendar, half of my work is done in Google Docs and, if I'm lost, I'll invariably turn to Google Maps. I research on Google News, and I read blogs on Google Reader. On my laptop, my browser is Google Chrome.[2]

Hugo Rifkind, Edinburgh-born columnist for *The Times*

Few companies have as much influence over our lives as Google does—it is now difficult to imagine life without it. Yet, in China, the story is a little different. At one point, Google had to decide whether to stay there or leave. On March 22, 2010, just two months after it publicly announced it was contemplating leaving China, Google shut down its China site and redirected its traffic to Google.com.hk, its Hong Kong-based website, after an intense dispute over censorship with the Chinese government.

Google had thus failed to find an answer to its own question: How could it enter China without being "perceived as evil"?

Don't be evil

Larry Page and Sergey Brin, two Ph.D. students at Stanford University, launched Google as a research project in 1996. They went onto incorporate formally as Google Inc. on September 7, 1998.

The name Google originated from "Googol," which is a mathematical term for the number 1 followed by 100 zeros. It reflected Google's mission "to organize the world's information and make it universally accessible and useful."[3] Google was able to win its audience because of the quality of its search results and its do-no-evil, make-money-honestly philosophy.

As a young company experiencing hypergrowth, Google began to come up against the typical problems companies face as they transition out of the start-up phase. The early employees (mostly engineers) were resistant when staff with business skills began joining the technically driven company. They feared that they would be pressured into moving towards a more profit-driven mentality, which would ultimately affect the purity of the company's products. Page and Brin were also becoming concerned about the identity of the organization.

In 2001, some senior employees, under the guidance of the founders, gathered for a corporate soul-searching meeting to address the issue. Few would have imagined at the time that the three words that emerged from the meeting—"Don't be evil" would one day become three of the most important words in Google's history—the informal company motto.

"Don't be evil" not only sets the ethical boundaries of Google's internal company dealings but also directs its every business decision. To stick with and live up to it, however, has become increasingly tricky, especially since Google is in the business of being "a global arbiter of human knowledge and commerce."[4] Surprisingly, the more successful Google has become, the more it has found itself pondering its role as "the morality police for the global economy"[5]—a role that is too big for any company.

Battling with the "Great Firewall of China"

The first problem with the "Don't be evil" philosophy is how Google defines evil and what it meant for Google in China.

> They [Google] can't afford to not be in China ... They are facing a hard choice. They really don't want to be seen as doing something that is evil, but no one goes into China on their own terms.[6]

Self-censorship is one of the requirements of doing business in China for internet companies. Like many of its rivals, Google had wanted to prosper and grow in China, but it could not reconcile the regulatory requirement for censorship with its core value—"Don't be evil."

Ever since its formation, Google had been available, uncensored, to internet users worldwide, including China. In 2000, it launched a Chinese version of Google.com, news of which spread quickly by word of mouth among Chinese internet users. It worked well until 2002, when Google started to notice that its service was sporadically unavailable in China.

Then in September 2002, the "Great Firewall of China" blocked Google.*
At that point, Google faced two choices: (1) stay out of China, or (2) establish

---

* Also referred to as the "Golden Shield Project," a censorship and surveillance project operated by the Ministry of Public Security of China.

a local presence in the country, and adhere to Chinese laws and regulations. Either option would run counter to its stated corporate values.

In the end, Google chose to stand by its values, which it claimed "turned out to be a good choice."[7] Within about two weeks, access to Google.com had been largely restored and Google claimed that it had not been forced to modify its service. Although Google did not disclose how it worked with the Chinese government, according to John Battelle, author of *The Search: How Google and Its Rivals Rewrote the Rules of Business and Transformed Our Culture*,[8] some Chinese scholars in the United States believe that the Chinese government restored Google's services because of a strong backlash from Chinese citizens.

New problems soon arose, however. Access became slow and unreliable. Even though Google was not self-censoring, search results were still being filtered, which was crippling its service. Politically sensitive queries, in particular, were not reaching Google's server, and users were sometimes redirected to local Chinese search engines. Still, Google continued to offer its service from outside China while its major rivals were entering China and building a local presence.

Google found its market share in China was steadily declining and believed that the slowness and unreliability were the leading causes. Google then took a serious look at China, and over the next couple of years, reassessed its approach. This time, it redefined what was evil. According to Eric Schmidt, chairman and CEO of the company:

> We concluded that although we weren't wild about the restrictions, it was even worse to not try to serve those users at all. … We actually did an evil scale and decided not to serve at all was worse evil.[9]

Then, to add a bit of Chinese flavor to its forthcoming initial public offering (IPO) on Nasdaq, in or around April 2004, Google knocked on Baidu's* door—a Chinese start-up that was not yet well known outside its homeland. Two months later Google acquired a 2.6 percent stake in Baidu for US$5 million, followed by Google's IPO on August 19, 2004.

In January 2005, Google was granted the right to open offices in China. Several months later, Google introduced a new version of its search engine for the Chinese market by purging search results for websites that the Chinese government did not approve of. In January 2006, Google launched Google.cn and announced its Chinese name—Gu Ge—the first non-English name it had used anywhere in the world.† After the launch, Google decided to focus on its China website and, in June 2006, sold off its stake in Baidu for more than US$60 million, making a handsome profit.

---

* Incorporated in the Cayman Islands on January 18, 2000 as Baidu.com Inc., Baidu was China's Number-1 search engine—often referred to as "China's Google." The literal meaning of Baidu is "hundreds of times," inspired by an ancient Chinese poem and representing a persistent search for the ideal.

† Gu ge is a transliteration, literally meaning "song of grain," expressing the abundance of harvest or "song of the valley," a reference to Google's Silicon Valley roots.

The intention was that Google.cn would not be a replacement for Google.com, which would remain open, unfiltered and available to all internet users worldwide. Despite content restrictions (estimated at only 2 percent of all search queries in China), Google concluded that a fast and reliable Google.cn would more likely expand Chinese users' access to information.

A new approach to China

Despite entering the Chinese market late, Google was catching up and gaining market share at the expense of other major players in the market, with the exception of Baidu. Google had compromised in order to balance its own idealism with pragmatism. It turned out to be a sensible decision. The result: Google gained nearly one-third of the Chinese market, established an R&D and sales presence, and derived between 1 and 2 percent of its global revenues from the fast-growing Chinese market.

However, in January 2010, citing cyber-attacks originated from China (though lacking any concrete evidence) Google decided to revise its strategy and chose to declare publicly that it would no longer comply with China's censorship requirements for internet companies. Perhaps Google had hoped that Chinese government would give in. The tactic did not work. For Chinese people, face-saving and harmony is deeply rooted in the culture, "Google is not God" and public confrontation would never work.

Unable to resolve its differences with the Chinese government, Google decided to shut down the Google.cn service and redirected all its traffic to the uncensored Google.com.hk. On the surface, it appeared to be a "graceful" or "semi" exit, because theoretically it did not pull out of China completely (Hong Kong is one of the two special administrative regions of China). Technically, as Google acknowledged, China could still block the access to Google's Hong Kong site or censor the search results and thus affect Google's ability to do business there.

Still, Google claimed that it was a sensible solution and entirely legal to redirect its traffic to Hong Kong. The Chinese government did not respond to Google's new approach, nor did it take any further actions. However, according to David Drummond, Google's chief legal officer, "it is clear from conversations we have had with Chinese government officials that they find the redirect unacceptable."[10]

This time, Google had shot itself in the foot. Shareholders of Google started feeling the "pain." Google's share of the Chinese search market dropped 5 percent from its peak of 36 percent in the last quarter of 2009 in the first quarter of 2010 (the first decline since the second quarter of 2009), then continued on a downward trend to 19 percent in the second quarter of 2011.[11] This benefited its own competitor (Baidu's revenue in the first quarter of 2010 was up 60 percent, net profit more than doubled, the number of advertisers increased, and the share price soared by 14 percent to a record high,[12] its market share was up from 59 percent in the last quarter of 2009 to 76 percent in the second quarter of 2011);[13] and it became increasingly clear that advertisers were worried and turning to a safer choice like Baidu.

The fallout also began to spread to other Chinese partners. Tom Online Inc, a mainland Chinese internet firm controlled by Hong Kong tycoon Li Ka-shing, announced that it would stop using Google's search services after their agreement expired. China Unicom claimed that it would not use Google search boxes on its phones and would only work with companies that abided by Chinese law. Google lost some key talent to its local rivals. Within one month, two of its top executives jumped ship—one opted to join Baidu, and one went to another of Google's local rivals.

The compromise

Google needed a valid license to continue to operate in China, and its existing license was due to expire on June 30, 2010. To secure the renewal of its license, on June 29, one day prior to the expiration date, Google finally made a compromise by updating its approach. Users going to Google.cn were given a link to click through, if they wished, instead of being automatically redirected to Google.com.hk.

Although there were no material differences between the two approaches, the update was seen as a face-saving compromise and the Chinese government viewed it as a sensible improvement. Eventually, Google got its Chinese license renewed, thus ending a months-long saga that threatened Google's future in China. According to Reuters, shares of Google rose 2.4 percent, while Baidu dropped 1.6 percent upon the news.[14]

Yet, what is it all about?

China is not the only country that censors the internet; there are many other countries that do so. According to a report by two Harvard researchers,[15] Google had begun filtering its own servers, e.g. in Germany, France, Switzerland and even the US, where users are blocked from accessing sites carrying material likely to be judged racist or inflammatory in each country.

Meanwhile, shareholders of Google were wondering about their own rights and whether they too, had a say in the matter. Though Google did not ask for their "forgiveness," it decided that it would seek for their "permission" at last. In the midst of a review of its operations in China, Google, at its annual shareholders' meeting held on May 13, 2010, sought their approval for its proposal regarding the adaption of Google's human rights principles with respect to its business in China. More than 90 percent of the voters voted against the proposal, while only 1 percent voters voted for it.

Yet, what were the real motives behind Google's suddenly changing its approach to China?

Google claimed that the cyber-attacks on its site, which it believed to have originated in China, were the trigger, while admitting that there was no clear evidence that they were linked with the Chinese government.

One possible explanation, as some analysts pointed out, was that Google used it as an excuse to avoid looking like a failure. According to Morningstar Equity Research:

> While we recognize that Google's anti-censorship stance is genuine, we also think that Goggle struggled to gain traction in China, as Baidu remains the dominant search engine with about 65 percent market share compared with 30 percent for Google. We also estimate that Google's operation in China was unprofitable. Therefore, we think Google tried to use its political position partially as an excuse to close down its search engine in China without looking like it failed.[16]

Whether or not Google considered itself a failure in China with some 30 percent market share in China within four years, the decision to stop censoring the search results (which clearly went against the law of the land) appeared to be, at least, "irrational"[17] in the eyes of Steve Ballmer, the CEO of Microsoft. Even more so, according to Google's corporate blog, Google's employees in China did not have any knowledge of or involvement in the decision.[18] How odd is that? It is hard to imagine that a giant organization like Google could have made a decision to reverse its stance in one of the world's most promising markets without its team on the ground having the slightest awareness.

Another possible explanation, according to the mainstream Chinese media, was that it was a more political act than purely commercial.

> Google's case is in essence part of the U.S. Internet intrusive strategy worldwide under the excuse that it advocates a free Internet.[19]

First, Google had close links with the Obama administration and was one of the four major sponsors during Obama's presidential campaign. Second, coincidentally, US Secretary of State Hilary Clinton praised Google as one of the internet companies helping the Obama administration realize its foreign policy just a few days before Google's announcement, and subsequently gave a speech supporting Google's Internet freedom campaign.

A third possible explanation that may come as a surprise to many, was that Brin, one of the co-founders of Google, was actually instrumental in shaping Google's position on China.

> As a boy growing up in the Soviet Union, Sergey Brin witnessed the consequences of censorship. Now the Google Inc. co-founder is drawing on that experience in shaping the company's showdown with the Chinese government.[20]

The so-called Google triumvirate, Schmidt, Page and Brin, with nearly 70 percent of the voting rights due to the two-tier share structure,* essentially controlled the company. Each of them focused on the different aspect

---

* According to Google's March 2010 proxy filing, as of February 17, 2010, Page and Brin controlled 58.9 percent of the voting power. Although it was reported that the co-founders were to reduce their control of the company to 48 percent by 2014. Schmidt controlled 9.5 percent of the voting power.

of the business: Schmidt on finance and strategy, Page on products, while Brin concentrated on technology. Regarded as "Google's moral compass on China-related issues,"[21] Brin was able to impose his personal view on politics and policy matters on Google and defined "what is evil." In this case, it seemed as if Brin finally got fed up with the "self-censorship" requirements of the Chinese government.

While urging the White House to pressurize the Chinese government, Brin had hoped that other internet companies would follow suit. He was furious, however, when Bill Gates came out and criticized Google's decision:

> You have got to decide: do you want to obey the laws of the countries you're in or not? If not, you may not end up doing business there.[22]

However, Google had decided to make a U-turn in that it was no longer willing to continue self-censoring Google.cn, even though it meant shutting down the site and, potentially, its offices in China. Confucius said: "A little impatience spoils a great plan." Google could have been more patient. Despite the speed of development, China still decides its own pace for progress and has rarely made any rapid radical changes in the past. Nor was it likely to do so just because of pressure from multinationals. Google could and should have tried to influence the Chinese government through open dialogues instead of public confrontations.

The story is far from over

Google made a tough call by turning away from China, and in doing so, won praises from human rights advocates while also receiving backing from the US government. Was it the best that Google could do at that time? The answer was "No": a mere few months later, Google, facing the expiration of its license to operate in China, had to compromise to get the approval of the Chinese government for the renewal.

Yet, the Google story is far from ending. On June 1, 2011, Google again claimed on its corporate blog that the personal Gmail accounts of hundreds of users, including senior US government officials, journalists and Chinese human rights activists, suffered phishing attacks originating from Jinan, China. This time, China officially rejected Google's accusation. "Blaming these misdeeds on China is unacceptable," Hong Lei, Chinese foreign ministry spokesman told a news briefing in Beijing. He also stressed that "hacking is an international problem and China is also a victim. The claims of so-called Chinese state support for hacking are completely fictitious and have ulterior motives."[23]

"Don't be evil" was the ethical boundary that Google set for itself. That said, it went beyond the boundaries that China sets for companies to operate there. Google had taken a huge and calculated risk when it went into China.

Certainly, any number of large and important companies face conundrums like the China question, but Google sees itself as a different kind of company, one that makes its own way and refuses convention almost on principle.

We do not live in an ideal world and moral issues are not always black and white. There is no absolute right or wrong. Google had developed a sense of purpose—"Don't do evil," but it has yet to identify the parameters to measure it. By attempting to impose its own values on China, Google managed to get itself into a situation where neither side would win. Had Google stayed true to its own values by ultimately serving its users, it could have initiated constructive dialogues with the Chinese government, made sensible compromises, and thus achieved "win–win."

Google's rival, Microsoft, however, took a different approach. On July 4, 2011, Microsoft and Baidu joined forces to offer web services in English. There is perhaps no doubt that the new English-language search results will be censored and Microsoft was clearly aware of it. As a Microsoft spokeswoman said, "Microsoft respects and follows laws and regulations in every country where we run business. We operate in China in a manner that both respects local authority and culture and makes clear that we have differences of opinion with official content-management policies."[24] By following this path, Microsoft gained access to serve more Chinese users, while Baidu became able to provide better English search experiences and results to its users.

In September 2011, Chinese government renewed Google's Internet Content Provider (ICP) license in China for another year. However, Google's share of traffic and revenue in China continued to fall, partly because the Chinese government continued to censor the search results of Google's overseas websites for users in China. Access to Google's overseas sites and its Gmail service have become increasingly unreliable for users in China.

Harmony is deeply rooted in the Chinese culture, and is essential to successful partnerships in China. Yet, few Western companies have realized its importance. Some appear to have achieved certain level of peaceful coexistence with their Chinese partners, but most have faced troubles, which first appeared only as the tip of the iceberg.

2 A Bumpy Ride in China

Groupe Danone SA (Danone), the French food and beverage conglomerate, is a successful company in many ways, and has earned the respect of many in China. It successfully introduced yogurt to Chinese consumers, and a generation of younger Chinese grew up with an array of Danone brands. A French icon, the company even raised the French government's concern over national interests when it became the target of a hostile takeover launched by Pepsi in 2005.

Danone's business model is all about "accelerated growth";[1] growth is in Danone's genes and fundamental to its approach. Danone has had a run of successes in growing its businesses by acquiring companies or forming partnerships in emerging markets, including China, but it has also run into trouble with some of its many partners. For example, Danone had long-standing disputes with Britannia, its joint venture partner in India, and was taken to court in 2007 in a dispute over the copyright of Britannia's Tiger biscuit brand.

So, who is Danone and how did it come to China?

From container to content

Danone's predecessor, Boussois Souchon Neuvesel (BSN), was formed in 1966 by the merger of two little-known French glass manufacturers. Antoine Riboud (dubbed Old Riboud by Danone's Chinese partners) was appointed chairman and CEO of the merged company. Aiming to achieve global reach for the French glass industry, in 1968, Old Riboud launched the first hostile takeover bid in France for glass manufacturer Saint-Gobain. The bid failed.

However, Old Riboud reflected on the setback and then revised the company's strategy to expand downstream into the food industry. In 1973, BSN merged with Gervais Danone, to create the biggest food company in France, with an ambitious goal "to build a food group with the muscle to compete with international heavyweights, combining the Danone brand and products with the industrial knowhow and financial resources of BSN."[2] Subsequently, the company also shifted its focus to food by divesting its industrial glass activities and acquiring Italian and Spanish companies producing pasta, ready meals and fresh packaged foods thus establishing a strong base as a European company.

Adventure begun by father

Under Old Riboud's charismatic and visionary leadership, the company enjoyed tremendous growth. For three consecutive decades, it doubled or tripled sales every ten years by adopting a brand-focused strategy combined with decentralized operations, astute financial management and a steady stream of acquisitions in the world food industry. It began buying companies in Western Europe, before buying Dannon USA in 1981,* then moving on to the rest of the world, including China.

> Having long foreseen the emergence of China and Southeast Asia, Antoine Riboud made a personal visit to China in September 1983 and a Danone team arrived in the country one year later. The launch of Guangzhou Danone Yogurt Company Ltd in 1987 gave the group its first industrial presence in China ... [3]

However, in 1993, Danone experienced an unprecedented decline in sales after a prolonged recession in Western Europe. This, compounded by adverse exchange rate movements, led to a 10 percent drop in operating income. Danone's three most important markets—France, Italy and Spain—were among the worst hit. Partly to reinforce the management's faith in the value of its global brands, the company changed its name in 1994 from BSN to Danone—the group's flagship fresh dairy brand.

Danone then stepped up its pace of global expansion mainly through acquisitions and partnerships, focusing increasingly on Eastern Europe, Southeast Asia and Latin America. As a source of future profits, it targeted categories where it could rival or outperform the world's top contenders. Compared with its traditional rivals—Nestlé SA and the Unilever Group—Danone was a relatively late entrant in the international food market, had less experience and fewer historic links with many developing markets and a less international senior executive profile; they were mainly French. Yet, Danone had demonstrated a strong ability to be flexible, innovative, fast and adaptive to evolving local business environments.

Pioneering spirit carried on by the son

In 1996, Old Riboud stepped down and his son Franck Riboud took over as chairman and CEO of Danone. This led to accusations of nepotism as the family only held about 1 percent of the company's share capital. It was up to Riboud to prove the critics wrong, as he eventually did. Born in 1955, Riboud was an engineer by training and had spent 15 years working his way up through various positions within Danone.

---

* Dannon in the USA was sold off in 1959 and bought by BSN in 1981. In 2007, Dannon was one of the top two yogurt producers in the USA and the best-selling brand of yogurt worldwide.

Over the next 10 years, Riboud further shifted Danone's focus to fresh dairy products, biscuits and beverages. The company made more than 50 international acquisitions and strategic partnerships in these sectors and gradually divested itself of other activities. Riboud's view on strategy was very pragmatic:

> At Danone we don't talk about strategy, we react to the context around us. For me, it's like a Lego box that you buy for your children. They start to play, trying to find a way to build the image on the Lego box. At the end of the day, they give up, throw out the box, and put the pieces away. The next weekend you put all the Lego pieces on the floor and then the strategy starts. They try to imagine something. Not what was on the box, but what they have in their heads. That is strategy at Danone for me: It's Lego.[4]

Essential to this strategy was decentralization and the preservation of the autonomy of local management. Because of this, Danone believed it was able to stay close to consumers, develop products that differed from market to market and get them to the market faster than its competitors. An ex-windsurfer, Riboud's enthusiasm for sports had also influenced the way he managed the company and its flexible approach to dealing with many issues. His views on the company's relation to rules and processes were also specific:

> We definitely have to play by the rules, but rules are not the goal. Victory is the goal. Rules are here to allow the game.[5]

This distinguishes Danone from many Anglo-Saxon companies. Pierre Cohade,* former executive vice president of Danone's beverages business, a Frenchman, but a firm believer in Anglo-Saxon business values, commented on Danone's business mentality after a brief one-and-a-half-year career at Danone:

> Danone operates via a network. By this I mean, "Who do I know, and what network of friends do I have, within the organization?" ... . Danone seems at times to operate by inspiration.[6]

A long march in China

Following the same approach that it had adopted in other emerging markets, Danone had acquired or formed strategic partnerships with major players in the Chinese dairy, beverage and food industries, thereby gaining the rights to major Chinese dairy and beverage brands (see Exhibit 2.1).

---

* Cohade spent 17 years with Eastman Kodak prior joining Danone and is presently (2011) the president of The Goodyear Tire & Rubber Company's Asia-Pacific region.

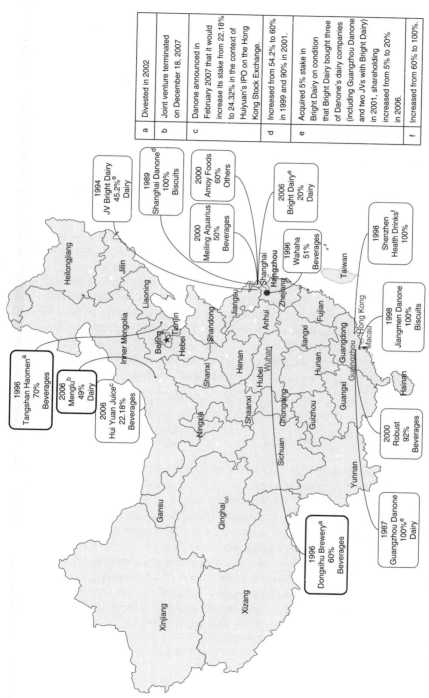

Exhibit 2.1 **Danone's major investments in China (as of December 21, 2007)**

Source: Developed from various company reports, announcements, press releases and media reports.

It [Danone] ... plays like a shadow to all the best Chinese companies in the dairy [and beverage] industry.[7]

In 1992 and 1994 respectively, Danone set up two joint ventures with Bright Dairy; in 1996 it formed a strategic joint venture partnership with Wahaha; and in 2000 it managed to acquire 92 percent of Wahaha's closest competitor, the bottled water manufacturer Robust.

Over the previous 20 years, Danone's accumulated industrial investment in China had reached nearly RMB5 billion (about $600 million). It had shown a strong appetite for acquiring sizeable interests in leading Chinese companies, which owned leading Chinese national brands that were already trusted by Chinese consumers. Some of them were direct competitors in certain segments, namely China Huiyuan Juice Group Ltd (22 percent), Shenzhen Health Drinks (100 percent) and Bright Dairy (20 percent). On 18 December 2006, it announced the signing of a 49 percent joint venture with China Mengniu Dairy Company Limited (Mengniu), a leading dairy company in China and Bright Dairy's direct competitor. Danone executives also assumed directorships in its many acquired companies.[8]

China had become increasingly important to the company's growth and was the largest market in terms of products manufactured and units sold.[9] In March 2006, Danone had moved the headquarters of its Asia-Pacific operations from Singapore to Shanghai.[10] The 2006 revenue of its China businesses reached €1.49 billion (US$1.97 billion),* accounting for 10.6 percent of the Group's total revenue (€14 billion or US$18.5 billion) and contributed over RMB1 billion (about $120 million) in taxes to the regional governments.[11]

Bumpy roads ahead

Over the years, Danone had demonstrated its strength in buying companies and cultivating strategic partnerships in China. However, despite handsome financial gains, Danone's track record of managing these acquired businesses, especially those with strong partners, had been poor. Often things started well but, somehow, at a certain stage in the co-operation, circumstances changed with unhappy consequences.

In chapters 3, 4, 5 and 6 we examine three major partnerships that Danone had formed in China, which started out as sweet co-operations, before resulting in bitter endings, namely the Danone–Wahaha joint venture, the Danone–Robust acquisition and the Danone–Bright Dairy co-operation. We hope that they will help illustrate some valuable lessons.

---

* Unless otherwise specified, the conversion rate €1 = US$1.32 has been used.

3 A Rising Chinese Champion

Wahaha,* a leading food and beverage company in China, had 2006 revenues of RMB18.7 billion (US$2.5 billion).[1] At the time, it was the fifth largest beverage company by revenue in the world, after Coca-Cola, Pepsi, Cadbury, and Gatorade. The company's main products, such as bottled water, fruit milk, and adult milk enriched with calcium and mixed *congee*† were leaders in the Chinese beverage industry. Wahaha's milk products and bottled water were in direct competition with its international rivals, which included Unilever and Nestlé.

Origins in a school-owned enterprise‡

Yet, Wahaha had humble origins going back to 1 May 1987, when Zong Qinghou—a school employee aged 42—together with two retired teachers and a loan of RMB140,000 (US$19,048)[2] started the sales department of an enterprise owned by the Primary School of Hangzhou Shangcheng District. They started selling beverages, ice cream and stationery on a commission basis. In 1988, Wahaha Nutritional Food Factory§ (WNFF) was founded and the Wahaha brand was formally created. WNFF was established to manufacture its first and only product—Wahaha Oral Liquid for Children—a kind of natural food with a medicinal effect based on the philosophy of Chinese medicine. It filled a gap in the fragmented oral liquid market by establishing a niche for children,** and earned WNFF and the Wahaha brand its first success. By 1990, WNFF's annual revenue had exceeded RMB100 million, profit and tax†† reached about RMB30 million, and the company was viewed as an "economic miracle rising from a school campus."[3]

---

* The name means "children's laughter" and was taken from a Chinese children's folk song.
† A type of rice porridge.
‡ Since the 1980s, the Chinese government had encouraged schools to run their own businesses in order to provide opportunities for pupils to learn practical skills and boost school funds.
§ Factories were treated like companies in China, i.e. as legal entities.
** None of the 38 companies then producing oral liquids in China was making them specifically for children.
†† In China, companies (especially state-owned and private companies), do not separate "profit" and "tax" in their reporting, the total of the two is shown as "profit and tax" as one item.

Small fish eats big fish

Soon WNFF's capacity could hardly meet the rising demand. In 1991, in a deal supported and arranged by the Hangzhou city government, WNFF acquired the state-owned Hangzhou Canned Food Factory (HCFF) for RMB80 million (US$10.9 million). WNFF had only 100 employees, but RMB60 million (US$8.2 million) in cash; HCFF had 2,000 employees (including over 700 retired workers) but a negative net worth (about RMB70 million of debt). The combined business was able to operate on a larger scale, and within three months, Zong had managed to make it profitable. In mid-1991, Hangzhou Wahaha Group Corporation (Wahaha) was formally incorporated.

As part of the commitment to the government for the acquisition, Zong had agreed to no employee lay-offs at HCFF. The acquisition thus increased the overhead of the combined businesses. Relying purely on manufacturing and selling Wahaha Oral Liquid for Children could not sustain the additional 2,000 employees. In addition, Zong felt that it would be difficult to sustain long-term growth due to the short life span of the original product, and the company would have to find other sources of revenue. Zong therefore decided to turn the company from a health drink manufacturer into a food and beverage manufacturer.

Diversification and expansion

In 1992, Wahaha raised RMB236 million (US$32 million) from employees and others in order to form the Hangzhou Wahaha Food City Co. Ltd (WFC). WFC was one of the first of nine joint-stock companies in Hangzhou with the labor union holding the employees' shares in the company. WFC's core business was developing commercial properties and it was charged with building a factory for WFC to prepare the company for an IPO. However, WFC missed the opportunity for an IPO as construction was delayed for six years, mainly due to cash-flow problems resulting from a lack of experience and expertise in project management.

Strategic partnership

In 1992, the same year, Wahaha formed a joint venture partnership with the Korea Hyonong Company Limited (Hyonong) to manufacture canned food products. It started as an equal partnership and the initial investment was US$490,000. Even so, the Korean party took the chairmanship and Zong the vice-chairmanship.

Due to intense competition in the domestic canned food industry, the joint venture looked to expand its manufacturing capacity and increase its product portfolio and exports. Thus, in 1994, the registered capital of the joint venture was increased to US$1.33 million (total investment was US$1.69 million). By then, Wahaha held a majority 65.8 percent equity interest. Despite this, Zong remained as the vice-chairman. However, the increased investment in the joint venture did not lead to immediate growth. Then in 1995, Wahaha embarked on a path of overexpansion. It launched more than ten new products during the year but almost all failed. This, coupled with the delay in the construction of WFC, strained the corporation's capital reserves.

Geographic expansion

In 1994, the central government encouraged companies in coastal cities such as Hangzhou to invest in inland China and to support the development of the Three Gorges area. In response, Wahaha started its first cross-provincial investment by acquiring three insolvent local companies* and setting up a subsidiary in Fulin, Chongqing municipality, about 1,500 miles (2,000kms) away from Hangzhou. This enabled Wahaha to reduce its distribution costs by having a manufacturing base in inland China. Wahaha Fulin Company became an important contributor to the local economy and one of the "15 leading corporations" of Chongqing.[4]

Subsequently, Wahaha further expanded across the country and set up about 20 subsidiary companies—especially in poor rural areas†—that accounted for one-third of the group's total production.[5] All of the subsidiaries made profits and became important local taxpayers and "locomotives" of local economies (see Exhibit 3.1).

At the time, Danone wanted to gain a strategic foothold in the Chinese market. In 1995, the so-called father of the Chinese private equity industry, Francis (Botao) Leung of Peregrine Direct Investment Holdings Limited (Peregrine), a Hong Kong-based investment company,‡ approached Danone. He proposed that Peregrine and Danone invest jointly in Wahaha for the purpose of developing and producing food and beverage products in China under the Wahaha brand, and introduced Zong to Danone.

From the outset, the proposal represented a good investment fit for both Danone and Wahaha. It made sense to Danone because the French company was looking for further opportunities to capture the great potential for growth in China. It also made sense to Wahaha, which was seeking foreign investments to overcome its capital and technology constraints and expand further.

After months of negotiations, it was agreed that Danone would channel its investment through Jinjia Investments Pte Limited (Jinjia)—an entity

---

* Wahaha and the local government each invested RMB40 million for the acquisitions.
† Hangzhou to Chongqing, Sichuan, and then further to Guangxi, Gansu, Henan, Hubei, Hunan, Anhui, Jilin, Liaoning, Hebei, Tianjin, Guangdong and Shandong.
‡ Peregrine was liquidated in 1998 following the Asian financial crisis, and was acquired by BNP Paribas and became its investment banking arm in Asia.

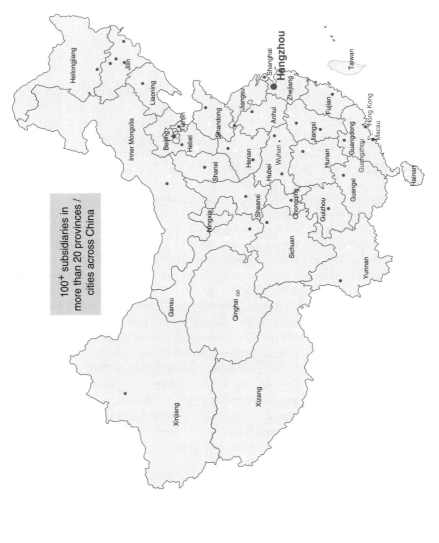

Exhibit 3.1   **Wahaha's national presence (as of December 21, 2007)**

Source: Wahaha company website.

established in Singapore with Peregrine. In 1996, it signed a joint venture agreement with Wahaha. The joint venture was made up of five subsidiaries companies (referred to as joint venture companies or JVs), mainly covering the manufacture of different product categories, e.g. food, health food, beverages and quick frozen food. These categories were already in existence and Jinjia gained rights via equity transfer agreements with the respective foreign partners of those companies, with the option to invest in five other existing companies in which Wahaha had an equity interest.*

At the beginning of 1996 (just before the JVs were formed), Wahaha decided to go into the water business. Subsequently, it launched Wahaha Purified Water, which became a huge success mainly due to its competitive pricing and effective advertisements. It went on to win the title of China's "Most Famous National Brand."[6] In the following year, Wahaha successfully launched Wahaha calcium milk enriched with vitamins A and D. This allowed the Group's revenue to exceed the RMB1 billion mark.

Challenging Coca-Cola and Pepsi

In 1998, after ten years of development, Wahaha believed that it was ready to compete directly with its international rivals. Despite strong objections from Danone, Wahaha launched the first Chinese cola—Future Cola (the Chinese name, *feichang*, means extraordinary or unusual and sounds similar to "future"), to compete directly with Coca-Cola and Pepsi in China. Future Cola was packaged in red, which gave it a patriotic appeal, and the writing on the packaging was similar to Coca-Cola's. It tasted sweeter than Coke or Pepsi, which appealed to its target consumers. Wahaha began marketing the product in the vast rural areas of China, where consumers had little knowledge of cola and their choices were more influenced by price than brand. In addition, Wahaha could leverage its extensive distribution network in areas where Coca-Cola and Pepsi had little presence. After dominating the rural market, Wahaha began to compete head-on with Coca-Cola and Pepsi when it began promoting Future Cola in big cities. To everybody's surprise, the launch of Future Cola was a huge success—first-year sales reached RMB100 million and exceeded RMB 1.5 billion three years later. It became number three in the carbonated beverage sector, after Coca-Cola and Pepsi.

Restructuring and further diversification

When the JV partnership was formed, Wahaha was a 100 percent state-owned company. With the continuing reform of Chinese state-owned enterprises (SOEs), however, the managers of these enterprises were allowed to

---

* According to Danone, Jinjia was unable to exercise the right due to certain complications.

receive incentive shares if the company met certain performance indicators.*
In August 1999, the Hangzhou city government issued interim guidance on
how the policy in Hangzhou was to be implemented.

Three months later, Wahaha's ownership restructuring plan was approved.
The State-owned Asset Bureau of Hangzhou Shangcheng district would own
51 percent (further reduced to 46 percent after transferring 5 percent of the
shares to the employee union two years later). Zong would receive 29.4 percent
of the company (worth RMB 150 million), which he acquired by borrow-
ing money from banks against his own personal credit; 38 senior executives
would receive 2.3 percent of the shares; and 1,885 employees received a total
of 17.3 percent of the shares (worth RMB 89.23 million) according to their
rank within the company. In 2003, the restructuring process was completed,
and by then, Wahaha had already been partially privatized, and transformed
from a 100 percent SOE into one where Zong and the employees owned the
majority of shares. The employees' shares were held by the employee union.

In 2003, Hangzhou Wahaha Guangsheng Investment Co. (Guangsheng), a
subsidiary of Wahaha, was established with registered capital of RMB50 million
(US$6.8 million), which increased to RMB80 million (US$11 million) the
following year. Zong held 60 percent of Guangsheng's shares, while the
employee union held 40 percent. Guangsheng made nine major investments that included Hangzhou Wahaha Children's Clothing Co., Changsha
Wahaha Beverages Co., Harbin Shuangcheng Wahaha Foods Co. and Jian
Wahaha Beverages Co., with Guangsheng's shareholding ranging from
39 percent to 65 percent.

In August 2003, Guangsheng transferred its 65 percent share in
Hangzhou Wahaha Children's Clothing Co. to Zong and three other individual shareholders later passed their shares on to Zong. The company was
thus 65 percent owned by Zong, 10 percent by Zong's wife—Shi Youzhen—
and 25 percent by Platinum Net Ltd† (a company registered in the British
Virgin Islands). Subsequently, Guangsheng gradually eased out of the other
eight investments it had made.[7]

Zong Qinghou

> Zong Qinghou was not only the founder and chairman of Wahaha, and the
> "head" of the "big Wahaha family," even more he was the spiritual leader of
> Wahaha! The core! The Soul![8]
>
> Luo Jianxin, former Wahaha employee

To understand the rise of Wahaha, it is important to understand Zong
Qinghou, the man behind it.

---

* For instance, if the net profit/asset ratio had been higher for three consecutive years than
the average of all state-owned or state-controlled enterprises in Hangzhou.
† It was reportedly owned by individuals associated with Zong.

Tough early days

Zong was born in 1945 in Hangzhou. He was the eldest son and a 36th generation descendant of Zong Ze, a distinguished, patriotic general of the Southern Song Dynasty. Despite the family background, Zong's family remained poor when he was young. To help relieve his family's financial burden, Zong stopped studying at the age of 17, after graduating from middle school and went to work on a state farm in Zhejiang where he spent 15 years as a laborer.

Zong returned to Hangzhou in 1979, when his mother retired and replaced her as an employee at a primary school (not as a teacher due to his low level of education). The next eight years proved to be difficult and unhappy years for Zong. Without much education or many connections, Zong was unable to find a job in which he would be able to utilize his talents. But, as the saying goes, "luck favors the prepared," and in 1987, an opportunity arose. Zong volunteered and was put in charge of the sales department of a school-owned enterprise—the precursor of Wahaha. Zong led and grew the company, and has exercised control over its day-to-day management ever since.

A self-taught entrepreneur

Zong was a Communist Party member and a delegate to the National People's Congress. A practical leader, he believed in a hands-on approach. Known as an extremely confident and hard-working man, Zong ran his company with an iron fist. To Zong, "work is life, life is work." He worked long hours, slept less than six hours a day and took almost no days off. Employees recalled that on every public holiday, Zong was either in his office or on a business trip. He spent over 200 days a year visiting markets, testing new products himself and leading his managers on market tours of street vendors to show them how beverages were sold. Thanks to those tough early days perhaps, Zong has maintained excellent health into his sixties (despite his heavy smoking habit), and he still has ample energy to devote to his company.

By and large, Zong was a self-taught entrepreneur and a self-made marketing genius. Although he had no formal training, he derived most of his marketing and management philosophy from reading books that were mostly about history and the military, books such as *Selected Works of Mao Tse-Tung* and *Three Kingdoms*. He applied his knowledge in his work and life, creating his own unique management philosophy.

Zong also read up on management theories. On his bookshelf sit books including Michael Porter's *Competitive Advantage*. His firm belief in management in practices coincidentally validated Peter Drucker's view on "management as practice." Not surprisingly, Zong did not like using consulting companies or market research reports. He wrote his own market bulletin every two or three days and made decisions based on his intuition.

His time in the market was time well spent as it gave him accurate insights into consumers and the business as well as helping him establish close relationships with his distributors (first-tier distributors met with Zong every year and any distributor/vendor could call Zong directly with any problem).

At Wahaha, Zong maintained a centralized, flat management structure, with all middle management reporting directly to him. He was both the chairman and general manager, and Wahaha was perhaps one of the few Chinese companies of its size that did not have a vice general manager. The simple, lean and stable structure enabled Wahaha to respond and react quickly to the market, something its international competitors were unable to do. However, it also made Wahaha highly dependent on Zong's personal leadership.

Zong led by example and cared for his employees with both firmness and love. He helped employees constantly improve their living standards. For instance, the company restaurant provided employees with three meals a day so that they were free of worries at work, and in the early years he even gave his own apartment away in order to retain a talented individual. However, sticks often came with carrots, and Zong had the absolute authority on rewards and penalties. Despite the fact that it did not take much to get fired or demoted, the turnover of middle management was extremely low and most of them had followed Zong for years.

As Sun Tze said, "Know yourself, know your enemy." To cultivate successful partnerships, you need to understand not only what you want achieve, but also where your partner comes from and what kind of personalities you are dealing with. Now that we have briefly looked at both Danone and Wahaha, we can take a closer look at how their partnership formed and evolved.

4   A Bittersweet Partnership

After nine years, what started out as a sweet joint venture partnership began to unravel amid a public dispute that led to bitter lawsuits and ended with Wahaha buying out Danone's interests in the joint venture and Zong eventually becoming the richest person in mainland China. The outcome of the dispute may not have been surprising, but the way it was handled was rather long and painful, and thus offers valuable lessons.

> The feud over control of the Wahaha empire offered a peek into the breakup of a major Sino-foreign joint venture. Danone's strategy to publicly confront its partner, and Wahaha's to respond with its own accusations, marked a break with prevailing business practice in China, where problems have usually been settled with face-saving, private negotiations.[1]

What happened? Why did a one-time showcase for Sino-foreign joint venture partnerships turn sour?

Formation of the Danone–Wahaha joint ventures (JVs)

The Danone–Wahaha joint venture partnership was essentially a restructuring of Wahaha's existing joint venture with its Korean partner, Hyonong. Jinjia, on behalf of Danone and Peregrine, acquired Hyonong's entire 34.2 percent interest in the Wahaha–Hyonong joint venture and the new partners agreed to increase the registered capital of the joint venture subsidiaries from US$1.33 million to US$29.1 million.

Ownership structure

On February 9, 1996, a joint venture agreement (its effectiveness still subject to relevant government approvals) was signed between Wahaha, WFC, and Jinjia. Following the completion of the capital injections, the two Chinese partners (Wahaha and WFC) held a 49 percent interest in the JVs, while Jinjia held 51 percent (see Exhibit 4.1 for the ownership structure of the Danone–Wahaha JVs).

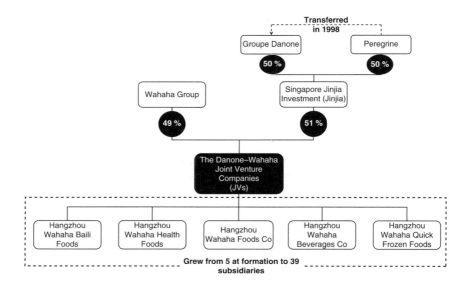

Exhibit 4.1   **Ownership structure of the Danone–Wahaha Joint Venture (as of December 21, 2007)**

Source: Developed from various company reports, announcements, press releases and media reports.

The JVs, together named Hangzhou Wahaha Food Company Limited (WFCL), were created based on five out of the then ten existing Wahaha group companies. Wahaha put the major part of its beverage business into the JVs, namely all prior knowledge, trade secrets and intellectual property associated with beverage products, as part of its capital contribution. Danone and Peregrine invested US$45 million as a first installment, followed by a further US$26.2 million.[2] Wahaha was therefore able to introduce advanced technology and bring world-class production lines from Germany, the US, Italy, Japan and Canada to its sites in China.

Trademark

The joint venture partners signed three agreements related to the Wahaha trademark at various stages following the inception of the JVs. According to the trademark transfer agreement signed in February 1996, Wahaha would transfer all rights in the Wahaha trademark to the JVs for a price of RMB100 million (US$13.6 million). Of this amount, half was considered as Wahaha's investment and Danone paid the other half as the registered capital.

However, in order to "protect national brands," the Chinese trademark authority did not approve the transfer. This failure would, in theory, have rendered the joint venture agreement ineffective immediately.

However, instead of terminating the joint venture agreement, both parties decided to sign a trademark license agreement with the JVs in May 1999 as a way to get around the regulatory barrier.* The license agreement gave the JVs "exclusive" rights to use the trademark for a list of specific products but still allowed Wahaha to use it for future products with the written consent of the JVs. In addition, as part of the agreement, both parties signed a short-form licensing contract solely for the purpose of registering with the trademark authority. In December 1999, the trademark transfer agreement was terminated, three and a half years after it was signed.

In October 2005, the joint venture partners signed an amendment to the license agreement, which allowed two types of Wahaha group companies to use the Wahaha trademark conditionally: (1) those that had manufacturing agreements with the JVs, and (2) (subject to the approval of the board of the JVs) those that manufactured different products (e.g. clothing, cosmetics, etc.).[3]

Management control

Once bitten, twice shy. Having learned lessons from his first unsuccessful joint venture experience with the Korean partner, Zong insisted on four basic principles to be implemented in the terms of its joint venture agreement with Jinjia. They were: (1) it would be strictly a "joint venture" rather than "joint brand"—in order to promote the Wahaha brand itself; (2) the Chinese partner must retain management control; (3) no employee lay-offs; and (4) the security of retired employees had to be ensured.

In addition, Zong was appointed chairman and general manager of the JVs, while retaining his role as general manager of the Wahaha holding company and other group operating companies. Danone held the vice chairmanship and supervised the JVs through the board of directors. The five-member board included two Danone representatives (one as vice chairman) and one from Peregrine.[4]

Because of Zong's experience and expertise, Danone felt that he could be trusted to run the JVs. It agreed to Zong keeping management control, responsible for the day-to-day management of the JVs. Two service agreements with Zong, dated February 29, 1996 and June 29, 2003 respectively, formalized such arrangement, ensuring that Zong continued to have management control of all the existing and future JVs between Danone, Wahaha and its affiliates. In Danone's view, Zong "operate[d] in a very entrepreneurial way, making a lot of decisions on his own."[5]

Danone's involvement in the JVs remained purely at the board level, even though it had the right to appoint its own people in key positions, e.g. the first financial director. Danone also sent several managers to work for the JVs, including a marketing director who only spent six months on site at

---

* Trademark usage rights were not subject to SAIC approval. (SAIC was the administrative authority for industry and commerce in China. The trademark office under SAIC was in charge of the registration and administration of trademarks nationwide.)

Wahaha in late 2003 and early 2004, and an R&D director, who was there from June 2004 to early 2006, to help Wahaha to set up its R&D center.

Their contributions to the JVs, however, remained controversial. Wahaha believed them to be insignificant, whereas Danone claimed that they had transferred technical knowledge and expertise. The only position that was retained by Danone until the disputes began was that of finance director. Danone argued later that Zong would not permit the finance director to participate in the management of the JVs or in any of the managerial or operational decision-making processes.

Noncompetition obligations

Both the joint venture agreement and the service agreement of 1996 stipu-lated that Zong and the Chinese parties involved would observe noncom-pete clauses with respect to the JVs.[6] In return, Zong wanted a similar understanding from Danone. Danone, however, managed to negotiate that no noncompete obligation would be applied to its side of the JVs. This was to ensure that there would be no impact on any of Danone's existing invest-ments in China and no impediment to its ability to make future investments in the Chinese food and beverage industry. As an alternative, Danone agreed that Jinjia would not harm the interests of the JVs.

Change of ownership

In May 1998, a Danone representative replaced the Peregrine-designated director on the board.[7] Only then did the Chinese partners find out—just before Peregrine's collapse—that Danone had bought out Peregrine's interest in Jinjia in late 1997, giving it 100 percent ownership of Jinjia and an effective 51 percent ownership of the joint venture.[*,†,8]

Achievements and rewards

The number of JVs increased substantially after the partnership was estab-lished, from five entities at formation to 39 entities,[9] with annual sales climbing from a few hundred million renminbi to RMB18 billion (US$2.5 billion) in 2006. Danone claimed that, according to "incomplete statis-tics," its cumulative industrial investment in the JVs had exceeded RMB2.5

---

* Although a transfer of shares in the Wahaha Group companies should have required state approval under the rules for protecting state assets in force at the time, the shares in Jinjia were not covered, since it was a Singapore-registered company.

† Danone claimed that its majority shareholding status was part of the agreement from the beginning.

billion (US$340 million).[10] The JVs' products ranged from bottled water and carbonated and fruit beverages to dairy products. Even after the dispute became public, Danone, in an official response to a *China Economic Review* article in October 2007, acknowledged Zong and the management team's "noteworthy contributions" to the business, while emphasizing that they had also received "significant financial returns"*.[11]

Non-joint-venture companies (non-JVs)

During its 2007 interim earnings conference call, Danone claimed, that beginning in 2000, the board of the JVs had agreed to start co-packer† operations (or subcontracting), as part of the global sourcing strategy for the joint venture business in China. Deutsche Bank estimated that about one-third of the JVs' production came from subcontractors, while the rest was from JV-owned plants.[12]

According to Danone it was only later that they discovered that Zong and his family members had gradually come to own companies in the same industry which were making products that competed directly with the JVs' products. Danone also claimed that Wahaha used the Wahaha brand and product formula owned by the JVs without proper authorization.[13]

> To our surprise, those co-packers [subcontractors] became related-party companies, and also took an increasing proportion… of the total industrial capacity of the Company, with a clear acceleration in 2004, 2005 and 2006.[14]

Danone believed that the majority of the non-JVs founded by Zong and his family members were controlled by offshore companies. Since 1998, using the name of his 25-year-old daughter, Kelly (a US citizen), and close friends and associates, Zong had registered 10 offshore companies and invested in 28 of the non-JVs, controlling 15 of them. The most important non-JVs were fully controlled by Zong and his family. For example, Kelly was the legal representative of Ever Maple Trading Ltd (Ever Maple) registered in the British Virgin Islands.‡ Wahaha employees were also shareholders of these companies. In addition, 22 of the non-JVs had no state/employee-owned shares, one had only a few state-owned shares, and 16 had no more than 25 percent shares owned by employees.[15]

However, according to Zong, all of the products produced by the non-JVs were distributed by the sales company owned by the JVs, and this was

---

* For indicative purposes only, these were in the tens of millions of US dollars, according to the authors' field research.
† A co-packer is a company that manufactures and packages foods that other companies market and distribute. A co-packer works under contract to the hiring company to manufacture food as though the products were manufactured directly by the hiring company.
‡ Ever Maple invested in six non-JVs, including the Hangzhou Hongshen Beverage Co Ltd, which enjoyed the highest sales volume among non-JVs.

reflected in the JVs' monthly accounting statements. In addition, these companies were mainly set up in western China, the Three Gorges area or poor rural areas, where Danone was not willing to invest. In 2006, the total assets of the non-JVs was RMB5.6 billion (US$762 million) and the annual profits reached RMB1.04 billion (US$141 million). In addition, Danone had appointed PricewaterhouseCoopers (PwC) as external auditors to audit the JVs semi-annually from the beginning, including related companies and related-party transactions, such as the non-JV co-packers.

Negotiations to gain a share of the non-JVs

In the summer of 2006, a year after Emmanuel Faber, Danone's former CFO, had taken the helm of Danone Asia-Pacific, Danone claimed that it had concrete evidence through an internal investigation that Wahaha was in material breach of the JV agreements. Danone held the view that Zong had breached the joint venture agreement by setting up the "competing" non-JVs. However, Danone did not take immediate legal action; instead, it looked to solve the issue through negotiations.[16]

Because of concerns over Zong's full control—operational, financial and managerial—over the JVs and fears of potential disruption to the joint venture businesses, Danone had been trying to settle the case throughout 2006, "in an amicable manner."[17] On December 9, 2006, after months of negotiations, Riboud arrived in Hangzhou and signed a legal agreement with Zong. It provided for the integration of the non-JVs into the JVs, i.e. Danone would acquire a 51 percent stake in the non-JVs for RMB4 billion (US$544 million). In Danone's view:

> Taking the loss[es] of the JV's into consideration, this agreement was a great compromise made by Danone to its Chinese partner.[18]

However, the negotiations did not end there. According to Danone:

> The few days, weeks and months that followed that agreement basically showed that our partner had a different view of his level of satisfaction about the agreement and basically tried everything he could not to implement it.[19]

In January 2007, however, Zong sent a letter to Danone rejecting Danone's proposed acquisition. As Zong said:

> The situation was simple—the price offered by Danone is too low and we (the shareholders) have rejected it.[20]

Some days later, Kelly registered Hangzhou Wahaha Food and Beverage Marketing Co—a sales company for the non-JVs. Zong's wife was a director.

All settlement negotiations with Zong having failed, Danone then decided to carry out a full-scale investigation and analysis.

The public saga

Intense public debate and the start of the legal dispute

On April 3, 2007, an article entitled "Wahaha Victim of Low-ball Buyout by Danone,"[21] published on the website of a government press agency, Xinhua, claimed that the shareholders had rejected Danone's attempt at a "hostile takeover" of Wahaha. The article was written by a journalist who would help Zong place the article in the so-called Internal Reference* in the hopes of influencing political leaders on Wahaha's fate.[22] The article immediately generated heated public debate, including a letter from Ye Hongyan—chairman of the Jianlibao Group†—voicing his support for Zong:

> I noticed that Mr. Zong protected a national brand and fought against the monopoly of the Chinese beverage industry by multinationals. At the same time, he actively proposed legislation to restrict foreigners from acquiring national brands. I fully support him.[23]

Even to Zong, the article came as a surprise. Zong's original plan was to print the article in the Internal Reference but he was surprised that the article went to the mass media instead. Zong took immediate action to withdraw the article from some of the related web pages. Two days later, Danone held a press conference in Shanghai saying that its proposed acquisition of 51 percent of the non-JVs complied with relevant laws and regulations in China. In the following days, Zong changed his mind, and all the web pages that had been removed were re-posted in the sina.com‡ web chatroom on April 8, 2007.

Zong said:

> Because of my ignorance of the importance of trademark and brand, the development of Wahaha fell into a trap elaborately designed by Danone. Also, due to my ignorance and neglect of duty, the growth of the Wahaha brand has been affected and blocked. Now, if I don't take measures to remedy this, I will betray Wahaha and my country.

> If Danone succeeds, then the Chinese parties will lose management control of Wahaha.[24]

---

* An "Internal Reference" is a publication that only high-ranking Chinese government officials are able to access.
† A leading food and beverage company in China, which had become a known brand after the famous gymnast Li Ning joined the company upon his retirement from sport.
‡ One of the three most popular websites in China.

On April 4, 2007, the Danone-designated directors called a board meeting in Hangzhou. The relationship between Zong and Danone, however, deteriorated rapidly and the dispute became public. On April 10, Danone issued a statement implying that Zong was in breach of his agreement with Danone by setting up businesses with other partners with the right to use the Wahaha brand. Danone accused Zong of selling identical products using the brand outside of the JVs, and demanded a 51 percent stake in these.[25] It even sent a warning letter to Zong (as chairman of the companies), giving 30 days for the non-JVs to stop illegally selling products that used the Wahaha trademark without proper authorization.[26]

Zong said that Faber had personally authorized the setting up of the units that were beyond the scope of the JVs.[27] Danone conceded that in or around 2003, it had allowed Zong to become a minority partner in businesses that made Wahaha products outside their joint venture structure because local governments often preferred to have Zong as a partner. By 2005, Danone realized Zong controlled as many as 20 external businesses making drinks and claimed that these represented approximately 25 percent of Wahaha products.[28] Danone estimated that Zong had established more than 80 unauthorized companies using the Wahaha brand name between 2001 and 2006.[29]

Zong set up externally owned factories to produce products identical to Wahaha's, and Danone alleged that dealers/distributors were asked to set up new bank accounts for their deposit payments in the name of Hangzhou Wahaha Food and Beverage Marketing Co. to enable them to buy products from these factories.[30]

In the time after the dispute erupted, many distributors and employees had come out in support of Zong, calling for a boycott of Danone and even of the joint venture products.[31] On June 8, 2007, Wahaha distributors filed an open letter on sina.com, thundering:

> Starting from today, we refuse to distribute anything from Danone so as to let Danone's product fade out from the Chinese market.[32]

Danone takes legal action

While Danone set itself to seek "justice" against Wahaha and Zong in the international arena, Wahaha engaged Danone on multiple fronts at a local level. Political leaders from both countries called for an amicable solution to the dispute.[33]

In accordance with the joint venture agreement, Danone filed a case for arbitration in Stockholm on May 9, 2007 that contained eight claims, the most important of which alleged the breach of the noncompete clause. On June 4, 2007, based on the "long-arm jurisdiction"* statue under US law,

---

* Long-arm jurisdiction is a statutory grant of jurisdiction to local courts over foreign defendants under the United States jurisprudence.

Danone filed suit in the Los Angeles superior court for damages of US$100 million against Ever Maple and Hongsheng, as well as Zong's wife and daughter, who ran the two companies. Ever Maple was the controlling shareholder of Hongsheng, which was the parent company of the sales company for the non-Danone JVs.

Zong resigned as chairman of the JVs the following day.

On June 8, Zong sent an open letter to Riboud, saying:

> It was very hard to work with people who do not understand the Chinese market and culture ... They only want to take the profits and benefits instead of taking on risks and carrying out their responsibilities. Therefore, I decided to resign from the joint venture companies ...[34]

Zong also accused Danone of "resorting to personal attacks when its buy-out attempt failed" by "hiring private detectives to keep him under round-the-clock surveillance." He wrote at the end of the letter,

> See you in Stockholm.[35]

Danone responded in a media statement on June 12 by welcoming Zong's "recognition of the validity of the Stockholm arbitration procedure." However, it also said,

> Other than that, the facts stated in his letter are incomplete, twisted, out of context or simply untrue.

Wahaha challenged Danone as to whether the JVs had ownership of the Wahaha brand. It made an application to the Hangzhou Arbitration Committee for arbitration of the dispute with Danone over the trademark; the application was accepted on June 17. Over the two months from April 6 to June 11, Danone's share price dropped by 9 percent.

On July 31, Danone announced that it was promoting Faber to be the Group's co-chief operating officer in addition to his current role as executive vice president for the Asia-Pacific area.

On August 31, Hangzhou Wahaha Food Company Limited (WFCL)—the leading JV company—sued the State Trademark Bureau (STB) over what it claimed had been "improper administrative behavior" in 1996 and 1997. However, the case was withdrawn the following day as STB filed a defense outlining that it had never received a formal application from Wahaha requesting the transfer of the Wahaha trademarks to the JVs. Therefore, there was no dispute over which to litigate, as STB had never had the chance to take any administrative action.

With the aim of preventing Wahaha from transferring any assets to foreign countries during the legal process, Danone filed substantive actions, based on various tort* theories, against ten entities it believed to be linked to Wahaha in Samoa and the British Virgin Islands (BVI). The BVI high court placed eight companies registered there into receivership and froze their assets on November 9, 2007; the supreme court of Samoa issued a similar order for two entities on November 22. The international auditing firm, KPMG, was appointed as receiver for each of the BVI companies and another receiver was appointed for the two Samoan entities. Under the court orders, the receiver's primary role would be to identify, locate and secure the assets of these ten Wahaha-linked companies.

On November 10, the Hangzhou Arbitration Committee ruled that Danone had failed to file a lawsuit within a reasonable time† to settle the dispute over the trademark transfer. The Wahaha labor union, citing fears of some 300 job losses, also joined the legal fight against Danone. The union accused Danone of holding shares in companies that competed with the 39 Danone–Wahaha JVs.

On December 18, partly due to the dispute, Danone announced the "automatic termination"[36] of an agreed joint venture partnership with Mengniu Dairy Group (Mengniu) because some of the conditions and pre-requisites were not met within the agreed timeframe.

The increasingly bitter public dispute cast doubts on the fate of what was once a showcase joint venture partnership. The antagonism between Danone and Wahaha led to legal fights in the courts, prompting the Chinese and French presidents to call on both companies to resume "peace talks" and find an amicable solution (the dispute was on the agenda of French President Sarkozy's official trip to China from November 26 to 28). On December 21, under political pressure from their respective governments, Danone and Wahaha agreed to suspend their legal battle and resume negotiations, as set out in a joint statement:

> Complying with the expectation of both Chinese and French governments, both Wahaha Group and Groupe Danone agree to finish antagonism and return to peace talks. Both parties agree to temporarily suspend all lawsuits and arbitrations, stop all aggressive and hostile statements and create a friendly environment for peace talks.

> Both parties agree to carry out the talks on the basis of adhering to the principles of equality and mutual benefits, to seek common grounds by tolerating minor differences, to reach mutual understandings and to strive for the success of peace talks. Both parties will work together to further develop all entities operating under the Wahaha brands and contribute to develop Sino-French friendship and promote co-operation between the companies of the two countries.[37]

---

* Tort: a civil wrong, or wrongful act, whether intentional or accidental, by which injury occurs to another. Torts include all types of negligence cases as well as intentional wrongs that result in harm.
† The time limit for beginning an action based upon a contract dispute was two years in China.

It was easier said than done. If both parties had worked with the principles from day one, perhaps their match would never have been troubled. The real question was how would the two parties proceed from here?

The announcement came as the first sign of a truce. Danone had "signaled its willingness to end hostilities and try to bring Wahaha back to the negotiating table after losing several court rulings in China and facing pressure from the joint venture's [labor] union."[38]

According to a Société Générale report[39] before the joint announcement on December 21, 2007, Danone had proposed several different solutions to the Chinese government, including:

1. a merger with a competitor;
2. an IPO (of either the current group or a new group created after a merger);
3. an unchanged organization, but with a government representative alongside Zong;
4. a financial stake for Danone.

Société Générale believed that:

> Danone would like to improve operations at its subsidiary [the JV] before selling it in order to obtain the best price. Wahaha's book value is around €300 million. Danone is thus hoping to be able to announce a solution at Wahaha in the coming weeks. If there is not a quick solution, the group is expected to focus on its Chinese development in the fresh dairy sector from Shanghai where it would be operating on its own.[40]

Even though both Danone and Wahaha had agreed to return to peace talks, an imminent solution seemed less probable. Unsurprisingly, the ensuing back-and-forth negotiations were anything but smooth.

On March 9, 2008, Wahaha rejected proposals put forward by Danone that the two companies merge the JVs and non-JVs to form a new company that would list on the Chinese stock market. Danone and Wahaha would hold 40 percent each, leaving the remaining 20 percent as public shares. Danone wanted to ensure its stake was worth RMB50 billion (US$6.9 billion) in market value if its shares in the new company were less than 40 percent.[41]

In April 2008, Zong was being investigated for alleged tax evasion of up to RMB300 million (US$43 million).* He accused Danone and Qin Peng, the head of Danone's China business, of being connected to the probe because their negotiations had failed. Danone denied the accusation.[42]

On June 23, 2008, it was revealed that Zong and his wife were holders of United States Permanent Residence Cards—Green Cards—and had been

---

* Before the case could be formally filed, Zong quickly paid more than RMB200 million in overdue taxes to the relevant authorities, thus ending all inquiries into the matter. Source: authors' field interviews.

since 1999. This generated public controversy, partly because Zong was a representative to the Chinese National Congress.

On June 30, 2008, Wahaha Shenyang won its suit against Danone executive Qin Peng, who was fined RMB400,000 (US$57,000) for serving as director and senior executive of rival companies. This was the second case that the Danone executive had lost, with one more still pending.

On July 11, a panel from the Arbitration Institute of the Stockholm Chamber of Commerce rejected Danone's plea for interim measures to restrict Wahaha from forming new companies outside of their JVs and from increasing the production capacity of other units making products under the Wahaha brand. A final decision was yet to be given regarding the disputes in the original filing.

On July 30, the Hangzhou Intermediate People's court rejected Danone's appeal against Wahaha's use of the Wahaha trademark. Danone said that it would continue its fight in the higher courts.

Danone was asking Wahaha to pay a price for its shares ranging from RMB17.6 billion to RMB20.9 billion (US$2.5 billion to US$3 billion), whereas an independent appraisal (by an evaluation company hired by Wahaha) was between RMB2.3 billion and RMB3.2 billion (US$330 million and US$460 million).

The dispute had led to at least 25 lawsuits and legal proceedings in five countries.[43]

While Danone and Wahaha were still battling on a legal front across several continents, uncertainties remained about how the situation would play out eventually and where the joint venture partnership was headed. One thing was certain—the possibility of Danone remaining part of the JVs would be very low. The real question was how Danone would eventually exit, and at what cost.

The settlement

With "the support of both the Chinese and French governments," on September 30, 2009, one day before the 60th anniversary of the People's Republic of China, Danone finally reached an "amicable settlement" that it would sell its 51 percent share in its JVs to its Chinese partner, ending a decade-long joint venture partnership. Zong said in the announcement:

> China is an open country. Chinese people are broad-minded people. Chinese companies are willing to cooperate and grow with the world's leading peers on the basis of equality and reciprocal benefit.[44]

No financial terms were disclosed, but China's *Caijin Magazine* reported that Danone sold its 51 percent stake in the JVs back to Wahaha for €300 million (US$438 million), which was close to Wahaha's offer, but far less than the amount initially sought by Danone.[45] For years, Danone had been enjoying billions in sales through its China venture with Wahaha, which accounted for about 10 percent of its global revenue in 2006. The decision to pull out had left Danone with a much smaller footprint in China despite its "longstanding commitment" to China.

The settlement also put an end to all legal proceedings related to the disputes between the two parties.

5 A Controversial Acquisition

During the public dispute, Danone claimed that Wahaha had breached its noncompete obligation in the joint venture agreement. Yet, as Zong and Wahaha employees pointed out on different occasions, Danone formed partnerships with other major industry leaders in China, including the acquisition of Wahaha's closest competitor Robust despite strong objections from Wahaha. The fierce price war waged by Robust in the purified water business following the takeover almost wiped out margins, hurting both companies financially. According to Danone, however, Zong was personally involved in their acquisition of Robust, and he had received "handsome" compensation (reportedly over US$1 million by means of share buyback from an overseas subsidiary[1]) from Danone for the "services" that he provided.

The verbal battle had certainly piqued the interest of the Chinese media and the public in finding out more about what had happened behind the scenes. They started tracking and mapping out the history of Danone's China expansion, or "invasion." The story behind Danone's acquisition of Robust began to emerge.

For Danone, the Robust acquisition was a defensive move—to prevent it from being bought by a competitor. This was evident in the timing, in the way Danone approached Robust and in the way the subsequent negotiation process went. In order to gain access to Robust, Danone promised and, indeed, did bypass its team in China to ease the concerns of He Boquan (cofounder and president of Robust) about commercially sensitive information being exposed to its direct competitor—Wahaha.

Wahaha and Robust were initially two companies in the same league. Robust was at one time a leading beverage brand, second only to Wahaha in China. However, since the acquisition, Robust had been on a downward trend and the brand was gradually fading from the public eye. Only a year or so after the acquisition, the cofounders exited the company (even though they had kept management control) citing differences with Danone over the management philosophy and strategic direction of the company. The general view of the media and the Chinese public, including some Wahaha employees, was that the decline was mainly due to Danone's mismanagement of Robust after taking over the company. This tied in with Danone's claim later on that they had actually made some mistakes in using the wrong people. A series of scandals surrounding the acquisition were also revealed, especially Danone's collusion with Robust's former president, He Boquan,* and allegations of tax evasion surrounding the transaction.

In this chapter, we explore what had happened and just what Zong's role was in Danone's acquisition of Robust.

Robust† and He Boquan

Born of the soil of entrepreneurship

In 1989, the same year that Wahaha launched its first product—Wahaha Oral Liquid for Children, He Boquan and four cofounders (mainly friends and relatives) started Robust, which later became Wahaha's strongest competitor, in their hometown of Xiaolan‡ in Zhongshan County, Guangdong Province.

By and large, Robust (formerly known as the Zhongshan Robust Health Products Company or the Guangdong Nowada Group§) was a direct beneficiary of the local government's pro-business attitude and its support in promoting entrepreneurship. More importantly, it also benefited from the rapid growth of the Chinese economy. With an initial capital injection of RMB950,000 (US$115,000) from the town government** and a license to the Robust brand from Guangdong Provincial Health Products Company (a company that produced a health tonic that did not taste good), the cofounders embarked on an adventure in the Chinese beverage industry.

Robust in the making ...

He Boquan, born in 1960, dropped out of school at the age of 15 but later graduated from the China Central Radio and TV University with a major in management. Prior to 1988, He worked for a local pharmaceutical company and headed a government youth organization. His pharmaceutical background and concern for China's youth led him to consider health products for children. He discovered that of the hundreds of nutritional products that

---

* He had been the president of Robust until November 2001.
† The Chinese name of "Robust" is *Lebaishi* in Chinese, meaning "delighting the people."
‡ Xiaolan Township is on the periphery of Zhongshan, Guangdong Province (Guangdong). With a population of more than 110 million, Guangdong is the most populous province in China and home to Guangzhou and Shenzhen. It has been known for its relatively liberal government policies since the late 1980s, when China first opened up. It has also benefited from its geographic proximity to Hong Kong and Macau.
§ In October 1992, the company was renamed Guangdong Nowada Group (the Chinese name *jinri jituan* means the Today Group). Nowada was chosen because the word "Nowaday" could not be trademarked.
** The cofounders took a 55 percent majority stake in the company, while the government took a minority stake of 45 percent.

were on the market for children, few were actually nutritious. Based on his analysis, he concluded that what was needed was a health tonic that was not only good for children but also tasted good.

In a rented 10-square-meter office, the company launched its first product—lactic acid milk,* which combined the Robust health tonic with powdered milk and other ingredients. It was hard going during the first few years, as the company had limited resources for advertising. However, the cofounders did not give up. Instead, they were forced to be innovative and use whatever means were available; these included going around pasting the company's handmade posters all over the township.

After the first year, the company expanded from its home base of Guangdong province into two neighboring provinces in southern China, and by late 1991, it had expanded into all provinces south of the Yangtze, including large cities such as Shanghai and Nanjing. By 1992, the company's lactic acid milk had become a nationwide hit. From 1993 to 1997, it was number one in sales in its category and the company had grown to more 4,000 employees with various subsidiaries.

In 1997, Robust bought the Robust brand from the Guangdong Provincial Health Product Company for RMB100 million (about US$12 million) and finally owned the trademark. The company's product portfolio also expanded from lactic acid milk to other milk products, including UHT pasteurized† milk, Vitamins A and D and calcium-enriched milk, sweet milk, fruit-flavored milk and "Student Milk,"‡ bottled water (mineral, purified and distilled) in 1996, fruit-flavored jellies§ targeted at children in 1997, and tea beverages in 1998.

In just ten years, He took Robust to become second only to Wahaha in China. He was also renowned as one of the top ten entrepreneurs in China under the age of 40. The company was honored with a number of national government department and industry group awards, such as the All-China Branded Food Products Award, Star of the Chinese Health Products Industry, Exemplary Chinese Brand and China's Most Competitive Domestic Brand.

Dare to be innovative

Compared with a traditional state-owned enterprise, Robust was young and flexible in the way it was managed and was especially known for its daring

---

* A "health-oriented milk product" made from milk powder, added vitamins, calcium, flavoring and a nutritional formula derived from animal products.
† UHT (ultra-high temperature) pasteurization enables milk to last in its package for six months without refrigeration.
‡ A product with nutritional additives such as DHA and vitamins, based on a formula created by the National Commission on Student Nutrition.
§ With added nutritional elements, the candy-like jellies were sold in small, thimble-shaped plastic containers.

and ability to innovate. It had pioneered a few business practices that were still relatively new to the Chinese business community.

It was among the first of many private companies in China that started on-campus recruitment of employees with higher education. The "Nowada" name of the company was actually coined by students at Peking University in 1992.

In 1994, Robust spent RMB10 million to acquire the formula for "Ener-G" health tonic, which had been developed by the famous Chinese track and field coach Ma Junren.* At the time, it was the largest intellectual property transaction between an individual and an enterprise in Chinese history.

In 1998, Robust became a pioneer among Chinese private companies when it engaged Mckinsey & Company (Mckinsey) for a strategy review, spending about RMB12 million (about US$1.5 million) on the consulting firm's services.

In August 1999, Robust relocated its headquarters from Zhongshan to Guangzhou. Two months later the group formally changed its name to Robust.

Robust was essentially led by a team of five, dubbed the "four dragons and one phoenix" within business circles. The cofounders were close to one another, had clearly segregated roles and responsibilities and worked well together as a team. Like Wahaha, Robust had also created a family atmosphere. The difference, perhaps due to the founders' ages and management style, was that Robust employees felt that He and his cofounders were more like brothers and sisters, while Zong was regarded as the head of the Wahaha family.

Preludes to an acquisition

An inviting target for investment

Robust's products were trusted for their value-for-money, quality and consistency. Its strong presence in the low-price, mass-market segment, especially in urban areas, as well as its strong brand recognition with Chinese consumers made it an inviting target for investments.

Back in 1994, Goldman Sachs, for instance, had already approached He and offered RMB70–80 million (approximately US$10 million) for a 30 percent stake. A year later, Nestlé became the first multinational player in the industry to knock on He's door. Many other leading international financial investors and industry players followed. Despite all the proposals or offers, He was not tempted, as he had no intention of selling the company.

---

* Ma trained several world-class middle- and long-distance female runners in China.

Contemplating discussions with potential investors

Selling the company—how could it ever be an option? Like many other Chinese entrepreneurs of his generation, He and his cofounders had built the company from the ground up. It was their baby, and it was still at the very early stages of its success. Besides, the company did not need additional capital, so He had no reason to sell. Even if he were to consider selling the company, He preferred to find good "in-laws" for the company, someone with capital, management know-how and innovation. In He's view, this would rule out financial investors, since they would only be interested in reselling the company for a higher price at a later date.

Nestlé seemed an interesting possibility. However, He was reluctant to consider its offer for two main reasons: Nestlé had demanded at least a 51 percent stake in the company; He knew that Wahaha was in discussions with Danone and had the patience to wait for the outcome so that he might be able to use it as a benchmark to secure a better deal.

Nevertheless, He was smart and did not close the door on discussions immediately. After all, it would be a learning experience for him and his team to go through the exercise with potential investors and get a sense of how much the company was worth. It was, in fact, during the back-and-forth discussions with Nestlé that He figured that it was only a matter of time and price before he would give in on the ownership control—something that Nestlé seemed really care about. However, as soon as he discovered that Nestlé's China business was still experiencing losses, he became hesitant— he was not sure how Robust would be treated if it were in Nestlé's hands. Besides, He was certain that there would come a point when multinationals would be willing to pay even more than they were currently.

He remained open-minded, and neither Goldman Sachs nor Nestlé gave up their pursuit. They kept in regular contact with He and persistently tried to persuade him to sell part of the company.

While He was contemplating discussions with potential investors, news broke that Wahaha had made a first move by forming a joint venture partnership with Danone, bringing in not only US$45 million in real money but also management knowhow and advanced technologies.

Obstacles to future growth

Against this background, in terms of day-to-day operations, however, it was not all plain sailing. Robust had made a series of wrong moves that resulted in bottlenecks to its future growth.

Over-expansion compounded by market downturns: the jellies were essentially a straight copy of a competitor's product.* As already mentioned,

---

* Jellies were copied from Xizhilang, a leading local company, which originated jellies in 1992.

He quickly introduced a Robust brand of jellies in August 1997. The market rose sharply in early 1998, which proved that his initial intuition was correct. To seize the opportunity, Robust quickly installed several more production lines for jellies. However, the market collapsed, at around the time that Robust's production lines came into full operation. As a result, Robust incurred losses of several hundred million renminbi on capital investments. In 1998, the health tonic market also took a downward turn and the production of Ener-G was put on hold.

Inappropriate choice of advertising media: Robust had spent more than RMB300 million in advertising on CCTV (China Central Television). Despite CCTV's strong influence across the country, the results of the advertisements were disappointing for two reasons: (1) consumers from Guangdong (Robust's home market) did not normally watch CCTV; (2) Robust did not capture areas where CCTV had a strong influence, especially in the massive rural markets where there was real potential for growth.

Wrong market focus: Instead of focusing on its home market of Guangdong, Robust had ventured into markets further afield in China. Compared to Wahaha, which had more than 10 percent of its revenue coming from its home market of Zhejiang, the percentage of sales coming from Guangdong for Robust was almost negligible.

Missing the boat on new product development: Robust had missed the right timing for launching carbonated beverages even though it had planned to launch them for some time (the company even had chosen a name for its cola product). However, Robust eventually chose tea beverages over carbonated beverages, whereas Wahaha successfully launched Future Cola in 1998. The tea beverages did not take off because the market was not ready, and it was too costly to promote the products and educate the market. Also, the organizational structure had become a barrier, as employees were not motivated or given sufficient incentives to promote new products.

Capital constraints: Robust had financed its growth with debt. Eventually, it encountered capital constraints on financing for future growth to keep the debt/equity ratio at a healthy level.

Lack of skilled labor: Even though Robust was proud of its highly educated labor force—about 1,000 of its 4,000-plus employees were college- or high-school-educated or technical specialists—it lacked skilled labor with proper management training, especially in marketing and finance.

Growth, therefore, had slowed down significantly by 1998. Except for bottled water, the growth of all other product categories had experienced huge setbacks resulting from changes in the market situation as well as Robust's own constraints. Revenue growth slipped to 33.3 percent in 1998, down from 85.3 percent the previous year. In contrast, Wahaha had maintained a growth rate of several times that of Robust, and the gap between the two companies had further widened. He therefore, felt not only the increasing competitive pressure but also the rising capital constraints and other bottlenecks to the company's future growth.

The Mckinsey diagnosis

Despite all the setbacks and constraints, He and his management team remained confident and planned to turn Robust into the number-one health beverage producer in China within five years. Robust needed a strategic breakthrough.

In 1998, Robust engaged McKinsey to review its market position and formulate strategies for its future growth. The McKinsey study pointed to an influx of foreign competition in China and concluded that, unless Robust expanded into new product categories, improved its management skills, and secured additional capital, the company risked being marginalized in China.

McKinsey mapped out the following competitive landscape for Robust:

▷ **National:** Except for Wahaha, Robust had few strong competitors at the national level.
▷ **Local:** Robust faced intense competition at the local level—generally from smaller local players, such as smaller town and village enterprises (TVEs) (Robust was a TVE itself). Although these small local players lacked sufficient capital or management skills to support national expansion, they had good connections and reputations within their own territory.
▷ **Foreign:** Foreign competitors with deep pockets had begun to enter China and were a great threat because of their strong marketing, financial and management skills. Consumer goods was one of the most deregulated industries in China, so it was a relatively level playing field for foreign competitors as they could both set up joint ventures and operate fully owned subsidiaries.

McKinsey also identified the need for Robust to move away from its "follower's strategy" to become a brand leader with its own new product development capabilities, since expanding into new product categories would be essential for its future growth. The capital constraints would have to be overcome.

The consultants concluded that Robust needed to develop world-class best practices to avoid being pushed aside like some of its smaller, local competitors. Foreign companies were rapidly building skills and brands for China, while consumers were becoming more demanding and quality-conscious. In addition, its main local competitor—Wahaha—was beginning to upgrade its skills. For instance, Wahaha had diversified its portfolio from health beverages by launching its first non-health beverage—Future Cola—thereby competing head-to-head with strong foreign contenders, such as Coca-Cola and Pepsi.

The interaction with McKinsey was informative and educational. He learned that there was nothing right or wrong about selling the company.

He also learned that the more control he gave up, the higher the price he would get in exchange. His decision to sell part of the company gradually became firm.

McKinsey was then mandated to help He identify a suitable buyer. After a careful and thorough review of the industry, screening of major industry players and a comparison of recent transactions, McKinsey recommended that Nestlé would be the best suitor. Even though He personally favored Danone in spite of its joint venture partnership with Wahaha, he followed McKinsey's advice and resumed negotiations with Nestlé.

Shortly after in July 1999, Nestlé signed a letter of intent with Robust for a possible joint venture in which Nestlé would have at least a 60 percent interest. It then entered into a three-month exclusive negotiation with Robust to complete its final round of due diligence. Two months later, in or around September 1999, Danone found out about Nestlé's discussions with Robust and came forward with a higher bid.

Acquisition at last

Although Wahaha had gained the "first-mover" advantage by bringing in foreign capital, He's hesitation (or patience) eventually paid off by attracting the highest bid ever. Danone with a 51 percent share in the largest beverage company in China, had been enjoying the rapid growth of the Chinese beverage industry through its Wahaha JVs. For some reason Robust had never appeared on Danone's radar screen, even though it had been highly sought after by other investors. In Danone's view, Robust on its own was not a concern. However, the situation would be different if it were to be acquired by a major competitor such as Nestlé. Obviously, Danone did not want to see this happen and had to take action.

Once Danone found out that Nestlé was in negotiation with Robust, it approached He directly through its regional headquarters in Singapore. This was done deliberately to ease He's concerns about the possible leak of commercially sensitive information to Danone China or Wahaha. To gain He's trust, Danone further promised that the discussion would be strictly with Danone's headquarters in Paris and/or with its regional headquarters in Singapore. Neither Danone China nor Wahaha would be involved in the discussion. In addition, Danone also indicated that it was willing to take a minority stake and was willing to exclude Ener-G from the deal.

All of this sounded appealing to He, not only because Danone was initially his preferred choice as an investor, but also because he knew that Danone would value Robust more than Nestlé, given its existing joint venture partnership with Wahaha. Besides, He had nothing to lose and would be free to discuss with Danone in a month's time when the exclusivity agreement with Nestlé expired. He formally declined the RMB1.5 billion offer from Nestlé and, shortly afterwards, started negotiations with Danone's Asia-Pacific headquarters in Singapore.

From the outset, Robust seemed to be the one dominating the negotiation process. With annual profits for the past three years of RMB110 million (1998), RMB130 million (1999) and RMB160 million (2000 projection), He gave progressive quotations proportionate to the control he would relinquish: RMB1.2 billion for a 49 percent stake, RMB1.6 billion for a 51 percent, RMB1.9 billion for a 70 percent or RMB2.3 billion for a 92 percent. Danone's starting position was to acquire 100 percent of the company. However, this was not acceptable to He, since his "emotional attachment to the company was priceless." Danone then made a counter-offer of RMB0.5billion for 92 percent of the company. Whether it what Danone thought the company was worth or merely a negotiation tactic, it did not work. Not only was it far from He's expectations, but he also knew how much other potential buyers were willing to offer based on his previous negotiations. He then laid down the rules for negotiations stating that the starting point should be Robust's quoted price.

Unlike the discussions with Nestlé, the back-and-forth negotiations with Danone focused on price. Danone also indicated its willingness to give up management control of the company. A few months later, after several rounds of negotiations, the two parties agreed that Danone would acquire 92 percent of Robust for RMB2.3 billion. The deal excluded the ownership of the Robust brand trademark, which alone was thought to be worth around RMB2 billion at the time, and Ener-G, while the cofounders kept management control of the company. Due to differences over performance projections for 2000, the cofounders agreed that RMB0.3 billion would be held back as a guarantee that Robust would meet certain performance targets in 2000. If the targets were not met, Robust would not receive the money that had been held back. In the end, the cofounders not only received the RMB0.3 billion in full but also an additional bonus of RMB80 million. In total, Danone paid RMB2.38 billion for 92 percent of Robust, which was 50 percent more than Nestlé's offer and more than four times Danone's original offer.

Post-acquisition

Post-acquisition integration and reorganization

Since its inception, Robust had maintained a centralized structure based on the main functional areas (such as manufacturing, logistics, marketing, distribution and regional sales companies), under the direct management of the cofounders. The cofounders and employees had worked together to create the company culture. This contributed to the initial success of the company. However, as the organization grew, the downside of the system was gradually exposed, especially after Danone acquired a 92 percent stake in the company. For instance, it was not clear who was responsible for profitability. The manufacturing department was only responsible for costs and quality, while sales was responsible for revenues and expenses. In reality, nobody was responsible for profitability except for He. In addition, in order to achieve sales targets, regional sales companies tended to focus more on the company's bestselling products, such as water and lactic acid milk, instead of promoting new products, such as tea beverages.

In a move to change the situation and dilute the power of He and his cofounders, in August 2001, Danone initiated its first reorganization, despite the agreement that He and his team would retain management control. He remained as the president of the company, and three-quarters of the employees changed positions, including He's four cofounders. Under the new structure, there were five business units, eight functional departments, and one sales company under He. The five business units were five separate profit centers, namely bottled water, milk, lactic acid milk, packaged water and tea beverages. Thus, Robust's management team was enlarged from the initial five people to fifteen.

A few months after the reorganization, in November 2001, He* and his cofounders left the company suddenly, citing differences with Danone over the strategic direction and management philosophy. Danone's China president, Qin Peng, took over Robust.

In March 2002, with Qin at the helm, Danone conducted its second reorganization of Robust. This time, the business-unit-based structure was converted to an area-based structure. The company was reorganized into five geographic areas, namely southwest, central south (central China and southern China), eastern China, northeast and northern China with the intention of better utilizing the manufacturing and sales resources and further leveraging Robust's strong distribution network for other Danone family products (including non-Robust products). Under this structure, each area could react to the market more swiftly and in a more flexible manner.

In March 2003, Danone appointed Zhang Jiwen, a former Pepsi executive, and a Hong Kong citizen, to head Robust. In September 2005, Zhang was replaced due to his mismanagement of the company. During Zhang's short tenure, many Robust employees left the company. Again, Qin took over as president. After March 2006, when Qin's focus gradually shifted to Danone's strategic acquisitions in China, the company was effectively run by the vice president.

In September 2006, for the first time since the acquisition, Danone sent a French executive to take over the presidency of Robust while remaining as head of Danone's regional beverage business. A third round of reorganization started the day the new head was appointed, which resulted in at least one-third of the employees being let go. By this time, there were only a few employees left from the old days at Robust.

---

* He became an angel investor after leaving Robust, splitting his time between investing in companies and pursuing his hobby—photography. He is founder and chairman of Guangdong Nowaday Investment Co., Ltd. and 7 Days Group Holdings Limited, cofounder and director of Noah Holdings Limited, and was vice chairman and director of Beijing Ikang Guobin Co., Ltd.

Mission impossible—aligning the Chinese "Coca-Cola and Pepsi"

The competition between Wahaha and Robust was akin to that of Coca-Cola and Pepsi, but now both companies were controlled by Danone. Through the acquisition of Robust, Danone had further strengthened its number one position in the bottled water and dairy beverages industries in China. The combined Wahaha and Robust businesses had enabled Danone to hold nearly 50 percent of the Chinese market for bottled water. In addition, Robust was particularly well established in urban areas.

As the market grew and matured, the water business went through a period of consolidation in 2001. The post-acquisition performance did not live up to expectations, mainly due to difficulties in developing a group strategy for Robust and Wahaha and aligning the two companies. For instance, Danone had attempted to coordinate two price increases with Robust and Wahaha on their purified water products in May 2000 and 2001, respectively. Both attempts failed because Wahaha decided not to pursue the agreed price increases at the last minute. The existing balance between Wahaha and Robust was disrupted and Wahaha was able to win over some of Robust's distributors when Robust went ahead with the price increase as agreed. Danone's attempts failed mainly due to Zong's unwillingness to cooperate. Consequently, Danone failed in its attempt to increase its pricing power in the water industry by trying to align the top two players in the industry. The problems increased and the two companies even entered into a price war.

Still, the company enjoyed some brief successes because of Danone's strong financial backing and marketing know-how. In 2003, Robust launched Maidong (Mizone in English), an innovative energy drink for sports enthusiasts created by Frucor,* a New Zealand-based beverage company that Danone acquired in 2002. The product was specifically adapted for the Chinese market and soon became a nationwide hit, taking the top spot in the energy-drink segment and earning the title of China's beverage of the year. Despite this success, the post-acquisition performance was far from satisfactory.

---

* Frucor had the number one market share position in the Asia Pacific region for energy drinks.

6 A Chinese Perspective

Four years before Danone inked its joint venture agreement with Wahaha, it had already formed a joint venture with Shanghai Bright Dairy & Food Co., Ltd (Bright Dairy).* Bright Dairy was once a leading Chinese company that was initially state-owned and then partially publicly listed.

A 15-year cross-border love affair

From 1992 to 2008, Madam Wang Jiafen, a professional woman who did not have any stake in it, managed the company. Over the years, Danone's partnership with Bright Dairy had evolved and taken different forms. It started out as joint venture partnerships, then it took more than 10 years for Danone to gain a small shareholding in the company, until eventually Danone gained further ownership and management control, and finally it exited from the partnership and went on cooperating with Bright Dairy's direct competition.

Wang played a key role in making the cooperation happen. Back in the early 1990s, the question of how to attract foreign capital was still a sensitive "political topic."[1] But, Wang embraced the idea of foreign cooperation because she saw it as an opportunity to learn from foreign partners and then surpass them. Further, through the cooperation, Danone also opened a whole new world to Wang. However, Wang's attitude towards Danone had shifted over time.

> Wang had strong feelings about Danone's desire [to increase its equity interests in Bright Dairy]. Initially she embraced Danone, later she became cautious, suspicious and worried.[2]

Despite all the obstacles, problems and issues, the first few years (at least between 1992 and 1995) of cooperation between the two companies had turned out to be a success. In Wang's own reflection, she described it as a "cross-border love affair" and the initial period of success as the "sweet honeymoon."

> On cooperation with foreign companies, I'm a firm supporter and doer. Since day one, I have positioned it as a process of cooperating, learning and surpassing. The 15-year cross-border love affairs between Bright Dairy and Danone have also been a unique journey to the success of Bright Dairy.[3]

---

* "Bright" (*guangmin* in Chinese) was a recognized brand of the Shanghai Milk Group in the Shanghai area, and it was often associated with quality. For simplification, "Bright Dairy" has been used throughout the book instead of Shanghai Milk Group.

Wang also placed trust in Old Riboud and He Yi—Danone's first designated general manager of their joint venture. However, the situation changed around the time that Old Riboud retired and there was an internal shakeup at Danone. Subsequently, Danone had started more aggressively pursuing its goal of owning and gaining control of Bright Dairy. And to make things worse, Danone had openly displayed distrust of Wang and her management team. On several occasions Danone had expressed, to Wang or to major shareholders of Bright Dairy, its view that it could manage the company better than Wang and her management team.

Standing next to global giants

To understand how to work better with your partners, you need to understand where your partners come from, who they are, and what they expect to get out of the partnership and from you.

Before Bright Dairy's cooperation with Danone, Wang had had little experience in dealing with multinationals. For Wang, a visit to Danone's headquarters in France and a glimpse of how a world-class company worked, was an eye-opening experience. Despite the equal ownership, Bright Dairy agreed that the joint venture be operated by Danone in order to gain management knowhow and increase the venture's profitability.

Wang also understood the importance of not seeking to reinvent the wheel and tried to learn from foreign partners where possible, including suppliers, distributors, partners and customers. "Aiming higher" had been the motto of Bright Dairy, and the company was set to fly higher. With such an open mindset, Bright Dairy had not only worked with many foreign companies but also learned how to manage them. All these had contributed to Wang's belief of "gaining a global vision" by "standing next to global giants."[4]

As a Communist Party member and a professional manager of a then state-owned company, Wang believed that it was her duty to safeguard the interest of state-owned assets, to learn and succeed, and to make Bright Dairy a Chinese company with international competitiveness. It had never occurred to Wang, that one day Bright Dairy might become the subsidiary of a multinational company. However, Danone had hoped that one day it might be able to own and control Bright Dairy. Besides, Danone had always believed that it was superior to Bright Dairy in many ways, such as capital, branding, management knowhow, and technology. What's more, Danone had even tried to remove Wang from her post because Danone believed that they could find the best manager in the world to run the company instead of Wang. It was as if two partners were running in opposite directions. There could be no doubt that Danone was set to fail.

Excited by their initial success, the two companies went on to set up a second joint venture. The brief sweet honeymoon period was soon over, however. Danone started to become more open in its intention of gaining ownership and management control of Bright Dairy. It started lobbying relevant government authorities and Bright Dairy's major shareholders, but encountered strong resistance from Wang and her management team. Wang managed to gain support from the Shanghai municipal government by putting forward convincing arguments and persuading it of the strategic importance of keeping Bright Dairy as one of Shanghai's showcase companies. Meanwhile, Bright Dairy further elaborated the "noncompete" clause that it initially had with Danone, adding such restrictions as forbidding any entities in China in which Danone held a controlling stake to conduct dairy businesses, including fresh milk, yogurt and milk beverages.[5]

Perhaps Danone thought that "it may not be a wise course" if it "want[ed] to prosper in the Chinese market" to be "only a strategic shareholder, lacking management control."[6] Finally, after all Danone's attempts to gain a controlling stake and management control in Bright Dairy had failed, it managed to gain rights to cooperate with third-party companies.

In a sudden move, Danone went on to cooperate with Bright Dairy's direct competitor, Mengniu. It came as a shock to Bright Dairy since it only found it out two days before Danone signed the agreement with Mengniu. The partnership thus came to an end. As Wang reflected,

> To many Chinese companies, what does "multinational company" mean? Are they giants? Are they wolves? Are they opportunities? Or are they banes? I have concluded from the cooperation between Bright Dairy and Danone that multinationals are not here [in China] for charity, they are catfish, but at the end, they will become shark. Over the process of change, Chinese companies and Chinese brands can only survive by continuous growth, continuous learning, selectively tolerating and growing.[7]

Details matter

Wang concluded from her own experiences in cooperating with Danone that details mattered. Even though a deal was conceptually agreed, the way it was documented and carried out mattered. In 2000, when Bright Dairy was preparing for its public listing, Danone finally grasped the opportunity and managed to lobby and persuade the two major shareholders that Danone's strategic investment in Bright Dairy would be of great help in promoting the company's image externally. It seemed inevitable that Danone would become one of the shareholders. Wang raised the bar for Danone to acquire a 5 percent shareholding in Bright Dairy by laying out four more conditions. To Wang's surprise, during the final round of negotiation, Danone agreed all four conditions on the spot and even, right in front of her, asked for permission from its headquarters in Paris to acquire its shares at a price twice as high as other investors.

Perhaps Danone's representatives were so immersed in the victory that they were unable to focus on the follow-up discussions. Even Wang was surprised that nobody had ever raised any questions on her proposals related to other important matters, such as packaging and product positioning. The meeting soon ended due to time constraints. In Wang's view, Danone may have come to regret some of the details agreed or allowed by default in the meeting, and this may have partially triggered the "divorce" of the two companies.

Despite all the difficulties and obstacles, for Wang, Danone was still Bright Dairy's "primary teacher of marketization, internationalization and scientization."

> It was a 15-year "love affair" [between Bright Dairy and Danone]. We mutually influenced, we fought while we cooperated, we benefited from our fights, we hurt each other even though we appreciated each other.[8]

Business is business, but in a way it is also personal, as individuals have impact on the cooperation, the events and the people, and thus shape the partnerships. Among all the Danone executives that Wang* had worked with over the years, she thought highly only of two people, He Yi and Old Riboud. Even though each executive or manager has his or her own employer to serve, it is people who, eventually, will make or break the business. Qin Peng, a long-time employee of Danone who has had two-decade career with Danone and Danone in China described in just three words his experiences—"respect, persistence, courage."[9] Whether it was perceived this way, it was a separate question. People matter, style matters and communication remains vitally important to cultivate a win–win partnership.

---

* Wang joined GGV Capital's Shanghai office as a partner in May 2008 after stepping down from her post as the chairman of Bright Dairy. GGV Capital is an expansion-stage venture capital investment firm in the USA and China.

Pause for Reflection

Go to China with an open mind. The Great Wall of China not only exists in physical form, but also in minds. It is a misperception that China needs you more than you need China. Therefore, do not assume your way is the only way of doing business and that China has to adapt to your way of thinking and conducting business there. This is especially the case with successful companies, for instance, reflect on the case of Google. Overconfidence, built upon the successes in your home market or other parts of the world, sometimes hinders your ability to grasp reality. Long term, if you think that you can be revolutionary with China, whether it be in policy making, developing a new industrial model or modifying consumer behavior, then you are likely to be disappointed. Hence, Google, inevitably, bumped into the walls by confronting the Chinese government directly.

Retail companies, however, faced with different set of problems, retreated. The struggles and setbacks of Best Buy Co., Inc. (Best Buy), the US-based electronics retailer, and the Home Depot Inc. (Home Depot), the US home improvement retailer, for instance, highlighted the challenging tasks of making revolutionary changes in China. Both Best Buy and Home Depot were leaders in their own sector, and perceived as the industry standard. Yet, both have closed shops recently in China, proving once again that foreign companies must adapt when they operate in this market, with its vast opportunities, yet full of challenges and difficulties. Fortunately, both companies reflected on their setbacks and took them as an opportunity to step forward. Despite closure of their respective retail shops in China, both companies reaffirmed their determination to invest in the market, to refine their approach and make it work in China.

Mini-Case: Best Buy—A tough sell in China

We are very committed to China, and we are trying to figure out the business model that is going to work for China.

Kal Patel—president, Best Buy Asia[1]

We're trying to understand China in our own way, and offer an entirely different experience.

John Noble, CFO, Best Buy International[2]

China, with its attractive market potential, was always on top of Best Buy's agenda for its international expansion, and it didn't go to China unprepared. Best Buy ventured into China first in 2003, by locating its global sourcing in China—starting in Shanghai. The main functions of the 25-person sourcing office were to source products at lower costs and to reduce the time to market by being closer to its manufacturers. It then also provided a window to understand and learn about the Chinese market in preparation for opening its own stores. By the time Best Buy announced its plan to open its trial store in China in early 2005, it already had three Chinese sourcing offices, based in Shanghai, Beijing and Shenzhen.

Canada had been Best Buy's first international venture. It entered Canada in 2001 by acquiring Future Shop, the leading consumer electronics retailer in the country. It was renamed Best Buy Canada, but continued to operate Future Shop as a distinct brand. The acquisition enabled Best Buy to leverage on its own operational experience and the leading position of Future Shop in Canada. It also marked the launching of a dual-brand strategy that would allow Best Buy to target different customer segments by maintaining the brand equity of the acquired brand and attracting new segments of customers to its own-branded stores. As a result, it had garnered Best Buy a combined market share of 34 percent (compared with Future Shop's 15 percent).

Drawing from its successful experience, Best Buy adopted a dual-brand strategy in China. In June 2006, Best Buy acquired a 75 percent stake for US$180 million in Jiangsu Five Star Appliances (Five Star)—the then fourth-largest retailer of appliances and consumer electronics in China. Five Star had 136 stores in seven of the 34 provinces in China at the time. The main reason for the acquisition was to obtain an immediate retail presence in China and gain knowledge about Chinese customers. In parallel with Best Buy's own branded stores, Five Star would serve different segments of customers—it would focus on the less-developed, second-tier cities, while Best Buy targeted higher-end customers in the more affluent east coast, top-tier cities. The investment in Five Star illustrated Best Buy's international growth strategy, and allowed the company to increase its knowledge of Chinese customers, preparing its path for future further expansion in the Chinese markets. Yet, what worked in Canada may not work in China.

In December 2006, Best Buy opened its first flagship store in Shanghai, occupying 87,000 square feet spreading across four floors—the company's largest store anywhere in the world. Further expansion, however, did not go according to plan, due mainly to some delay in receiving government approvals. Consequently, Best Buy was only able to open its second store in August 2008. Somehow things were straightened out and soon after, Best Buy announced that it had received approval for opening four more stores in China. By the time Best Buy announced the closing down of its stores in China, it had in total nine stores.

Conventional wisdom has it that Best Buy failed in China because its model did not suit the highly price-conscious Chinese customers. Some observers said that the Best Buy concept was too "advanced" for the price-conscious Chinese customers. That may be true, but equally, Best Buy may have taken their previous success for granted, believing that it could adapt its way of working to meet the circumstances in China.

Best Buy chose a dual-pronged strategy that it hoped would allow it to adapt to the unique qualities of the Chinese market, and at the same time, bring into play its domestic strengths. Best Buy's acquisition of Five Star almost caused panic and fear throughout the industry by offering the Chinese public a revolutionary shopping experience. But despite these efforts, it did not become an immediate threat to its local rivals.

Why? The Chinese retail market had its own characteristics. First, it was highly fragmented. The top five players together held less than 20 percent of the market share (compared with Future Shop's 15 percent at the time of the acquisition in Canada). Second, there was a ferocious price war. In certain categories, such as TVs and white goods, excess manufacturing capacity had squeezed profit margins to less than 3 percent, the lowest in the world. Third, there was ongoing consolidation of the industry, with a potential new wave of mergers and acquisitions in prospect. Fourth, approximately two-thirds of the sales staff were on the payrolls of suppliers. Last, but not least, the growth of sales lagged far behind that of "other income," such as rebates and listing fees.*

In theory, Best Buy's dual-pronged strategy should have worked. In practice, it was easier said than done. For instance, for retailers, economies of scale are important for a profitable venture not only for reasons of operational efficiency, but also for building a following among consumers. However, Best Buy's planned second shop was behind schedule, mainly due to a delay in obtaining government approvals. According to Kal Patel (president, Best Buy Asia), if Best Buy were to launch a China strategy now, it would try out "fast, quick and cheap"[3] ideas.

Still, with hindsight, Best Buy may have done its best. It prepared itself to enter the market for several years and took a number of incremental steps to get there. It started off with a sourcing office on the ground. Then it took several years to study the market and customers and prepare for the challenges. However, the process had been too slow and its plans for store openings were probably too optimistic.

When Best Buy entered China, on one hand, it had to compete head-on with the much more agile and aggressive home-grown rivals. The biggest challengers were Gome, the number one player in the market, and Suning Appliance Co, the second. Shortly after Best Buy's acquisition of Five Star, Gome completed its acquisition of the number three player, China Paradise Electronics Retail Limited. Best Buy was struggling and captured less than 1 percent market share. On the other hand, however, Chinese companies are quick learners. They quickly adopted the best of Best Buy's model, such as the flagship stores and providing consumers with improved shopping experiences. The problem

---

* Retailers in China usually do not or cannot make money from price mark-ups, but instead rely on fees. These fees include store entry fees, display fees, promotion fees, annual rebates based on sales volume and sometimes even take the form of under-the-table kickbacks. According to Mckinsey, some 20 years ago, suppliers typically paid retailers a "commission" or "rebates" of 4 percent on the sales of their goods. Today, they are paying 10–15 percent. In some cases, such as Carrefour, it can be even higher than 20 percent. Source: Knowledge Wharton. "Carrefour in China: When the price isn't right." http://www.knowledgeatwharton.com.cn/index.cfm?fa=viewArticle&articleID=2379&languageid=1 (accessed August 31, 2011).

for Best Buy, however, compared with its Chinese rivals, was that it offered the same products at higher prices. No wonder it didn't work out.

Key points

- ▶ Best practice in other markets does not always equal success. There is a need to adapt to local conditions.
- ▶ While there is no scientific method for determining an appropriate strategy, companies have to choose one, test it out and refine it where necessary along the way. It is essential that the financial aspects of the business model stack up—as they did not for Best Buy.
- ▶ The devil is not so much in the detail but in the execution. Speed, quality and low costs are crucial.

Partnerships

Partnerships between international and Chinese companies have rarely worked in the long run. We have yet to see a persuasive example of so-called "long-lasting" and "win–win" partnerships. Distrust and conflict can threaten the very survival of a partnership, as can compromise and surrender.

In a *Harvard Business Review* article "Collaborate with Your Competitors—and Win,"[4] the authors, drawing on their research on partnerships between Western companies and their Japanese or Korean rivals decades ago, concluded that companies could win from strategic alliances by adhering to a set of simple yet powerful principles. However, twenty years later, we still find many international companies, despite financial gains, exiting their partnerships in China in surrender, bitterly and sometimes miserably. This prompted us to dig deeper in the hopes of finding the success formula that might enable Western companies to make long-lasting yet win–win partnerships with their Chinese partners.

We examined the development of Danone's string of partnerships in China. Perhaps, instead of asking how to make partnerships work, we might consider operating on the basis of "hope for the best, but plan for the worst." That way, if your partnership ends, you can still win by walking away contented. The question is how?

Lay a solid legal foundation

The failure to transfer the Wahaha trademark to the Danone–Wahaha JVs was a major flaw.

The trademark was valued as part of the investment of the JVs. When the trademark authority declined to approve the trademark transfer, or did not even receive a proper application for the approval of the transfer,* the economics of the transaction immediately changed. If the latter case were true, even though the Chinese partner was responsible for securing the trademark transfer, in terms of the joint venture agreements, Danone failed to oversee the processes. In the former case, Danone had the right to decide whether to raise the issue with the Chinese authority or to restructure the deal. Either way, the key issue of trademark ownership jeopardized the venture from the outset.

The choices Danone made were not atypical. Pending the approval, Danone and Wahaha proceeded by finding a way to get around the regulatory barrier. They signed an alternative trademark license agreement that only required registration (but not approval from the authorities) and even created a short-form licensing contract solely for this purpose. This alternative solution created the conditions for confusion. Further exceptions, allowing Wahaha use the trademark for other products under certain conditions, compounded the problems.

Admittedly, Danone and Wahaha were creative in finding an immediate solution. It was perhaps the best choice for Danone in the circumstances. However, it did not solve the fundamental problem that trademark ownership was not transferred to the JVs. This increased the risks for Danone if things did not go well.

The battle to gain control (ownership or management) is never-ending

Both Western and Chinese managers tend to be obsessed with ownership and management control. The battle to gain control is a never-ending process.

In the Danone–Wahaha case, the confusion between ownership and management control was a major contributing factor to the dispute. The ambiguity existed from day one when the partners agreed the structure of the deal. The question was whether setting up Jinjia with Peregrine in Singapore was a legal maneuver to allow Danone to gain ownership control of the JVs, or whether Wahaha fully understood Danone's intention that it would eventually be the sole owner of Jinjia. It appears, at least, that there might have been some confusion, even if there was no intention to mislead.

In addition, the change in ownership of Jinjia was effected offshore, without the need for any Chinese government approval or any requirement to inform Wahaha. Wahaha felt it had been misled from the outset: it only realized that Danone had "taken over" the JVs when a Danone representative replaced the Peregrine-designated director on the board.

---

* Danone claimed as much based on a formal statement issued by the trademark authority to Danone in 2007, which we have never seen.

This undoubtedly sowed the seeds of future resentment. When asked in an interview in July 2007, what he would change in retrospect, Zong said without hesitation:

> For sure, I'd insist on having 51 percent ownership or more; having the controlling stake ...[5]

The Robust and Bright Dairy cases were different even though Danone never hid its intention to gain ownership control, and if possible, management control. For Robust, ownership control was a bargaining chip to allow He to extract maximum value from the acquisition. Danone paid the price while Robust retained management control. For Bright Dairy, as soon as Wang realized Danone's real intention, she and her management tirelessly fought to safeguard the state-owned assets or interests. After several attempts to extract some concessions from Bright Dairy, Danone finally gave in.

Foster a culture of learning

It has been argued that ownership structure is perhaps much less important than the extent to which each partner can learn from the other. Research shows that alliances between Asian companies and Western rivals seem to work better for the former, mainly because of the Asian companies' willingness and ability to learn.

Consider Danone's partnerships in China. Danone was looking for ways to effect quick and low-cost market penetration. It chose to work through partnerships. Danone's Chinese partners, however, entered into the partnerships with the aim of gaining access to capital, technology and/or management knowhow. In particular, as Wang of Bright Dairy spelled out, she was determined to learn and excel.

Chinese are fast learners. In the Bright Dairy case, despite the initial success of the joint venture managed by Danone, Bright Dairy was soon able to buy back and run the joint ventures itself, and produce a better performance than Danone had. In the Wahaha case, Danone's involvement in the JVs gradually reduced, partly because of Wahaha's resistance and partly because of Danone's lack of ambition. Over time, the two partners became polarized, with Danone becoming increasingly dependent on its Chinese partner, while the Chinese partners worked steadily towards gaining independence.

Fostering a culture of learning from your partners is essential to build up corporate capabilities and win the race with your partner. It should be at the top of your corporate agenda, together with a willingness to commit the necessary resources. It is also essential to get trusted executives with proven track records to manage the partnerships and provide necessary oversight and guidance.

...learning within an alliance takes a positive commitment of resources—the travel, a pool of dedicated people, test-bed facilities, time to internalize and test what has been learned.[6]

Compromise is a fact of life, but protect it proactively, constantly and rigorously

A strategic alliance is a constantly evolving bargain whose real terms go beyond the legal agreement or the aims of top management.[7]

Partnership negotiations do not end with the initial legal agreements. The balance of power will probably shift over time. Consider the Danone–Wahaha case. It appeared to be balanced at the outset—Danone got the majority stake, control of the board and the ability to appoint the CFO, while Zong was appointed as the first general manager with the provision that the role would rotate between the partners. Wahaha would have management control. Over time, Wahaha managed to acquire and internalize certain skills, while keeping Danone in the dark. Danone, as a consequence, failed to protect its own position, and did not acquire any new skills from Wahaha.

By contrast, Robust, even though it held management control, decided to surrender when the gap between strategic direction and management philosophy widened. The cofounders also failed to find their own compromise and handed the company to Danone. The Danone–Bright Dairy case illustrates clearly the constant need to defend the strategic compromise between two partners. Danone tried to gain ownership and management control of Bright Dairy on every possible occasion. To safeguard the state-owned assets and interests, the management of Bright Dairy tirelessly repelled Danone's attempts.

Mini-Case: CICC—A true success?

In 1995, Morgan Stanley and China Construction Bank (CCB), together with other Chinese and international financial institutions and corporations, joined forces and created China International Capital Corporation Limited (CICC), the first Sino-foreign joint venture investment bank. CICC also later became the first true investment bank in China. It was a perfect match, since China wanted to attract foreign capital and financial knowhow, while Morgan Stanley gained what looked like an unrivalled access to China's investment banking market.

However, the joint venture partnership had been problematic almost from day one. James McGregor, in his *One Billion Customers: Lessons from the Frontline of Doing Business in China*,[8] has told the behind-the-scene stories of how the two parties almost clashed on all fronts, from the structure of the deal, through organizational differences, attitudes and even to the personalities and leadership styles of key players.

The financial industry in China was highly regulated. Consequently, a joint venture was the only way for a foreign financial institution to gain access to the market. Even more important, a controlling stake was not negotiable. To get into the market, Morgan Stanley went into the partnership with a view that it would tap into the huge Chinese market and build its own capabilities there. In exchange, it offered its Chinese partner capital and financial knowhow.

Morgan Stanley had wanted an equal partnership of the joint venture, but was simply not negotiable, and so CCB held the largest stake in CICC, followed by Morgan Stanley. To maximize benefits from the joint venture, CCB compromised and gave Morgan Stanley management control as well as the right to appoint the head of CICC. In the early years, both parties worked on the basis of mutual trust and respect. While cooperating on several other projects with its other Asian operations, Morgan Stanley saw CICC as a platform for developing its business in China. It sent over many managers to introduce advanced investment banking technologies and practices to CICC.

Later, however, conflicts arose over issues such as compensation, management, and strategy, as well as a difficulty in achieving consensus. By 2000 when Elaine La Roche, the last Morgan Stanley-appointed head of CICC, stepped down, Morgan Stanley withdrew its management from CICC and became a passive investor, only participating in the dividend distribution. At this point, the partnership had almost failed miserably. Still the second biggest shareholder of CICC, Morgan Stanley competed with the Chinese bank over several other projects.

When China further opened up its securities sector to foreign capital, Morgan Stanley started to look for ways to forge new partnerships. Since foreign players were only allowed one joint venture at a time, Morgan Stanley was obliged to give up its stake in CICC.* For several years thereafter, Morgan Stanley attempted to sell its 34.3 percent stake in CICC. In December 2010, the Chinese regulatory authority finally approved the transaction.

The sale meant that a 15-year partnership of China's first Sino-foreign joint venture investment bank had finally come to an end. Morgan Stanley expected to realize a pre-tax gain of approximately US$700 million when the deal closed, a handsome profit over its initial investment of US$35 million. Despite its huge financial success, Morgan Stanley's exit marked a bitter ending to a once-sweet joint venture partnership. Shortly afterwards, the China Securities Regulatory Commission (CSRC) approved Morgan Stanley's application to form a new joint-venture partnership with the Shenzhen-based Huaxin Securities Co. Ltd (also known as China Fortune Securities Co., Ltd).

Key points:

▶ Financial gains are not the only measure of success. By failing to find a way to maintain a consensual relationship with CICC, Morgan Stanley lost a lot of management time that could have been put to better use. It also led to a decade-long hiatus when they were unable to progress much in China.
▶ Always keep the ends in mind. Did Morgan Stanley have a clear objective or exit strategy? A lack of either can lead to major setbacks.
▶ The better and faster learner wins. The Chinese banks learned more and faster from their foreign counterparts than vice versa. That resulted in them becoming much stronger competitors.

---

* Morgan Stanley had intended to set up a joint venture with Fortune back in 2007.

To take, first you have to give—make sure you always offer something distinctive

Many Western companies have entered into partnerships because of complementary needs. They were comfortable that they were usually on the offering side of capital, technology and/or management knowhow, while their Chinese partners were on the receiving end.

Consider the Danone–Wahaha JVs. Danone sent an R&D director and a marketing director to help Wahaha establish an R&D centre. Both positions were short-lived because Wahaha believed that they made little contribution, though Danone thought the opposite.

While it is difficult to quantify Danone's contribution in this case, a safe assumption is that Danone must have made a certain contribution to the JVs. However, Wahaha learned fast and soon felt that there was no need for the Danone representatives to stay if they did not have any distinctive skills to offer. Besides, this meant that Wahaha did not have to be very transparent with Danone.

What is perhaps less open to doubt, is that, from then on, Danone made rare contributions. Besides, Danone did not have much urge to learn. It let Zong to do all the work, sat back and enjoyed its fair share of the growth. As Danone contributed less and less to the partnership, the balance of power shifted and it had to surrender more and more control to its Chinese partner. Thus, the partnership weakened.

Respect is the ultimate currency

Nobody likes conflict, especially in China; there is even a Chinese saying that one should play down serious conflicts, or ease them away.

What was supposed to be a purely internal commercial dispute between partners escalated into a public saga. Be aware that the public in China today are more sophisticated. As it turned out, the Chinese public was divided, by no means unanimously supporting Zong. His supporters echoed the sentiment of wanting to protect a national brand against a monopoly of the multinationals, while his critics believed that the situation should have been handled in a purely commercial manner.

At this point, Danone could have calmed things down. Instead, it issued a public statement claiming that Zong was in breach of noncompete obligations. To add insult to injury, it issued a warning letter threatening to start legal proceedings. This kicked off the public debate and a Chinese "patriotic element" entered the scene.

Had Danone reacted differently, the story might have had a happier ending. Instead, Danone turned on Zong's wife and daughter, which, in our view, did not help to solve the problem. Aggression and hostility can hurt, and such personal attacks escalate the problems. In the Chinese context, this would often give rise to questions of patriotism or nationalism.

Understand the external forces that may affect your
partnerships and respond proactively and swiftly

External forces, for example, political, social, legal and cultural aspects,
may affect your partnerships in China. In the 1990s, China was still under
transition from a planned to a market economy. Thus, depending on the circumstances, government approval, for example was necessary before Chinese
companies could enter into commercial agreements with foreign partners.
In the Danone–Wahaha case, the approval from the relevant government
authorities was required before the JVs could come into effect.

Later, as private companies prospered and reforms continued, Wahaha
came to be owned by Zong and Wahaha employees, with Zong having effective control of Wahaha. Did the change in Wahaha's ownership constitute
a change of ownership of the JVs? Perhaps. But Danone did not immediately
question or take any action against Wahaha.

Therefore, a thorough understanding of such external implications is
essential. So, too, is the need to respond to them by mitigating or appor-
tioning the risks through contractual arrangements.

In China, entrepreneurs do not have to be directly involved in politics
(although some are), but it is important to understand the political implications and manage them. Zong had a strong political sense. He saw the
opportunity to support the government's call for the development of the
poor areas of inland China. As a result, Wahaha was able to receive government funds, enjoy favorable tax treatment, and reduce distribution
costs. As a result, Zong also became a preferred partner of many local
governments.

At first, such investment opportunities may or may not have seemed
attractive to Danone, but Wahaha went ahead. Once these investments were
working, Danone wanted to be included. Despite the different attitudes to
risks and growth in multinationals and emerging Chinese companies, the
partnership was not limited to the initial five JVs and the number grew.

This could have worked if both parties were relaxed about it and there
remained a balance of obligations and responsibilities. However, as we have
seen from the way the case evolved, at some point during the cooperation
the balance was lost.

Legal action may help you reach a settlement, but is rarely
a desired outcome

Legal action in China often drags out and does not necessarily lead to a
desirable outcome. Before starting any legal proceedings, Western executives need to be clear about what they seek to achieve. Over the course of
the dispute, Danone first threatened and then took legal actions, seeking
"justice" against Wahaha and Zong (including Zong's family) both in China
and internationally.

If they [Danone] take this to court in China, I doubt that they would win. Or at least they're not going to get what they want.

Teng Binsheng—professor, Cheung Kong Graduate School of Business[9]

Indeed, such legal proceedings did not help Danone get what it wanted—the 51 percent share of the non-JVs. Furthermore, the distributors, the employees and the labor union all came out in support of Zong. And, finally, the turn of events may have led the "automatic termination" of Danone's joint venture partnership with Mengniu in December 2007.

Perhaps Danone chose to take legal action merely as a tactic in the hope that Wahaha would give in. Such a costly act, both emotionally and financially, might have worked in the past, as most Chinese companies did not have the experience or resources to fight international legal claims. However, Danone underestimated its strong Chinese counterpart—fuelled in part by patriotism, Wahaha and Zong were ready to fight every legal battle against Danone.

In addition, Danone did not just pick a fight with Wahaha, Zong, and his family; it also went against Wahaha's employees, who were shareholders in the Wahaha group of companies. Did Danone have any back-up plans if it did not win? Even if it had won, would it have been able to win back the loyalty of Wahaha employees and carry on the businesses? "Know yourself, know your enemy." Danone should have at least tried to understand its counterpart better before kick starting the legal disputes.

In the end, Danone lost ground on its legal claims for reasons related to the trademark transfer, which perhaps proves again that a valid legal basis is really just the starting point in making an investment work.

Mini-Case: Yahoo!'s Alibaba Dilemma

On May 10, 2011, Yahoo! Inc. (Yahoo!) stunned the stock market with the disclosure in its regulatory filing that Alibaba Group Holding Ltd (Alibaba)—the largest e-commerce company in China,* in which it held a 43 percent stake, had transferred the ownership of its online payment company Alipay to a Chinese domestic company majority-owned by Alibaba's CEO Jack Ma. Alibaba claimed that this was necessary to expedite the obtaining of an essential regulatory license for Alipay to operate its payment business in China. Yahoo!'s surprise announcement led to the revelation of an even more complicated situation.

In 1999, Ma, together with 17 others, founded Alibaba in Hangzhou. In 2005, Yahoo! paid US$1 billion in cash for a 43 percent stake in Alibaba. In exchange,

---

* Alibaba's core businesses included: Alibaba.com, the group's flagship company and the world's leading B2B ecommerce company; Taobao, China's largest online retail website and a one-stop platform for shopping, socializing and information sharing; Alibaba Cloud Computing, a developer of advanced data-centric cloud computing services; and China Yahoo!, one of China's leading Internet portals.

Alibaba would run Yahoo!'s China site. In recent years, the two companies had fought over several issues, such as Internet censorship in China and the number of seats that Yahoo! should have on Alibaba's board.* In addition, Alibaba, had been trying to reduce the foreign shareholdings in the company. According to Ma, the increasingly strict Internet regulations in China made it difficult for Alibaba to operate as a company majority-owned by foreign investors. In 2010, Alibaba tried to negotiate a buy-back of part or all of Yahoo!'s stake. The attempt failed because the two parties could not agree on a price.

According to Yahoo!'s disclosure, the transfer of the ownership of Alipay occurred in August 2010 and the deconsolidation was effective in the first quarter of 2011. However, Yahoo! claimed that, it, together with Softbank, a Japanese major shareholder, were not aware of the transfer until March 31, 2011 and the transaction occurred without the knowledge and consent of the Alibaba board of directors and shareholders. Alibaba disputed these claims, saying that the possible transfer had been discussed at several board meetings over the previous two years as changes in the Chinese regulations regarding foreign ownership that would require the divestment of Alipay had been anticipated.

Yahoo!'s shares plunged upon the news of the dispute as investors feared that the surprise shift in ownership had eroded the value of Yahoo!'s stake in Alibaba. Yahoo! also claimed in its disclosure that it was negotiating with Alibaba and Softbank to resolve the issue. On Yahoo!'s investor day held on May 25, 2011, Yahoo!'s management were vague when questioned on the progress of negotiations with Alibaba. The following day, Reuters reported that Alipay had received a license from China's central bank to operate an electronic payment system in the country.

Although there had been reports that Yahoo! and Alibaba were close to settling the matter, pending Softbank's approval, on June 1, 2011 at the AllthingsD conference in California, Ma said he was optimistic about the negotiations despite some complications and the slow-moving process. However, while Yahoo! was negotiating with Alibaba on a possible settlement for the spinoff of Alipay, Softbank, according to the Chinese press, was taking a hard-line and refusing to participate in the negotiation. Without Softbank's consent, the settlement seemed unlikely to happen.

On June 6, 2011, investors in US launched a class action against Yahoo! alleging that it had failed to disclose the transfer of Alipay in time.

At the center of the dispute was the timing of just when Yahoo! and Softbank were informed about the transfer of ownership of Alipay. It is not possible for outsiders to judge what had happened or to know for sure whether such transaction would require the approval from Alibaba's board of directors and shareholders. In any case, Alibaba decided to go ahead with the transaction and Alipay did receive the license. For Yahoo! and Softbank there were lessons to learn.

Although the dispute became very public very quickly, both Alibaba and Yahoo! took the right actions by first calming down the situation, then trying to find a

---

* Yahoo! currently held one of the four seats of the Alibaba's board of directors. The four members were: Ma, Joe Tsai (Alibaba's CFO), Masayoshi Son (chief of Softbank Corporation (Softbank), a Japanese technology company and a major shareholder of Alibaba) and Yang (cofounder and ex CEO of Yahoo).

resolution through negotiations, in marked contrast to Danone's approach with Wahaha.

On July 29, 2011, Alibaba settled its dispute with Yahoo! and Softbank, over the terms of the ownership change of Alipay and an appropriate compensation of the value of Alipay. The agreement guaranteed Alibaba 37.5 percent of the totally equity value of Alipay, subject to a floor amount of US$2 billion and a ceiling amount of US$6 billion, in case Alipay goes public or another liquidity event takes place. It also requires Alipay continue to serve Alibaba and other group companies (including Taobao) on preferential terms and pay Alibaba royalties for software services and 49.9 percent of its consolidated pre-tax income.[10]

Key points:

▶ Remedy is good, but prevention is better.
▶ A clear shareholders' agreement from the outset should prevent such problems arising.

Harmony is not the most important measure of success, but true harmony is definitely the highest level of success

Harmony is not the most important measure of success.[11]

Yet, we would argue, without harmony, any collaboration is doomed to fail. In the case of Danone and Wahaha the two joint venture partners had peacefully coexisted for more than a decade. The non-JV entities had existed from the day that the JVs were formed. The real question was—why now?

Over the years, there were many occasions that Danone could have raised the issues of the non-JVs. First, Danone had reflected the contribution from its JVs with Wahaha in its annual report. And, according to Zong, Danone received monthly accounting statements for the JVs and appointed PwC to audit the JVs semi-annually. In addition, PwC, in return for payment by Danone, sent separate sets of reports solely to Danone. Furthermore, the Danone directors, holding the majority of seats on the board, including the vice-chairmanship, approved and signed the accounts.

A couple of questions arise here. First, had PwC, the board or Danone ever raised a red flag over the years? If so, why hadn't Danone acted? If not, what had triggered Danone's claim after ten years of growing contributions from the JVs? Second, if Danone's claim were legitimate, why did it choose to solve the issue through negotiations and eventually, an arbitrary "agreement" (which Zong later claimed was only a letter of intent) with Wahaha to acquire a 51 percent stake in the non-JVs for RMB4 billion (US$544 million)?

Ask the following questions before you forge a partnership:

▷ What do you want/expect to achieve (strategic intent)?
▷ What can you give (contributions—resources or capabilities)?

▷ What can you take (learning—capabilities)?
▷ What can or cannot you do (external forces or boundaries)?
▷ Are you content? What about your partner?

And make sure that you adhere to the following principles:

Do unto others as you would have them do unto you

The breach of the noncompete obligations by the Chinese partners was central to the Danone–Wahaha dispute. Surprisingly, as the dispute evolved, it turned out that Danone had no such obligations. One has to question how it was possible for the partners to agree to such asymmetry of obligations and responsibilities. One explanation could be that, at that time, most Chinese companies were still not very familiar with international commercial practices and were inexperienced in dealing with their foreign counterparts. However, we found out during our research that Zong did try to negotiate a reciprocal noncompete deal with Danone, but somehow Danone managed to get away from it. A reasonable explanation could be that both parties conceded on certain issues in order to make the deal. Such imbalance undoubtedly sowed the seeds of future dissent.

Seek common grounds, manage the differences

Zong maintained that "the Wahaha–Danone match was troubled from the start," adding that the partners were like couples in the "same bed," but with "different dreams."

> Whenever we wanted to expand the business, they said no. They refused to invest more. But they let us spend the money and then when the ventures made money they wanted in ... They don't understand the Chinese market ... Culture is a very big problem. There is a very big gap between East and West.[12]

Zhu Xinli, chairman of China Huiyuan Juice, a leading Chinese beverage company, also expressed his view on foreign partners:

> To foreign capital, all partners are transitional. They cooperate with you when you are useful and quit on you when you are useless.[13]

It is true that the gap between the East and West is big, and each partner may have different agenda. Conflicts are inevitable and at times, you need to make or defend your compromises. The key, however, is to find common ground and work with the differences.

7 All at Sea

Derivatives are financial weapons of mass destruction, carrying dangers that, while now latent, are potentially lethal.

Warren Buffett[1]

The bar on what constitutes effective risk management is constantly being raised. Most institutions have an unfinished agenda.

Financial Times[2]

On the evening of October 7, 2004, the last day of the Golden Week holiday in China, Jia Changbin, chairman of China Aviation Oil (CAO), received a call from the CEO and managing director, Chen Jiulin. Chen told Jia that CAO had incurred paper losses on its futures trading and was requesting his instructions and possibly seeking financial support from its parent company in Beijing.

CAO was the largest jet fuel supplier in China and the largest Chinese corporation listed on the Singapore exchange. It was the only publicly listed subsidiary of China Aviation Oil Holding Company (CAOHC),* which held a 75 percent stake. In addition to their responsibilities at CAO, Jia was president of CAOHC and chairman of its executive committee and Chen was one of its three executive vice presidents.

Chen told Jia that the paper losses had amounted to US$180 million. Chen asked Jia whether to stop loss or to hold the positions as the board had not specified the stop-loss limit for options trading.† Jia told Chen then that they had to wait for Hai Liancheng (party secretary of CAOHC), to return from his business trip in Europe, then further discuss. Jia then asked Chen to talk with Li Yongji (nonexecutive director, member of the audit committee and head of CAOHC's Asset and Financial Management division).‡ Jia also called Li and directed him to find out from Chen what exactly had happened and report back to him.

Chen called Li immediately. Li broke into a cold sweat when he hung up the phone. "We have lost Singapore," he thought.

---

* CAOHC was created on October 11, 2002, based on China Aviation Oil Supply Corporation (CAOSC). For simplicity, CAOHC has been used throughout the book instead of CAOSC.
† Stop-loss limit for other transactions was US$5 million.
‡ Li was also responsible for monitoring the budget and financial statements of CAO.

Strategic evolution and main turning points

A chronological review of CAO's overseas adventure shows that the company had made several strategic choices and experienced two major turning points. It started out as an equal-partnership shipping agency in Singapore, a joint venture by CAOHC and two other partners, then turned into an international oil-trading company, and finally transformed itself to an integrated oil company.

Due to lack of clear strategy, limited market knowledge and management expertise, CAO's business did not take off and incurred losses of about S$190,000 (US$114,000) in less than two years.[3]

CAOHC was the largest integrated aviation oil supplier in China, covering jet fuel procurement, storage, transport, distribution, and refueling. It had the sole authorization from the Chinese government to allocate import quotas for jet fuel imports into China. CAOHC originally purchased its fuel through third-party trading companies. Despite steady demand for China's jet fuel imports at the time, CAOHC had plans to set up an overseas subsidiary to source jet fuel on its own behalf, to cut out the middle-men and reduce business costs. In 1995, the strategic focus for CAO became clear when bought out its joint venture partners with a view to utilizing CAO as its overseas procurement arm. CAO thus became CAOHC's first wholly owned overseas subsidiary.

However, it took CAOHC more than two years to plan the relaunch and obtain the requisite approvals from the Chinese authorities. Consequently, CAO remained dormant between 1995 and June 1997.

Building CAO: "King of jet fuel procurement"*

In July 1997, CAO relaunched its business. But it was not until February 1998 (due to various obstacles) that it gradually began its jet fuel procurement business by sourcing from the international oil markets for distribution to the Chinese civil aviation industry through CAOHC and its group companies. Chen took the helm of the company with one assistant,[4] no office, no trader, and no creditworthiness whatsoever.

Building up creditworthiness

After paying off the debts it had inherited from the joint venture and buying out its two partners, CAO was left with just S$384,000 (US$219,000) cash in hand. It could not afford even a fraction of a single cargo of jet fuel, normally worth about US$6–10 million. The Asian financial crisis,

---

* As dubbed by the media.

which took hold as the company was setting up, had further worsened the market situation, as the banks increased the country risk and reduced their credit lines for Asian countries. As a result, CAO was unable to secure either banking facilities or trade credits.

Chen resolved the issue through a creative idea of a "transfer account" (see Exhibit 7.1). This meant CAO could leverage the creditworthiness of other domestic Chinese enterprises by using them as the intermediary to buy the jet fuel from international oil suppliers, then buy it back at a certain mark-up. Although CAO had to give away most of its margins, the volume grew and the company gradually established its own creditworthiness in the Singapore oil market.

Then in 1998, CAO secured its first credit line of US$10 million from the French bank BNP Paribas, which CAO used to help improve its creditworthiness with its oil suppliers. BNP Paribas chose to grant the credit line to CAO mainly because Chen spoke fluent English. CAO was soon able to secure more banking facilities and trade credits.

As its creditworthiness improved, CAO gradually phased out the "transfer account" approach to achieve greater profitability.

Creating a level playing field

Nonetheless, CAOHC and its group companies could bypass CAO and purchase jet fuel directly from more established third-party trading companies and oil corporations. CAO was struggling because of its limited knowledge of the international fuel market, constraints on resources and banking facilities, and the lack of a business network. Turnover was low—about S$11 million (US$6.6 million)—and it reported losses of approximately S$0.3 million (US$180,000) at the end of its first year.

Chen then convinced CAOHC to purchase jet fuel via open tenders, in line with international practices, so that CAO could compete directly with

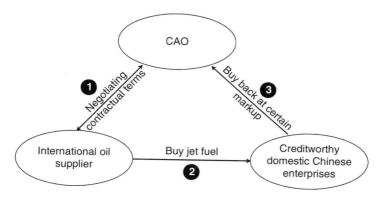

Exhibit 7.1 **Transfer account**

other trading companies and oil corporations. CAO procured jet fuel via competitive tender after receiving an order based on "cost-plus" from its customers. This model enabled CAO to offer its domestic end-users competitive prices and still make a nice profit. It also meant that there was little trading risk for CAO as it did not have to hold any fuel inventories, and CAO was cashflow-positive.

CAOHC conducted 26 public tenders in 1998. CAO won 21 and lost the remaining five by only US$0.05 per barrel. CAO made profits of US$299,000 on its first cargo of jet fuel procured.[5] CAO was able to buy and ship in bulk and offer better prices on higher volumes.

To further lower costs, Chen suggested CAOHC adopt a new model of "bulk purchasing and bulk transportation." After nearly one year of active lobbying and internal analysis, Chen finally gained the approval of CAOHC and, as a result, CAO not only lowered the costs for its parent company, but also gained a price advantage when volume grew.

Gaining AOT/GTP status

In 1998, CAO's total revenue amounted to about S$171 million[6] (US$103 million). It just met the minimum requirements (annual turnover of US$100 million) to be eligible for Approved Oil Trader (AOT) status (later known as the Global Trader Program (GTP)) awarded by the Singapore government. The award not only entitled CAO to enjoy a low concessionary tax rate, but was also an endorsement of CAO's performance and contribution to the Singapore economy. The Singapore Trade Development Board reviewed the GTP award every five years: CAO's GTP status was extended in 2003 for another five years and modified so that it became eligible for an even lower concessionary tax rate.

However, the terms of the GTP required CAO achieve a minimum cumulative turnover for physical trades of US$4.547 billion and derivatives trades of US$13.641 billion and employ at least 15 international professionals by the end of December 2008. In other words, such a requirement meant that the minimum cumulative turnover of derivatives trades be three times that of physical trades.

Benefiting from the "China growth story"

CAO benefited from the fast-growing Chinese economy and the rapid growth of the Chinese civil aviation industry.[7] By 2001, China was importing one-third of its jet fuel requirements.[8] The demand for jet fuel was expected to grow by 16 percent per annum, outstripping domestic supply, and was projected to grow to twice the level of domestic supply by 2011, and to three times by 2020.[9]

Exhibit 7.2   CAO's major awards and accolades

1998	Awarded Approved Oil Trader (AOT) status (later renamed Global Trader Programme, or GTP) by the government of Singapore
1999	Called "King of Jet Fuel Procurement" by Singapore's main Chinese daily, *Lianhe Zaobao*
2001	Listed on the main board of the Singapore Exchange with gross proceeds of S$80.6 million, subsequently ranked first in terms of economic performance among IPO companies listed on the Singapore Exchange in 2001.
2002	Won the "Most Transparent Company Award" from the Securities Investors Association (Singapore) out of newly listed companies on the Singapore Exchange.
	Ranked 26th most transparent company of those listed in Singapore by *Business Times Index*.
	Ranked top company listed on the Singapore Exchange in 2001 according to Singapore 1000, a report by the DP Information Network and compiled in conjunction with the Registry of companies and businesses
	Ranked 127th out of other big multinational corporations, the highest ranked company that had an IPO in 2001, and 26th among oil companies and 2nd among overseas Chinese companies in Singapore.
2003	Granted five-year extension to GTP membership by International Enterprise Singapore.
	Ranked 3rd in "Specialty for Niche", 4th in the "Improved" and 5th in the "National Oil Co." Categories in the Sixth Annual Industry Perception Survey by Applied Trading Systems Inc.
2004	Acknowledged for its outstanding risk management structure and procedures by China National Enterprise Federation at China's Tenth Annual Creative Management Awards. CAO was the only overseas Chinese-funded enterprise accorded the honor.

Source: Public company announcements.

Through successful tendering and bulk purchasing operations in the first few years, CAO had become the de facto sole jet fuel supplier of CAOHC. To secure this status, in the second half of 2002, Chen managed to lobby CAOHC to issue two management directives, instructing all its group companies to procure their imported fuel from CAO on a long-term basis. Thus, CAOHC explicitly sealed in writing CAO's status as the de facto monopoly importer of jet fuel into China.

CAO further secured competitive trade financing facilities (granting a shorter credit period to its customers than it had from its suppliers), and Chen lobbied to apply international industry standards for jet fuel.*

---

* China in the past had applied different standards for jet fuel, which few other countries applied, and this had made it too costly to procure jet fuel that met these different standards.

Through these efforts, CAO's share of tenders for China's jet fuel industry grew from less than 3 percent in 1997 to approximately 83 percent in 1999, and virtually 100 percent by 2001.[10] It had achieved its original mission of ensuring cheaper and more stable jet fuel supply in China and was labeled the "King of Jet Fuel Procurement" (see Exhibit 7.2 for CAO's major awards and accolades).

Forming a second strand of growth: International oil trading

CAO started its international oil-trading business in 1999, and at the start the volume was low. The board and CAOHC had set increasingly higher expectations on CAO's profitability. However, CAOHC also continuously lowered CAO's commission on jet fuel procurement. CAO then began to build up a second string of growth by expanding its international oil-trading product portfolio (see Exhibit 7.3 for CAO's revenue breakdown by product segment) and geographic coverage. The objectives were to achieve economies of scale, enhance profit through multiple income streams, and position itself to exploit opportunities as China opened up to the international markets. CAO's geographic reach extended beyond China and ASEAN,* then to the Far East and United States.

However, despite higher volumes and turnover from the jet fuel procurement and physical oil trading, CAO's gross profits and margins were in general decline from 2000 to 2003 because of highly volatile oil prices. This

Exhibit 7.3 Reported revenue by product segment

S$ million	1999	2000	2001	2002	2003
Clean petroleum products	342.1	811.4	751.6	821.8	1,432.7
Black petroleum products	64.8	115.1	290.3	572.7	540.6
Crude oil	–	40.4	–	278.8	388.8
Petrochemical products[a]	4.2	9.1	15.8	14.8	34.8
Others	–	–	0.3	0.7	1.7
Total	**411.1**	**976.1**	**1,058.0**	**1,688.9**	**2,398.8**

[a] Mainly plastic resins.

Source: Public company reports.

---

* Association of Southeast Asian Nations, a geopolitical and economic organization of 10 nations located in Southeast Asia, formed on August 8, 1967 by the five original member countries—Indonesia, Malaysia, Philippines, Singapore and Thailand—with Brunei Darussalam, Vietnam, Lao PDR, Myanmar and Cambodia included later on.

coincided with a period when CAOHC voluntarily lowered CAO's commissions for jet fuel procurement by 40 percent after CAO achieved higher volumes and profitability as a result of economies of scale.[11] CAO then placed more emphasis on its other areas of business such as oil derivatives trading and strategic investments.[12]

Faced with higher risks because of the highly volatile nature of the business, CAO had started mitigating the risks through hedging and rigorous risk-management procedures. In 2002, it won the "Most Transparent Company Award," endorsed by the Securities Investors Association of Singapore (SIAS), out of all the newly listed companies on the Singapore stock exchange (SGX).[13]

Thus, CAO had transformed itself from a shipping agency to an international oil-trading company with a focus on jet fuel procurement and international oil-trading businesses. It was also the subject of an MBA case study at the National University of Singapore (NUS) and became "the first overseas Chinese enterprise that had been publicly recognized for its exemplary success by an internationally-acclaimed university."[14]

Adding a third strand to the strategy: Strategic investments

To gain a foothold in the international market, Chen believed that CAO had to start to move along the value chain, possess some industrial assets, and make strategic investments. CAO's vision was to be a dominant player in the global oil industry. To this end, it added a third prong to its strategy for long-term growth—strategic investments in oil-related assets.

Going public

To materialize its three-pronged long-term growth strategy, CAO started the third step of its development strategy through an initial public offering (IPO). CAO hoped that it would be able to use the proceeds from the IPO for investments in oil-related assets, and therefore, to increase its revenue as well as profitability.

On March 27, 2001, CAO received the approval for an IPO of 25 percent of its shares on the Singapore Exchange (SGX). This would allow CAO to raise capital from the Singapore financial market and benefit from Singapore's sound corporate governance system.[15] Thus, CAO also transformed from a wholly owned overseas subsidiary of a Chinese state-owned enterprise (SOE) to a publicly listed company on the SGX, although majority control stayed with its Chinese parent. CAO's IPO prospectus stipulated speculative oil derivative trading as one of its businesses and listed the associated risks as the number two risk factor for the company (second only to the departure of the management). It then filed the prospectus at the Chinese Securities Regulatory Commission (CSRC).

On December 6, 2001, CAO went listed and became the largest IPO of the year in Singapore. Although CAO's shares were more than eight times oversubscribed[16] at both the retail and institutional level, and volume on the first day was the heaviest on the market, CAO's share price went "underwater" (the first day closing 45 percent below its IPO per share price). This was mainly due to generally weak market sentiment and some concern about the risky nature of CAO's trading business. CAO was sensitive to this point and aimed to raise its profile with analysts and investors. As DBS Vickers* commented, "the best work for the company is to boost public recognition."[17]

By the end of 2001, CAO's turnover exceeded S$1 billion (US$0.6 billion) and it ranked 127th of the top 1,000 companies in Singapore—the highest ranking for any company that had an IPO in 2001.[18]

The jewels in the crown

CAO made two acquisitions in 2002 partially using its IPO proceeds.

First, on July 23, 2002, CAO acquired CAOHC's 33 percent stake in Shanghai Pudong International Airport Aviation Fuel Supply Company (SPIA/AFSC) through a share transfer agreement.[19] CAO financed the total transaction—RMB370 million (US$44.7 million)[†]—in cash.[20] As a result, CAO could integrate SPIA/AFSC into its global infrastructure and network while using it as the springboard to further develop its business in China. Thus, it created a "win–win–win"[21] situation for all parties involved.

Then, on July 31, 2002, CAO acquired, a 5 percent stake in Compania Logistica de Hidrocarburos CLH. SA (CLH), a Spanish oil logistics and facilities company, through an exclusive tender exercise. This allowed CAO to interact as an equal with international oil majors as it held the same stake as Shell and BP, plus a seat on the board.

> CAO has constantly pointed out that they were on equal shareholding footing with companies like BP and Shell. Perhaps the investment [in CLH] was a cheap way to get regular meetings in front of the oil majors. CLH's supersized 17 seat board reads like a Who's Who in Spanish oil, with directors from Repsol and Cespa plus heavy representation from Enbridge and seats going to BP and Shell.
>
> DBS Vickers[22]

CAO has begun building a new pillar of sustainable growth for the future. These strategic investments also support the other two divisions availing round-the-clock energy-trading opportunities, to take advantage of market opportunities

---

* DBS Vickers Securities is a leading securities and derivatives brokerage firm in Singapore (also CAO's issue manager).
[†] Unless otherwise specified, the conversion rate US$1 = RMB 8.28 has been used.

in the global oil markets. CAO has established a strategic foothold in two continents, Asia and Europe, and is now looking beyond the horizon to more opportunities, even as far, possibly, as the Americas.

The Business Times[23]

These two investments immediately became CAO's main source of earnings, and they would account for 68 percent of its profit before tax for 2003.[24] CAO, therefore, transformed itself into "an integrated enterprise encompassing jet fuel supplying, trading and investment-related activities with emphasis on oil industry related investments."[25]

Building and managing investor relations

Even though CAO's earnings grew from mid-2003, its share price continued to languish (see Exhibit 7.4 for CAO's share price movement). As Chen said:

While CAO has a good business model and strategy, and continues to show fast and steady growth, investors may not be immediately aware of CAO's strengths.[26]

Endeavoring to further increase corporate transparency and improve investor relations, on May 11, 2003, CAO managed to recruit John Casey

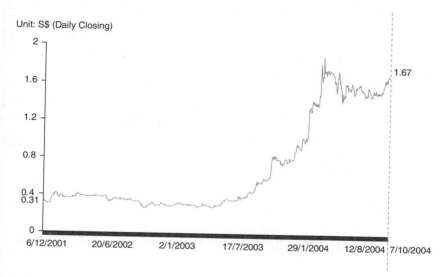

Exhibit 7.4   **Share price evolution**
Source: Datastream.

(a former security analyst at DBS Vickers* and an MBA graduate from Boston University), as deputy head of its internal audit and investor relations division.

More specifically, Casey's role was to facilitate better investor understanding of CAO by the local and international financial communities. In the months after Casey was hired, a series of analyst reports on CAO were published, each with a more positive tone. CAO's share price started to soar.

In October 2003, DBS Vickers recommended CAO's shares as a "Strong Buy":

> CAO has most of the characteristics investors look for, namely strong earnings growth, a secure earnings base, and a protected industry position with unusually low valuation and imminent price catalyst. The stock is relatively under-researched. We expect CAO to deliver strong earnings momentum in 2004. This will help to generate a wider base of interest in the stock.[27]

The day after CAO's analyst briefing on the release of its 3Q 2003 results (without material changes from the previous estimates), DBS Vickers reiterated its view and again raised its price target for CAO shares, adding:

> What is there not to love?[28]

The growing "war chest"

CAO had no interest-bearing debt until 2003 because it was not ready and was being cautious. In July 2003, it negotiated a favorable US$160 million[29] five-year syndicated loan facility with ten different—mainly Chinese—banks,[30] led by the Singapore-based Société Générale Asia Ltd. The unsecured facility, with an interest rate of only 80 basis points above the London Interbank Offered Rate (LIBOR), represented 158 percent of CAO's 2002 equity (S$176 million or US$106 million as of December 31, 2002).[31]

CAO now had a massive war chest (compared to its asset base) comprising the loan facility and cash, that could be used to invest in other businesses that would transform CAO's energy commodity trading and jet fuel procurement businesses into a more stable and integrated energy company. The idea was that the volatile energy trading business would contribute proportionately less to earnings, thus allaying some investors' fears.

Further on the acquisition trail

Between the middle of 2003 and the first quarter of 2004, CAO became one of the hottest stocks around, tripling in value as it embarked on an

---

* Casey was almost the only security analyst who had tracked CAO's shares since it listed.

acquisition trail and its sales soared.[32] In December 2003, it acquired its first controlling stake in oil-related, fixed infrastructure assets by purchasing 80 percent of the Shuidong oil storage facility (renamed China Aviation Oil Xinyuan Petrochemicals Co. Ltd). In February 2004, CAO announced its intention to acquire a 24.5 percent stake in South China Bluesky Aviation Oil Co. Ltd (Bluesky). Bluesky was perceived as becoming CAO's third "crown jewel" as it owned the entire jet fuel supply infrastructure for all 15 domestic and foreign airlines in central and southern China. The deal was suspended later that year, as the State-owned Asset and Supervision Administration Commission (SASAC) did not approve it.

One month later, CAO further expanded its horizons, this time to the Middle East by signing two memoranda of understanding with Emirates National Oil Company (ENOC)—an integrated oil holding company head-quartered in Dubai—and one of its subsidiaries. The intention was to forge a "strategic triangle"[33] and establish a supply chain running from the Middle East through Singapore and on to China.

Buying a "cow"

In August 2004, CAO hit the headlines with its intention to acquire from Satya Capital Ltd (a consortium of Indonesian businessmen) its 20.6 percent shareholding in Singapore Petroleum Company Limited (SPC). SPC was a major regional integrated oil and gas company.

CAO's management claimed that the deal was for strategic synergies and financial returns from SPC's complementary geographic footprint and capacity to refine jet kerosene would make it the first integrated oil company to operate overseas. But analysts questioned the justification for paying a high premium for the transaction, as well as suspecting ulterior motives. As DBS Vickers commented:

> Proverbially, CAO has bought one fifth of its neighbour's "cow" whose products are no cheaper than any of the milk, cheese, yogurt, or cream in the corner store.[34]

Thus, CAO had transformed itself from an international oil-trading company to an integrated industrial oil company.

Organization, process, and management

"Chinese Wisdom, International Expertise"

In September 2003, CAO changed its corporate slogan from "Leveraging on China, Going Global" to "Chinese Wisdom, International Expertise," centering on the fusion of East and West.

China is the beneficiary of a long history, wherein sages have successfully formalized the arts of war, business, strategy, culture and government, as well as those of peace and happiness. Western culture has developed science, economics, technology, and management theory at a remarkable pace.[35]

The concept was intended not only to reflect CAO's roots in China but also its status as a Singaporean company with operations and investments in China that had steadily grown more multinational. CAO also claimed that it brought together the Chinese concepts of *yi* (friendship and justice) over *li* (profit) and the Western emphasis on profitability by weighing each principle appropriately according to the situation. It believed in paying attention to *ren* (the Confucian concept of kindness and justice) in addition to making profits. In this way, it was able not only to create value for customers in the short term but also to forge key relationships with customers and partners to create even more value in the long term.

CAO hoped to become the bellwether* firm for overseas Chinese enterprises in terms of capital operations.[36]

Management concept and principles

CAO guided itself with a "One-Two-Three" concept of management and five investment principles based on combining all of CAO's available resources in a pragmatic fashion, in order to exploit opportunities as they arose.

The "One-Two-Three" concept stood for: One, aiming for rapid, continuous and steady growth; Two, advocating both systems and talent—in terms of systems, CAO emphasized the balance between incentives and restrictions, particularly for its risk management; and Three, following the "three-pronged strategy."

Its five investment principles comprised:

1. funding investments with controllable financial resources without over-stretching itself;
2. differentiating CAO by creating a strong brand name through quality, price, and service;
3. investing in asset-based businesses related to oil infrastructure;
4. creating economies of scale through its operations;
5. leveraging all alliances with multinational companies globally.

Management reporting structure at CAO

Much of Jia's (and his predecessor's) responsibilities as chairman of CAO were delegated to Chen right from the start. The chairman's control of the

---

* Leading indicator of trends.

company was mainly at the macro level and through the "eyes and ears"*
of the parent company. Ever since CAO resumed its businesses in 1997,
CAOHC had sent designated personnel to its Singapore subsidiary to balance
Chen. Over this period, CAOHC had sent three people as Chen's personal
assistants. However, several attempts to appoint a head of finance had failed,
as none of the candidates survived in the job for long, either because of the
language problem or lack of qualifications. For instance, Chen moved the
first finance manager to take care of travel and logistics after a few weeks.[37] In
October 2001, the independent directors recommended Peter Lim to be the
head of finance and Adrian Chang to be the head of internal audit. CAOHC
sent Zhang Zhicheng as the party secretary for the company† and deputy
CEO on May 15, 2002 (Zhang had the same internal ranking as Chen within
CAOHC and was Chen's former supervisor during his early days at CAOHC),
and Yang Bin (Yang had been internally identified as Chen's successor) to
assist the head of finance to strengthen its control over the Singapore entity
(see Exhibit 7.5 for CAO's management reporting structure).

In October 2002, Jia was promoted to president of CAOHC. In recognition of Chen's achievement in growing the Singapore business, SASAC
promoted him to one of the three CAOHC executive vice presidents—in
charge of CAOHC's international businesses. The three executive vice
presidents enjoyed equivalent status and privileges to a director-general of
a ministry of the Chinese government. Zhu Rongji, the then premier of the
state council of China, endorsed Chen's promotion.

CAO operated with a four-layer management structure. Staff reported
to managers, managers to department heads, department heads to Chen or
Zhang. Zhang and Yang reported directly to CAOHC, while Lim, Chang,
and Cindy Chong, the head of the risk-management committee and bank
relations, often reported directly to the independent directors. In addition, as
one of the major measures Chen undertook to integrate to the international
practices, CAO also recruited talent internationally. By May 2003, about 90
percent of CAO's employees came from the international community (including Singaporean employees), from at least six different countries. About 45
percent had prior multinational corporation experience—a major differentia-
tor CAO claimed from other Chinese companies. CAO also claimed that:

> It capitalizes on its multinational staff, as well as China's huge market and vast
> pool of human talent, to combine entrepreneurial spirit with the laws of nature
> and markets carved out by the ancient sages thousands of years ago.[38]

---

* Jia described this figuratively during the PricewaterhouseCoopers (PwC) investigation.
According to his representations to PwC and CAD during the investigation, all these "ears
and eyes" reported to the parent company and him directly so that the parent company and he
would have direct control over the Singapore entity.
† The Communist Party of China is the sole party in power in China. It exercises political,
ideological and organizational leadership through its organizations at both central and local
level. A grassroots party organization is always set up in enterprises or other organizations if
there are three or four full party members employed there.

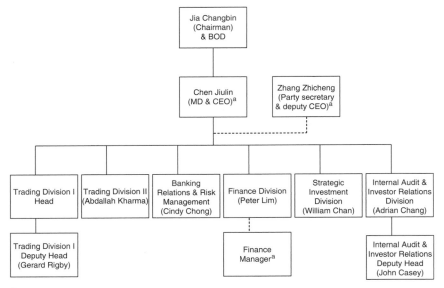

ªSent by CAOHC in Beijing.

Exhibit 7.5 **CAO's management reporting structure**

Source: Public company announcements.

There was a system of direct parallel reporting between the respective divisions in CAOHC and CAO. For instance, William Chan, CAO's head of investments, would report to Madam Gu, CAOHC's head of enterprise planning and development; Peter Lim, CAO's head of finance, would report to Li, CAOHC's head of assets and financial management. Similarly, CAO's risk controller Elena Ng would report to Li or his assistant.

CAO also had a "four-pen" system for all its expenditures, that is each expense required effectively four signatures—staff, department head, division head, then either Chen or Zhang, the final authority for approval. As Chen was often on business trips, most large expenditures related to letters of credit (LC) or matters that were submitted by the head of the risk-management committee and bank relations went to Zhang for his approval.*

Chen Jiulin: "the smart and bold"

Born in 1961 in Hubei province, Chen went to Peking University—one of China's top universities—in 1982. Although majored in Vietnamese, Chen

---

* Zhang was co-signatory with Chong in relation to all import and export documentation related to CAO, and was responsible for co-signing all application forms required for the issuance of any LC as collateral to support any margin calls. Yang was appointed by CAOHC to ensure financial control over the cash payments of CAO, and was signatory with Chen in relation to the operation of CAO's bank documents. He was responsible for all authorizations for cash payments made by CAO in excess of S$50,000.

had shown a strong interest in English. After his graduation in 1987, he joined the general manager's office at Air China Limited (Air China) as an interpreter. In 1989, he participated in negotiations for the formation of the first Sino-foreign joint venture in the Chinese aviation sector between Air China and Lufthansa Airlines of Germany.[39]

In 1993, Chen joined CAOHC, where he actively served as chief negotiator and project manager on various joint venture negotiations including Bluesky—a major milestone as it was the first regional project, and the largest joint venture project, in the Chinese civil aviation industry.

Chen later received his postgraduate diploma in law from the China University of Political Science and Law in 1996 and his Executive Master of Business Administration (EMBA) degree from the National University of Singapore (NUS) in 2001. Later, he also pursued a doctoral degree in law at Tsinghua University.

Within just four years, Chen turned CAO from a loss-making company into a successful publicly listed company. He was perceived within the parent company as one of "the smart and bold." His efforts and achievements were highly regarded and rewarded, so much so that he became one of the highest-paid chief executives in Singapore* and was recognized by the Singapore media as "the king of the working class."[40]

In 2003, Chen was voted one of 40 New Asian Leaders (renamed Young Global Leaders) by the World Economic Forum (WEF), the only one from China (excluding Hong Kong) and Singapore. The selection criteria included exceptional company performance and influence in the political, economic, or academic arena. The WEF found tremendous potential in Chen with his keen entrepreneurial spirit and strong management skills.

Chen soon became a rising star in corporate Singapore. Perceived as maintaining a "modest lifestyle"—and admired for it—he was outgoing, increasingly visible and gave his cell phone number to journalists.[41] Apart from delivering many key speeches at international forums, Chen had also published a book, *Leveraging on China, Going Global*,[42] and a number of articles in both domestic and overseas newspapers and magazines.[43]

Managing upwards

Due to constant interference and pressure from the parent company, Chen knew the ultimate importance of developing CAO's relationship internally with its parent group. This was even formalized in some of CAO's business arrangements. In 2000, CAO sponsored 18 CAOHC employees for the EMBA program at the NUS. Only three of them were directly involved with CAO, including Chen, Jia, and one of CAO's nonexecutive directors.

---

* Chen had an annual income of S$4.9 million (US$2.9 million) in 2002 based on a cumulative profit sharing scheme, although it was said that he may not actually have received most of the money.

> We had sponsored the courses for our parent group employees as part of our efforts to further develop our relationship with our parent group, who is our major customer. The sponsorship of these parent group employees could indirectly benefit our company as these are the key executives in our parent group who are in a position to make decisions that are beneficial to our company.[44]

Later that year, CAO also incorporated a wholly owned subsidiary under the name of Greater China Travel Industry (Singapore) Pte Ltd to meet its domestic customers' (including CAOHC's) regular international travel needs and thus improve its relationship with them.

The parent company

The management system in China is not the same as in other countries in the world. In China, the decision-making of subsidiaries was often not carried out by the entity board; instead the parent company takes the lead.

CAOHC had established a specific management system for overseas subsidiaries and had stipulated that all important items be submitted to CAOHC for decision-making. No less than 15 working days prior to a CAO board meeting, all the reports and materials that CAO management planned to submit to the meeting would have to be submitted to CAOHC first, going on to the CAO board only after approval or revision by CAOHC. Each year, CAOHC by-passed the CAO board and directly sent documents or directives through administrative management systems, while CAO managers were obliged to by-pass the CAO board and submit hundreds of reports or applications directly to the parent company. Any CAOHC executive could instruct CAO management directly at any time and ask the CAO management to execute. These instructions would not be discussed with the board, nor with other minority shareholders. As an expatriate from the parent company, Chen had to obey these instructions, otherwise, he could have been repatriated at any time. The parent company had already penalized him for not obeying instructions by not inviting him to attend an annual working meeting* and not purchasing jet fuel from CAO.

Board of directors

The CAO board comprised nine members, one of whom was an executive director. Six out of the nine members were nominated by CAOHC.

---

* CAOHC held a national annual working meeting, which it invited all overseas presidents (or CEOs) and party secretaries to attend.

None of the CAOHC-nominated board members had had any past, or even current, directorships with any publicly listed company in Singapore. Therefore, in accordance with the Singapore legal requirements, before or during the IPO process, these directors received formal training on corporate governance and directors' duties arranged by DBS Vickers and WongPartnership LLP, one of the largest law firms in Singapore, at the latter's office.The training was conducted by two seasoned lawyers (Raymond Goh and He Jun) in Chinese* in a closed setting. CAO also translated the IPO prospectus into Chinese and distributed it in the form of a formal document to the parent company and its designated directors for their comments. The parent company held various meetings to discuss the prospectus and gave their comments for revisions on the key issues such as directors' duties and jet fuel procurement. Even the company name in Chinese (*Zhong Guo Hang You*) was determined by the parent company after various discussions to avoid the confusion between a company from the mainland and Taiwan (CAO initially submitted its Chinese name as *Zhong Hua Hang You*). CAOHC then submitted the revised version to CAAC for approval. The latter consulted CSRC during its approval process.

To ensure the parent company fully understood the IPO requirements, Chen also invited Philip Tan, vice president of SGX, to go to Beijing and give a "lecture" to CAOHC and its designated directors. CAOHC also arranged for Yang Guoqin, vice director of CAAC, to meet with Tan. On the surface, it appeared that the board had seemingly delegated to Chen the training obligations, where "the directors, particularly the managing director and CEO, participated in seminars and/or discussion groups to keep updated on the latest developments that concern or affect the group." [45] However, in reality, CAOHC and the board were also actively involved in the IPO processes (including the training). Ultimately, CAO was CAOHC's first and only overseas subsidiary.

At the time of its IPO, CAO appointed three independent directors: two Singaporeans recommended by DBS Vickers, Jerry Lee Kian Eng and Tan Hui Boon, and Yan Xuetong.

Lee was chairman of the audit committee, an approved company auditor and liquidator under the Company Act in Singapore, and a senior partner of Ng Lee & Associates—DFK. DFK had been CAO's external auditor and tax advisor for three years before Ernst & Young took over in 2000. Lee also held directorships in various other companies and was chairman of the audit committee until March 2006.

---

* Chinese language: as a generalization, Singapore Chinese speak or understand Cantonese, but not Mandarin, or understand a little Mandarin, but not sufficient to fully understand or speak it. Most, if not all, CAO/CAOHC executives speak Mandarin, but not Cantonese. Although Chinese is one of the state's official languages, the (many) Singaporeans who grew up in an English-speaking environment tend not to speak either form of Chinese, or read even simplified Chinese, well.

Tan, a member of the audit committee, was a chemical engineer by education and former finance director—with no formal accounting qualifications—of Singapore Airlines. DBS Vickers had approached him after his retirement to take up a directorship in one of two Chinese companies. He chose CAO. Tan spoke some Mandarin, but was not fluent. He was a member of the audit committee and took over the responsibilities of the chairman for the remuneration committee in 2Q 2003.

Dr. Yan was the only non-Singaporean independent director. He was a director of the Institute of International Studies at Tsinghua University in China. He was a pure academic, albeit with much international exposure. He was chairman of the remuneration committee until March 2003.

To fulfill its responsibilities, the board had established an audit committee, a remuneration committee, and a risk-management committee, which were said to be "in compliance with the Best Practice Guide of the SGX."[46] The board did not have a nomination committee, even though it was a legal requirement, but said that "it would review the necessity."[47] Consequently, new directors were appointed by board resolution and there was no formal system for assessing the performance of the board.

The CAO board met twice a year. The meetings were hosted by the chairman. Chen spent half an hour reading the working report approved by CAOHC in advance and reviewed by the directors. The report was produced both in English and in Chinese. Proceedings and board papers were in Mandarin, and translated into English. While Chen was reading the report, a designated person illustrated the key points of the report in both English and Chinese in the form of a PowerPoint presentation. After Chen finished the report, the division heads also used PowerPoint to report to the board. CAOHC reviewed and approved all of the reports and materials submitted to the board in advance and, most of the time, the CAOHC-nominated directors shared Chen's views. At times, however, the CAOHC-nominated directors also had heated debates with Chen. All the minutes of the board meetings and the directors' reports were in both English and Chinese. Each board meeting was also filmed, recorded, and filed.

Risk management, governance and the regulatory environment

Risk management

For most of CAO's existence, risk was intuitively managed.[48]

On October 1, 2000, having incurred some losses in speculative derivatives trading (refer to Exhibit 7.6 for CAO's historical derivatives trading performance), CAO established a risk-management committee (RMC) to help monitor risk and formalize a risk-management system. The RMC comprised four full-time designated personnel including Cindy Chong,* chairman of the RMC and head of banking relations and risk management; Peter Lim, head of finance; Elena Ng, the risk controller and Eddie Heng, the finance manager† and three part-time employees. In addition to reporting directly to Chen, all members of the RMC also reported to the Internal Audit & Investor Relations Department (IAD‡), which in turn reported to the Audit Committee. The head of RMC, the risk controller, the financial controller and the head of each trading department attended every audit committee meeting.

Risk-management infrastructure

On July 1, 2001, CAO installed OilSpace, an oil-trading software program recommended by Ernst & Young (CAO's external auditor since 2000). Partly because of the program, all of CAO's traders were making profits. The business was so strong that the company employed two new "heavy-weight traders"—traders with the authority to take large positions.[49]

This software had a back-office risk-management add-on that warned the RMC once a trader had accumulated US$200,000 in losses and implemented an automatic stop-loss at US$500,000 for trades in paper swaps and oil futures. All open positions had to be closed once the stop-loss limit was reached, unless approval was obtained from Chen. However, DBS Vickers regarded it as a "highly redundant risk-management system":

Exhibit 7.6 CAO reported gain / (loss) on derivatives trading

S$ million	1998	1999	2000	2001	2002	2003
Paper swaps	(2.0)	3.4	(12.2)	(6.2)	(0.1)	12.7
Futures	–	0.0	(0.2)	(0.7)	(0.4)	3.9
Options	–	–	–	–	1.1	9.8
Total	(2.0)	3.4	(12.4)	(6.9)	0.7	26.3

Source: Public company announcements.

---

* On April 15, 2003, Chong was appointed chairman of the RMC. She had a bachelor of business degree (transport/logistics management) and had joined CAO in 2001 as head of the operations division in charge of supervising CAO's physical and derivatives trading operations after more than 14 years' experience with BHP Petroleum. Chong did not have the necessary qualifications or any previous risk-management experience.

† Heng was responsible for preparing the payment authorizations for cash payments to pay CAO's margin calls.

‡ It was not clear why CAO had a combined internal audit and investor relations function, even though it seemed that it had recruited the right people to be head and deputy head of the department.

This system worked fine but it was not a cutting-edge risk-management product because it did not account for dynamic risk of different commodities and changing market environments.[50]

In 2003, CAO upgraded to a trading software called Kiodex, which had the capability to value options. The Kiodex system used integrated market information, valuation models, risk-balancing algorithms, and deal capture.

While the traders' skills ultimately drive the company's trading profits, it is reassuring that CAO finally has an appropriate risk-management infrastructure.[51]

However, the RMC believed that the system was "unreliable" and therefore had not used it for its options trading.[52]

The Risk Management Manual (RMM)

Due to the high risk associated with the highly volatile international trading business, CAO placed much emphasis on its risk-management procedures in its IPO prospectus. Moreover, it clearly stated that the company might suffer huge losses due to poor judgment or misconduct on the part of the traders. It had also engaged Ernst & Young to develop a comprehensive Risk Management Manual (RMM), which was said to be modeled on the best industry practices of major international oil companies. The RMM was developed during the course of 2002.

At the March 14, 2002 board meeting, representatives from Ernst & Young and the then-current chairman of the RMC (Chong's predecessor) presented and explained the background and content of the RMM to the board. The board approved the RMM on a "test-run" basis because it did not have the time or expertise to digest the content and comment on the figures.[53] CAO stated in its 2002 annual report that it had adopted the RMM, but there was no indication that this had been done on a provisional basis. The same year, CAO won the "Most Transparent Company Award," endorsed by the Securities Investors Association of Singapore, out of all the newly listed companies on the SGX.[54]

According to the RMM, the board should approve entry into new businesses. It delegated the day-to-day risk-management responsibility to the CEO, who sub-delegated his responsibility to the RMC. The RMM also gave the CEO authority to approve any trading or credit risk exposure in excess of authorized limits, up to a maximum of US$5 million, and also set a trading limit of 2 million barrels for all products to restrict the volume of open positions.

The RMM did not address options trading, nor had any trading limits for options been set. The board had signed seven resolutions and documents related to options trading, but none had set trading limits, not even at the audit committee meeting on February 28, 2004, when speculative options trading was specifically discussed.

Enhanced risk-management framework

The 2003 annual report noted that the risk-management framework had been further enhanced with a "three-layer control system": (1) the divisional heads, the "independent" RMC, and the internal audit division; (2) the audit committee; and (3) the board (see Exhibit 7.7 for more details). Adrian Chang had been the head of internal audit and investor relations since 2001. He had an MBA in international business and was a certified public accountant in Singapore as well as an Australian chartered accountant. The audit committee consisted of CAO's two Singaporean independent directors and one CAOHC-nominated nonexecutive director, Li Yongji (head of the assets and financial management division at CAOHC).[55]

Within the first layer, the division heads and the RMC reported directly to Chen. Furthermore, the RMC had not reported any issues regarding the company's options trades to the internal audit division—to which it was meant to report—until it was asked to do so in May 2004.[56]

Despite all this, CAO became the only overseas Chinese-funded enterprise to receive an award for its risk-management structure and procedures at China's Tenth Annual Creative Management Awards in 2004. The award was given by the China National Enterprise Federation (CNEF), a quasi-governmental body with nationwide scope and influence, and all of China's top enterprises were members. CNEF's influence was such that it hosted and organized the China Business Summit 2003 in Beijing, together with the World Economic Forum. On June 11, 2004, Li accompanied an eight-member delegation consisting of officials from SASAC, the Chinese Ministry of Commerce, and CSRC, to examine CAO's nonphysical oil-trading

Exhibit 7.7   **Enhanced risk management**

Source: Public company announcements.

activities. During the course of the delegation's visit, the RMC specifically gave a two-hour presentation on CAO's option trades to the delegation.

The regulatory environment in Singapore and China

As a publicly listed company in Singapore that was majority owned by a state-owned Chinese company, CAO was directly or indirectly regulated by different entities in Singapore and China. The main ones were the SGX (as both a regulator and marketer) and the Monetary Authority of Singapore (MAS) in Singapore; and the China Securities Regulatory Commission (CSRC), the Civil Aviation Authority of China (CAAC) and the State-owned Asset Supervision and Administration Committee (SASAC) in China.

The Singapore Exchange Limited (SGX)

SGX is a self-regulatory, for-profit organization formed in 1999. On November 23, 2000, SGX became the first listed exchange in Asia-Pacific. It offered a diverse and exciting array of securities and derivatives products via a global network of broking members who provided access to these products through various channels.

SGX had a dual function, as the market regulator and a commercial entity committed to maximizing shareholder value. SGX positioned itself as the "Asia Gateway," and most of the foreign-listed companies were from Greater China,* Southeast Asia, and North Asia.

> SGX remained an attractive listing venue for foreign issuers, especially China issuers, which accounted for 7 out of the 11 foreign listings during the first quarter of FY2005 (SGX Q1 FY 2005 was from July 1, 2004 to September 30, 2004).
>
> Hsieh Fu Hua, CEO SGX[57]

It also adopted more market-oriented listing rules to provide flexibility for foreign companies with diverse backgrounds to secure financing in Singapore.

> SGX has looked to Chinese listings as a way to generate higher trading volumes. The 68 Chinese companies listed in Singapore account for about 10 percent of total listings.[58]

The Singapore securities market operated a disclosure-based regime, on the principle that informed investors can make their own investment decisions. It therefore required full, frank, and timely disclosure of information to investors.

---

* A term commonly used to refer to commercial ties and cultural interactions among ethnic Chinese. In geographic terms, it often refers to mainland China, Hong Kong, Macau and Taiwan.

In 2003, SGX introduced a new set of securities trading rules to reflect current market practices based on an earlier public consultation. In March 2004, SGX also held its first interactive orientation session for newly listed companies to help familiarize them with their listing obligations. The session provided companies with an overview of SGX's listing rules and featured discussions on topics including directors' duties, directors' and officers' insurance, and investor relations. Such orientation sessions were planned to be held approximately every quarter.[59]

In May 2004, SGX provided further guidance on the general duties of due diligence by sponsors, allowing for investigative reports to be commissioned, requiring post-listing sponsorship disclosure and directors' training disclosure and clarifying rules for foreign companies regarding "connection" to Singapore "to ensure sufficient local representation and the ability to take steps in the event of a problem."[60]

Monetary Authority of Singapore (MAS)

MAS is the de facto central bank of Singapore. It administers the various statutes pertaining to money, banking, insurance, securities, and the financial sector in general, as well as issuing currency following its merger with the Board of Commissioners of Currency on October 1, 2002.

MAS is SGX's regulator. It has the authority to issue directives to SGX—with which SGX has to comply—if MAS thinks it necessary or expedient in order to ensure fair and orderly securities and futures markets, or to ensure the integrity and proper management of systemic risks in the securities and futures markets.

From July 1, 2005, MAS started to levy a supervisory fee to meet the costs of regulating and supervising SGX and its clearing-house. The charge to SGX for fiscal year 2006 totaled S$1.39 million (US$834,000).[61]

China Securities Regulatory Commission (CSRC)

As a publicly listed company in Singapore, CAO was, in theory, not under the direct supervision of CSRC. However, CSRC governed all overseas futures transactions of Chinese SOEs.

Because of the losses incurred from speculative derivatives trading by some SOEs in the 1990s, CSRC in general prohibited SOEs from engaging in speculative trading of derivatives, and only permitted trading in futures for hedging purposes where licenses were granted. Even so, the regulations did not cover over-the-counter (OTC) trades.

Civil Aviation Authority of China (CAAC)

CAAC was an administrative body under the State Council of China that oversaw civil aviation activities in mainland China. CAAC was formed on

November 2, 1949 to manage all nonmilitary aviation in China. It was initially managed by the People's Liberation Army Air Force, but was transferred to the direct control of the State Council in 1980.

CAAC emerged as an international airline operator following a 1980 instruction from chairman Deng Xiaoping to begin planning for civil flights. On March 5, 1980, CAAC formed an airline operation division with six offices.

In 1987, the aviation regulation division and the airline operation division were separated, and the airline division further divided into five airline groups, to reflect the location of their headquarters and main areas of operation.

In 2002, CAAC underwent another major restructuring and part of its responsibilities were given to CAOHC and reported directly to the SASAC of the State Council.

State-owned Asset Supervision and Administration Commission (SASAC)

SASAC was a special organ of the State Council, replacing CAAC as CAOHC's regulator in October 2002.

In 1998, SASAC was set up based on the principle of separating government administration from enterprise management and ownership from management power. SASAC invested on behalf of the state; supervised and managed the state-owned assets of enterprises; guided and pushed forward the reform and restructuring of SOEs.

SASAC appointed and removed top executives of all enterprises under the supervision of the State Council, evaluated their performance, and rewarded or punished them as necessary.

The crisis

Derivatives trades had been part of CAO's business since 1998. Initially CAO started trading for hedging purposes to mitigate the high volatility risk of the oil price.

To ensure a wider business scope, at the time of the IPO in 2001, CAO noted in its prospectus its engagement in opportunistic or speculative trading:

> Besides hedging, we also engage in opportunistic trading by taking open positions in derivatives instruments when our traders, based on their experience and analysis of the market were of the view that the open positions would likely gain from the expected market movement.[62]

This had attracted CSRC's attention.

The board approved the opening of a broker account for the purpose of trading options and other derivatives on an exchange. A board resolution was passed by Jia, among others on February 20, 2002, resolving that Gerard Rigby (deputy head of Trading Division I) and Abdallah Kharma (head of Trading Division II) were authorized to enter into option contracts, Elena Ng (risk controller) and Eddie Heng (finance manager) were authorized to execute confirmations of options contracts, and to receive statements from the counterparty relating to these contracts.

On March 20, 2002, CAO began its options trading with "a casual exchange of e-mails between Rigby and Chen."[63] Initially, these were back-to-back trades* with airline companies. The background of the transaction was that Air China requested CAO to provide "back-to-back" support to its options trading with international companies and traders. The transaction was introduced by CAOHC.

In the same month, CSRC censured CAOHC for CAO's trading in derivatives without prior approval and instructed CAO to cease its specula-tive derivatives trading, to restrict its derivatives trading to hedging, and to apply for approval to trade in futures for hedging purposes. CAO was first directed by CAOHC to submit a self-criticism report to CAOHC for its onward transmission to CSRC. Then, in or around October 2002, CAOHC filed an application with CSRC for a license for futures trading for hedging purposes. The license was granted in March 2003, and subsequently, in a letter, CAOHC granted CAO a sublicense.

After explaining to CSRC, confirming with CAOHC and gaining board approval, CAO began speculative options trading on its own account on March 28, 2003, while continuing the back-to-back options trading with airline companies. The speculative options trading was restricted to the heads of its two trading divisions including Rigby. Rigby did most of the trading as he was regarded as the most experienced in options trading. He had worked at Ampol Australian Petroleum, Caltex Australia and in Singapore before joining CAO in 2001. It was understood that none of the independent direc-tors was informed of or consulted on the CSRC incident, nor was CSRC informed that CAO's speculative derivatives trading activities continued.

On September 1, 2003, the board signed an ISDA Master Agreement for the trading of OTC options with Bank of America (BOA), and later entered into similar agreements with Mitsui Energy Risk Management (MERM), the oil derivatives unit of Mitsui Corp, J. Aron and Company (J. Aron), the commodity division of Goldman Sachs., Société Générale Group, MSCG, Standard Bank, Macquarie Bank, HETC, and Air China. These ISDA Master Agreements set out the terms for all closed-out netting and the use of margin and collaterals between CAO and the respective counterparties.

Ernst & Young was informed by Peter Lim (head of finance) and Elena Ng (risk controller) that CAO only began speculative trading in options in 3Q

---

* "back-to-back trades: a pair of transactions that requires a counterparty to receive and redeliver the same securities on the same day." Source: Bank for International Settlements, Committee on Payment and Settlement Systems (2003) *A Glossary of Terms Used In Payments and Settlement Systems.*

2003. Ernst & Young did not question or verify the validity of the information, even though the fact that it had begun speculative trading was evident in CAO's open disclosure in its annual reports and in discussions that took place at the board and audit committee meetings from 2002 to 2004.[64] Therefore, from the outset, the independent directors were aware of the speculative derivatives trading but had never heard that CSRC had censured CAOHC for CAO's trading in derivatives without prior approval (though CSRC had never actually prohibited such transactions). It was obvious that CAO had carried on with the speculative derivatives trading. In addition, Ng, Chong and Lim attended various CAO audit committee meetings and reported on CAO's option positions and marked-to-market (MTM)* exposure directly to the members of the audit committee[†]. However, none of the independent directors, nor Ernest & Young, questioned the "1 to 5 healthy hedging" concept[‡] brought up by Lim and Rigby at the audit committee meetings.[65]

From 2002 to 2004, CAO's derivatives trading volume increased significantly. To keep up with the growth and also to meet the requirements of the GTP status, by November 2004, CAO had a total of nine oil traders.

A wrong bet

CAO's options trading strategy was based on its view of the oil price trend. Until the last quarter of 2003, CAO had taken a bullish view, which had largely proved accurate and yielded a profit.

In 4Q 2003, CAO changed its options trading strategy fundamentally as it switched to a bearish view of the trend in oil prices. It had taken more open positions, assuming that oil prices would fall and its counterparties would not extend the options, which would therefore lapse to the benefit of CAO.

However, the oil price did not fall in 4Q 2003. The options that CAO had bought thus had a negative MTM value of US$1.2 million in 4Q 2003. The rise in the oil price resulted in the counterparties extending the options contracts that had been sold in 3Q 2003 and CAO therefore faced the real risk of having to sell the contracted number of barrels at the agreed price. CAO would have had a net exposure on these options at maturity and faced the real possibility of realizing substantial losses in 1Q 2004.

CAO also regarded the MTM value of an option as the price difference between the agreed price and the forward price without considering the time value of the options, which did not reflect the industry standard that prices might be volatile over the period of the option.

---

* Marked-to-market (MTM): an arrangement whereby the profits or losses on a futures contract are settled up each day.
† Chen was not a member of the audit committee and never attended its meetings.
‡ Lim and Rigby proposed that if the volume of derivatives trading remained within five times the volume of the actual commodity trading, then it was "healthy hedging"—a nonexistent concept.

One of CAO's counterparties, in an e-mail, had tried to question CAO's valuation of certain outstanding options.[66] The e-mail did not reach Chen, and the RMC and traders did not realize that their valuation methodology may not have been correct.

At the mercy of counterparties

CAO traded mainly in over-the-counter (OTC) options. These were customized options, not traded on any major energy exchanges. The counterparties were banks and energy companies.

Depending on its exposure, CAO was required to place deposits or margins with its counterparties as collateral. The amount required varied or fluctuated from day to day based on the oil price. CAO was constantly facing calls from the counterparties to top up its margins.

After consulting J. Aron, Rigby, in his e-mail to Chen, Chong and Ng dated January 21, 2004, recommended that J. Aron's written proposal to restructure CAO's option positions be adopted "as it eliminates the immediate loss making positions and replaces with small volume exposure that is further out to 4Q which gives time to manage... Overall it is a more manageable position."[67] This was reiterated by Chong in her e-mail dated September 6, 2004, stating that "if we didn't restructure, we would take in the realized losses for this year. If we restructured, we would be extending (or transferring) the MTM negative value to the later periods. However, the margin calls would still be required based on the prevailing oil prices against the new strike prices."[68] Therefore, CAO first restructured its options portfolio on January 26, 2004, and subsequently twice more, on June 28, 2004 and in September 2004.

The two later restructurings were of the same nature, that is closing out the loss-making near-date options and replacing them with longer-tenure ones and in greater volumes to cover higher negative MTM, transaction costs and higher cash flow requirements to meet margin calls.

Based on the projections made by 21 international oil and financial institutions on the oil market, the traders at CAO and the RMC made the judgment that the market would eventually turn to the advantage of CAO. CAO, therefore, extended its options portfolio three times to avoid realizing the losses and in the hope that the situation could be managed. The first and second restructurings were carried out with J. Aron, while the third was carried out with five different counterparties (this time excluding J. Aron) between August 31 and September 27, 2004. Further, CAO did not book the losses that were realized upon the restructuring when closing out the loss-making near-dated options. In fact, CAO only started to prepare daily MTM reports to track its options trading losses from July 9, 2004. Both Chen and Lim received the reports and were aware of the losses. However, the accounting methods that the auditor and the audit committee used only recorded realized profits and losses in the quarterly reports, while unrealized profits and losses were only recorded at the end of the year. This method was stated in the 2003 annual report.

Knowing that the company had lost at least US$155 million from speculative oil derivatives trading, Rigby personally sold his 16,800 shares using an account at DBS Vickers on August 19, 2004.[69]

The "*Yin* and *Yang*" financial statements

According to Mr Jia, Chen, who denies this, always submitted two sets of financial statements and used them to disguise CAO's open positions in option trades. One set, for submission to the board for approval, only showed one line of futures transactions, while the other set released to the public showed both futures and options in two separate lines. However, since only one set was sent to the board prior to the release, none of the directors actually spotted the "*Yin* and *Yang*" of the financial statements.[70]

Based on the disclosed accounting method, CAO took the view that unless the losses were realized, there was no requirement to account for them in its financial statements. Hence the phrase "gain or loss on financial instruments for hedging purposes are recorded off balance sheet."[71]

Each auditor held different views on this. PwC believed that for the year ended December 31, 2002 and onwards, the financial statements were incorrect in that the MTM value of the options transacted by the company were not duly accounted for. The errors in the company's reported profit before tax (PBT) in the first three quarters of 2004 were as follows:

	1Q	2Q	YTD June 04	3Q	YTD Sept. 04
Reported PBT(S$ million)	19.0	19.3	38.3	11.3	49.6
"Corrected" PBT(S$ million)	(6.4)	(58.0)	(64.4)	(314.6)	(379.0)

Moreover, when the RMC provided reports on its derivatives trading to the audit committee, it concealed the losses the company had faced with regard to its option trades. Also, the RMC did not inform the board of the losses associated with the option trades.

The SOS

Between July and October 7, 2004, oil prices increased steeply—by more than 50 percent—from US$36 to US$54 per barrel.* Based on CAO's calculation, its lowest MTM loss was reported on July 13, 2004 at about US$28 million, while the highest MTM loss was reported on October 7, 2004 at about US$180 million.[72]

---

* The price of crude oil traded on the New York Mercantile Exchange was used as a measure.

CAO's cash position had been deteriorating severely as it constantly had to meet margin calls. After exhausting all the company's financial resources, including using the syndicate loan proceeds and delaying payment to CAO's trade partners, Chen called Jia on the evening of October 7, 2004, in the hopes that the board and the parent company would make a decision to help CAO through the crisis.

What next?

Chen's call came as a surprise. Jia could not think of any financial difficulties that CAO might have faced, nor could Li. The extent of CAO's financial problem was not yet clear to Jia. He did not proactively look into the situation, nor did he call for an urgent board meeting or ask the party members to find a solution. Instead, he was still enjoying his Golden Week holiday and was waiting for Li to come up with his report before reviewing the options for both CAO and CAOHC. Li was also enjoying his travelling during the rest of the Golden Week. Despite the fact that Chen had emphasized the urgency of the situation, Li asked Chen to send a written report so that CAO and CAOHC could hold a meeting to discuss their options in accordance with normal procedures when Golden Week ended and Hai Liancheng (party secretary of CAOHC) returned from his trip in Europe.

8 Stormy Waters

On the evening of Sunday November 28, 2004, Jia and his team flew from Beijing to Singapore. The following day they filed an application with the Singapore high court for the suspension of trading in CAO's shares and the restructuring of the company.

For nearly two months, ever since Jia had been informed of the problem, a rescue effort had been under way. CAO had incurred substantial losses due to speculative trading in oil derivatives, and faced bankruptcy if it failed to satisfy the margin calls.

A number of possible solutions to the company's financial problem had been explored, including selling shares in the company. A number of parties had been approached, including major Chinese petroleum companies, Chinese banks and international oil majors. However, none of the solutions proved to be sufficient and workable. At the same time, the estimated MTM losses were mounting on a daily basis because of the all-time high oil prices. They had escalated from the initially estimated US$180 million in CAO's report submitted to CAOHC on October 8, to US$550 million on November 29.

On November 30, the losses were announced to the public and hit the headlines as "Singapore's biggest corporate scandal since Barings.*" Presumed (or convicted) as the central figure of the scandal, Chen, the once regarded as a high flyer in both Singapore and China, was now referred to as the "Chinese Nick Leeson."

The extent of the problem

Li stepped into Jia's office first thing on the morning of October 8, 2004. He told Jia that the losses were too big to swallow. When Jia asked why, Li briefed him on his follow-up conversations with Chen. Jia asked Li to investigate the matter further and report back to him and then left on a prearranged business trip. Hai was still travelling in Europe even though he had received the urgent call.

According to an urgent report that CAO had submitted to CAOHC on October 9, CAO had incurred at least US$180 million of paper losses on its

---

* Barings Bank was the oldest merchant bank in Britain until 1995, when it collapsed after one of its employees, Nick Leeson, lost US$1.3 billion in speculative investing at the bank's Singapore office.

over-the-counter (OTC) options trades because of the record high oil prices in 2004. CAO was unable to meet the demands for margin top-ups, and it was likely that the shortage of funds could be as much as US$200 million. The options trading counterparties might even take legal action if CAO failed to top up the margins in time. CAO also further went on that it was due to release its 3Q financial results and had to make a public disclosure on the losses in accordance with the Singapore Exchange (SGX) requirements.

CAO also proposed in the report either a "back-to-back" arrangement to transfer the options positions to CAOHC, so that no losses would be shown on CAO's accounts and CAOHC could monitor the market and take appropriate measures to reduce the losses (in case of profits from the positions, the profits would go to CAOHC), or, if realized losses were unavoidable after CAOHC took over the position, CAOHC could sell some of its shares to strategic investors while maintaining a majority shareholding and lend money to CAO. Chen signed the report on behalf of CAO, which highlighted three key points: (1) CAOHC must take over the positions; (2) only after CAOHC took over the positions and the losses were realized, could CAOHC then sell some of its shares to make up the losses; and (3) the shares could only be sold to strategic investors instead of the public. Chen was trying to find strategic investors such as Exxon Mobile or BP to be shareholders of CAO and help to improve its management.

None of CAO's independent directors were informed of the derivative trading losses before October 9, 2004.

In the urgent report, CAO also stressed that the situation was critical and pressing, and if it was not handled properly, CAO could become insolvent. The impact on the reputation of Chinese SOEs, on CAO itself as a reputable company in Singapore, and on the Singapore financial markets would be unthinkable. There was an urgent need to salvage the situation.

Initial crisis management

While Jia was on his business trip and Hai was travelling abroad, the three executive committee members of CAOHC* who remained in Beijing decided that the problem was too serious to handle on their own and that they should report to SASAC. Meanwhile, they started to try to find a solution internally.

On October 10, a CAOHC† crisis management team (the CMT), headed by Chen, was set up to deal with the crisis. Other team members included

---

* CAOHC's executive committee comprised Jia; Hai Liancheng (Party secretary); Li Chunjian, Gong Feng and Chen Jiulin (vice presidents); and Dang Kou (vice secretary). Source: Field research.

† Including CAOHC's designated personnel to CAO based in Singapore, namely Chen, Zhang and Yang.

Madam Gu,* Zhang Lianxi (non-executive director and deputy director of CAOHC's procurement division), Bian Hui (Jia's secretary), Zhang Zhicheng (CAO's Party secretary and deputy CEO) and Yang Bin (Chen's personal assistant).† Both Zhang Zhicheng and Yang were CAOHC's appointed supervisors over CAO's finances.

Li also forwarded Chen's report to the members of CAOHC's executive committee, Madam Gu and Bian. In addition, upon Li's request, Jennie Liu e-mailed Li a draft back-to-back agreement prepared by CAO's solicitors.

The same day, Chen sent another report—Chen's self-criticism report—to CAOHC stating that disclosure of CAO's losses (realized or unrealized) would thwart any attempts to salvage the situation, as CAO's share price would collapse and the company would then face liquidation. Chen urged CAOHC not to disclose the losses and to restrict discussions of the matter to CAOHC's executive committee and finance department.

On October 13 or 14 two members of the CMT in Beijing, Madam Gu and Li, arranged for staff in Beijing to draft a report and submit it to CAOHC's executive committee. It explained how the losses had arisen, the crisis CAO was facing, and the proposed solutions. It also stated that CAO was due to announce its financial results and would be required to disclose even paper losses to comply with SGX regulations. If CAO reported accordingly, this would cause panic selling of CAO's shares, the banks' withdrawal of CAO's credit lines and CAO could face insolvency.

On October 15 Li submitted a situation report of the CMT to the CAOHC executive committee, Madam Gu and Bian, outlining what CAOHC had done since it received news of CAO's crisis. The CMT proposed two options: (a) let CAO become insolvent, ask to be delisted and apply to court for protection against creditors; or (b) have CAOHC take over all of CAO's positions and sell a 24 percent interest of its 75 percent shareholding in CAO (in order to retain a 51 percent majority stake in CAO), utilizing these funds to meet the margin calls and closing off some of CAO's option positions. The situation report also concluded that according to Singapore's listing requirements, even unrealized paper losses would have to be disclosed in CAO's 3Q report results, should the back-to-back agreement not be executed.

On October 16 CAOHC's executive committee decided, for a number of reasons, to save CAO instead of letting it become insolvent. First, CAO was the overseas subsidiary of a state-owned Chinese company and also a reputable company in Singapore. If the news leaked out, it would damage the company's corporate image and affect the stability of the Singapore

---

* Madam Gu was also responsible for all investment-related decisions that concerned CAOHC, including any investments that were proposed to be made by CAO. All of CAO's investment decisions had to be evaluated by Madam Gu's department before approval could be sought from the CAOHC executive committee.

† Yang was a professional who was once the general manager of the financial department in a large joint venture based in China, while Zhang was a senior officer whose power was similar with that of Chen.

financial market. Second, it would cost less to rescue the company than to let it become bankrupt. Most of CAO's open positions were taken during 2004 and would expire at the end of the year. All the international oil institutes were projecting that the oil price would fall in 2004 to about US$40 per barrel (average oil price in December 2004 was US$41 per barrel, while the average price for CAO's option positions was US$48 per barrel).[1] If CAO closed its positions at lower prices, then it would help to minimize its losses. Third, if oil prices stayed at around US$50 per barrel, CAOHC could still afford to save the company at this price level. To do so, CAOHC would have to take over all of CAO's open positions and meet the margin calls.

On October 18, Li, in his capacity as CAOHC's head of finance, wrote to Société Générale stating that CAOHC was supportive of CAO and would provide support to CAO for all outstanding payments upon approval being obtained from the relevant Chinese authorities.

On October 19 Jennie Liu informed Cindy Chong (chairman of the RMC) that Li had confirmed that CAOHC would pay RMB100 million to MERM as a guarantee for margin calls.

On October 24 CAOHC party secretary Hai Liancheng came to CAO's Singapore office and unilaterally took the decision to close out some of CAO's option positions, and all subsequent decision to square CAO's option positions were made by CAOHC directly.

On October 27 Li expressly set out in an e-mail to Chen, which was also forwarded to the CAOHC executive committee and the CMT, that as CAOHC had made the decision to rescue CAO, all payments made by CAO for sums less than S$5 million would require authorization from CAOHC's executive committee, and all payments by CAO for sums less than S$5 million had to be collectively authorized by Chen, Yang Bin and Zhang Zhicheng.

It was also decided at a CAOHC executive committee meeting on October 27 that CAO's positions with MERM had to be closed out, as MERM was threatening to declare an event of default, which would result in CAO's MTM exposure being realized and becoming actual losses.

The problem was that CAOHC did not have sufficient funds in its bank account. Where would the money come from? Selling shares seemed to be the quickest solution.

The quick fix

On October 10, 2004 (before CAOHC had decided to save the company) Gerald Rigby,* acting on instructions from CAOHC, had sent an e-mail on behalf of Chen to Oral W. Dawe, co-president and managing director of Goldman Sachs (Singapore) Pte (Goldman Sachs) stating that the options

---

* Rigby, the chief trader of CAO, independently proposed, advised on, and executed CAO's trading strategy in options, including the various restructuring schemes CAO entered into throughout the course of 2004.

positions which CAO traded with J. Aron (the commodity division of Goldman Sachs) "were actually traded on behalf of CAOHC." On other occasions, Chen had also instructed Peter Lim (head of finance) to inform counterparties who were asking for additional margins arising from the trading of options that the options belonged to CAOHC. At that time, Goldman Sachs and BNP Paribas had sent delegates to visit CAOHC in Beijing. When asked whether CAO's option positions were traded on behalf of CAOHC, none of the executive management members at CAOHC denied it. On the contrary, all the CAOHC top executives who received the delegates stressed over and over again that CAOHC would do its best to resolve the issue.

On the morning of October 14 Madam Gu called Chen and told him that CAOHC had decided to sell 24 percent of its shares in CAO. She also told Chen that SASAC had granted its verbal consent. Madam Gu then asked Chen to arrange for CAO employees to contact the local banks for the sale. Subsequently, Chen asked Lim to follow the instruction from CAOHC. Lim then approached Deutsche Bank, DBS, and ABM Amro to sound them out about the possibility of either a secondary sale of some of CAOHC's shares in CAO or a primary CAO share issuance. Initially, the three banks competed fiercely on the transaction. DBS declined, as CAO's share price had already gone up and there had been less demand for the stock in the market. Only Deutsche Bank decided to explore the possibilities further.

The same day, in the afternoon, Keith Magnus (head of Country Banking, Deutsche Bank AG, Singapore Branch) and other Deutsche Bank representatives met Lim. Instructed by Chen, Lim told Deutsche Bank that CAOHC needed the sale proceeds to buy a fleet of vessels.

After further confirming with Madam Gu on October 16, Lim, during a telephone conversation with Magnus, confirmed that CAOHC would proceed with the share placement, but CAO would not go ahead with the primary share issuance.

On October 18 Magnus and three other Deutsche Bank representatives met Lim again, to conduct due diligence in relation to the share placement. During the meeting, Lim told them that: (a) CAOHC would use the net proceeds for the purchase of the vessels and for investment purposes; (b) there were no material developments that would adversely affect CAO's prospects; and (c) there was no price-sensitive information regarding CAO that had not been disclosed to the market.

On October 19 Deutsche Bank representatives met with Chen and Lim. Chen made the same points as Lim had done the previous day. During the meeting, Deutsche Bank told Chen that point (a) how the proceeds from the placement would be used was actually not important. The reason why they asked the question was to have the answer ready for the institutional subscribers in case the question came up. While point (b) and (c) were all reflected in the Vendor Sales Agreement that were later signed between Deutsche Bank and CAOHC.

The same day, Madam Gu instructed staff in Beijing, on behalf of CAO, to draft a report to CAOHC proposing that CAOHC agree to sell its shares in CAO urgently. CAO suggested selling 24 percent of the shares in two phases of 15 and 9 percent. The report reiterated the urgency of the sale. Madam Gu then instructed the staff in Beijing to e-mail the draft report to Chen's assistant—Li Yan—to print it out for Chen to sign on behalf of CAO and then send it back to CAOHC. The report was numbered CAO Singapore [2004] 044.

On October 20 Madam Gu informed Chen that she had already received the approval from SASAC for CAOHC to sell its shares. Moreover, the joint conference between the party and the executive management* of CAOHC had also resolved to sell the shares. Again, Madam Gu instructed her staff in Beijing to draft a report to CAOHC, and then e-mail it to Chen for his signature. Since the sender of the email noted that "Madam Gu has already reviewed it, please sign,"[†] Chen then signed on behalf of CAO, and sent it to CAOHC. The report, numbered CAO Singapore [2004] 045, was faxed to CAOHC at the end of the business day in Beijing. The main idea of the report was that four counterparties had threatened CAO with legal action if it failed to make immediate payments. They were also threatening to disclose CAO's breach of contract to other Singapore financial institutions. Based on its own calculation, CAO was facing MTM losses of about US$271 million on October 20. Again, the report urged CAOHC to sell 15 percent of its interest in CAO and informed it that CAO was already in advanced discussions with Deutsche Bank for the placement of its shares and that lawyers[‡] had already reviewed the relevant documents.

The same day, CAOHC's executive committee passed a resolution to sell a 15 percent interest in CAO. On October 21 Jia flew to Singapore to sign the Vendor Sales Agreement. The shares were sold at S$1.35 (US$0.81[§]), a 14 percent discount on the previous day's traded price of S$1.57 (US$0.94). No prospectus was issued, as SGX did not have such a requirement for placements of existing shares. Deutsche Bank had not been told about the trading losses when it questioned CAO about its financial situation.

Keith Magnus said:

> The placement was executed within four hours and the shares were placed widely to institutional investors with a strong response from the market. This transaction is positive for the company as it diversifies its shareholder base. It also underlines the strength of Deutsche Bank's Equity Capital Markets platform in Asia and our ability to raise capital for [a] Singaporean corporate during difficult market conditions.

Rowena Chu (Deutsche Bank's head of Equity Capital Markets Asia) said:

> Deutsche Bank's ability to complete a transaction of this size, in a day when all Asian markets were down, speaks well for the franchise we have built across the

---

* This is a system by which the party participates in the management. Normally the conference is called by the party secretary at the branch level and all party branch members and top management would participate in the meeting.
† IMD field research.
‡ The report did not specify the lawyers. However, it was discovered later that the law firm that reviewed the share placement agreement was Stamford Law Corporation (Stamford).
§ Unless otherwise specified, S$1 = US$0.60 is used as the conversion rate.

region. The investor base was truly diverse, with over 50 accounts participating. Around 75 percent was from Asia, with the remainder coming from Europe and other offshore accounts.[2]

The net proceeds from the sale—S$196 million (US$118 million)—were credited directly to CAO's account on October 22 and 25, 2004. About 96 percent was used to satisfy margin calls from counterparties, namely Macquarie Bank Ltd, Mitsui & Co. Energy and Risk Management Ltd (MERM), J. Aron & Company (Singapore) Pte and Société Générale Paris; the remainder was used for working capital.

Oil prices climbed to a record US$55.65 per barrel on October 25, before falling back to US$51.76 by the end of the month.[3]

On October 28 CAO supplied further information in its announcement to the public that the share placement transaction had been made by its parent, CAOHC, and "CAOHC's independent decision to divest a stake was one in which CAO's role was limited."[4] It is worth noting that CAOHC had already decided in early October that any sensitive information (including announcements) regarding CAO could only be released to the public after CAOHC approved it. The October 28 announcement was approved by CAOHC.

In parallel, a search for strategic investors

Meanwhile, CAOHC had been looking for strategic investors to help relieve the situation. As it did not have sufficient cash on its own account, it would have to secure financing to meet the margin calls.

On October 10 CAOHC had asked CAO to provide a draft of the back-to-back agreement suggested by CAO. On October 14 CAOHC asked its regulatory authority for the following: (a) provision of funds to meet margin calls; (b) approval to sell up to 24 percent of CAOHC's shares in CAO; and (c) assistance in getting approval from the State Administration of Foreign Exchange (SAFE)* of the People's Bank of China (PBOC) for the remittance of funds abroad.

By October 25 CAOHC had been in active discussions with a number of institutions for further possible financial arrangements to meet the margin calls. It had approached SASAC-owned companies, including Chinese banks, Chinese petroleum companies, such as Sinochem Corporation (Sinochem)† and China National Offshore Oil Corporation (CNOOC), and international oil majors such as BP, the Vitol Group, and Fortune Oil.

---

* China still controlled the foreign exchange. SAFE was an administration tasked with drafting rules and regulations governing foreign exchange market activities, and managing foreign exchange reserves, for the People's Bank of China (PBOC). PBOC was the central bank of China with the power to control monetary policy and regulate financial institutions in China.

† Formerly known as China National Chemicals Import & Export Corporation.

Even if CAOHC had agreed to use its own assets as a guarantee, Chinese banks' approval processes for credit lines generally tended to be too slow to cope with such an emergency request. Likewise, it would take the Chinese petroleum companies a long time to secure funds, even though CAOHC had received approval from SAFE on November 2 to remit US$300 million to Singapore to help CAO to meet the margin calls.[5]

Chen used all his personal connections to find the rescuers. Both Sinochem and CNOOC expressed an interest in helping CAOHC with the rescue. Sinochem even sent a working team to Singapore for about a week to try to understand the situation. However, even though Sinochem could secure the funds that CAO needed, it requested Chen or CAOHC to procure the approval from SASAC for the rescue. Chen was unable to gain such support.

On November 5 Jia issued a letter informing Société Générale that CAOHC had the means to bear CAO's losses, and that CAO had the full support of CAOHC to overcome the crisis.

On November 8 Standard Bank (SBL) wrote to CAO stating:

> SBL continue to believe in the ultimate responsibility of CAOHC for the indebtedness of CAO to us. We know that there is a written agreement between CAO and CAOHC evidencing such obligation(s) in which we, along with a number of other financial institutions, are named. The agreement is executed by Chen Jiulin and Jia Changbin and is governed under Singapore law, with submission to the jurisdiction of the Singapore courts. We have seen a copy of this agreement. Further, its existence has been confirmed to us by a member of the board of CAO.[6]

By November 16 Chen had also found BP, which expressed an interest in helping CAOHC with the rescue. On November 19 CAOHC had more detailed discussions with both BP and CNOOC as potential strategic investors to take over the options positions.

Legal issues

CAOHC first realized on October 25, when it received the translated version of the share placement agreement with Deutsche Bank, that there might have been some potential legal risks associated with insider trading, and so started to look for international lawyers. It immediately approached an international law firm in Beijing with which it had worked before. However, there turned out to be a potential conflict of interest, since Deutsche Bank was one of the law firm's major clients. Believing that there was no such thing as a "Chinese Wall" within the same organization, the law firm decided to drop the case and recommended Stamford Law Corporation (Stamford). Stamford was a niche Singaporean law firm specializing in corporate law, which had a representative office in Beijing. Lee Suet Fern, senior director of

Stamford, is married to Lee Hsien Yang, the younger brother of Singapore's Prime Minister, Lee Hsien Loong.

On November 3, Madam Gu asked Chen to seek legal advice on SGX's requirements for disclosure of the actual losses in the 3Q results, and to reply to the query urgently within two hours.

> Now the company in Singapore incurred actual losses, is it necessary to make disclosure in the 3rd quarter report to SGX? What are SGX's regulations in this respect?[7]

As Chen was busy dealing with CAO's trading counterparts, he then directed one of his subordinates to reply to Madam Gu's inquiry as follows:

> There is no need to make external disclosure if the holding company takes over all outstanding positions. Some of the positions have already been closed and the remaining positions are still within manageable level for the holding company instead.[8]

It was only on November 8 that CAOHC made contact with Stamford in China and appointed the firm as its legal advisor. CAOHC wanted to know whether a back-to-back arrangement to transfer CAO's options positions to CAOHC could be a viable solution and whether there would be any potential legal problems in Singapore.

On November 21 BP informed CAOHC that it would not pursue the discussions about becoming a strategic investor, mainly because of its concerns about potential legal problems arising from the vendor placement of 15 percent of the shares with Deutsche Bank.* On November 26 CNOOC also informed CAOHC that it could not rescue CAO without the SASAC approval. Thus, the three cooperation agreements that CNOOC had prepared fell through.

The next day Jia and his secretary, together with Madam Gu, went to Singapore to prepare for insolvency. The search for strategic investors had failed. CAOHC was back to square one and had to decide whether to carry out a rescue or to let CAO go bankrupt.

The chosen option

Jia asked Madam Gu to stay in Singapore to work with the lawyers to find solutions. She met Temasek Holdings (Temasek), introduced by Stamford, for the first time on November 24, 2004. Temasek was the investment arm of the Singapore government (the equivalent of SASAC in China but not exercising the same governmental function) and 100 percent owned by the

---

* Specifically which could be considered as an insider trading.

Ministry of Finance in Singapore. It had actively been seeking investments and further strengthening its presence in China in recent years. Temasek was one of Stamford's key clients and its CEO—Ho Ching—is the prime minister's wife.

Madam Gu explained the crisis situation and invited Temasek to invest so that CAOHC could rescue the company. Initially CAOHC had hoped that it could sell shares to Temasek to generate sufficient funds to meet the margin calls. Temasek was a CAO shareholder, having acquired a 2 percent share during the Deutsche Bank vendor placement in October 2004.

Two days later, Temasek's senior management met Jia in Beijing. During the meeting, Temasek expressed its interest in assisting CAOHC with the rescue, but did not want to buy any more of CAO's shares. It was then that Temasek suggested that a third option might be available, apart from insolvency or rescue—restructuring. Stamford had also suggested this to Madam Gu in Singapore. CAOHC had never thought about it before and was not familiar with such international practice.

On November 27, at Temasek's Beijing office, the two parties officially discussed the issue.[9] On November 27 and 28 Temasek and Stamford sent people from Singapore to Beijing to explain to the team the basic concept of restructuring and how it would work, outlining the pros and cons. On November 28, at CAOHC's meeting on the restructuring, Madam Gu explained that according to Temasek, only US$20 million was needed to pay the creditors for CAO to get through the crisis.

After assessing the situation, CAOHC decided to go for restructuring.

The public is still in the dark ...

3Q 2004 financial results

Lim, CAO's head of finance, was aware of the need to disclose the losses in the 3Q 2004 results to be presented to and approved by the audit committee and then by the board. In fact, he had prepared two sets of results; one set reflected a profit after tax of S$8.8 million (US$5.3 million) (for 3Q only) and S$41.7 million (US$25 million) (year-to-date profits) and the other set showed the actual losses of S$360 million (US$216 million) (for 3Q only) and S$327 million (US$196 million) (year-to-date losses).

The audit committee meeting scheduled for November 8–10, 2004 was postponed by a day to November 9–11 because Lim said that the figures were not ready. Jerry Lee (one of CAO's independent directors and also chairman of the audit committee) was the only member of the audit committee present, as Tan Hui Boon (the other Singaporean independent director) had to go to Hong Kong on a prearranged business trip, though he dialed in for the meeting. The only Chinese director, Li Yongji, was not there. The independent directors found out that there were trading losses of about S$11 to S$12 million (US$6.6 to US$7.2 million). Tan asked whether the stop-loss limit set by the board had been exceeded. After being told that it had not, Tan accepted the losses. "It has happened before—in the trading business, you gain some, you lose some,"[10] he thought.

On November 12 Lim told Chen that he would resign without a back-to-back agreement signed by Jia. Feeling under enormous pressure, Chen—who later claimed that he had believed that Jia would eventually sign the agreement—said that he forged a document with Jia's signature and faxed it to Lim. After receiving the purported back-to-back agreement, Lim decided not to inform the audit committee of the derivatives trading losses or of the agreement.

On November 16 CAO released its 3Q results and announced that it would cease speculative trading by the end of November. The released 3Q results were based on the first set of results Lim prepared and showed an overall profit instead of losses. Based on the arrangement that CAOHC would take over the positions, the press release announced that CAO's prospects were "still highly positive." The announcement, in both English and Chinese, was sent to all nine directors in advance. Liu Jiahong, the investor relations manager at CAO, also called Jia to request his approval. Jia asked Liu to contact his assistant, Bian Hui. Bian asked Liu to delete one paragraph that Jia had remarked upon prior to the announcement and expressed no objections to the rest of the document. Even after the announcement was made, CAOHC also did not deny the errors in the announcement. However, the announcement did show around S$10 million (US$6 million) in trading losses, which confirmed earlier market rumors of trading losses. As DBS Vickers commented:

> In our mind, we find the trading losses surprising, disappointing, and regretfully large. In retrospect, we do not think the cumulative earnings aspect to the risk-management system was perfectly suitable since it allows successful traders to let their speculative positions "ride" instead of managing risk at an absolute basis or even on a VAR (value at risk) basis, but absolutely do not believe management was being deceptive, misleading or evasive. Rather, it is difficult to enumerate every single detail of the risk-management system ... We certainly did not begrudge them for making trading losses. He who has never lost money on a bet, bought high on an investment or incorrectly recommended a stock may cast the first stone.[11]

Despite the temporary impact of the trading losses, the market regarded CAO's announcement that it would cease speculative trading as "psychologically positive, as it eliminated the unpopular volatile trading business while fundamentally it was also negative as it also eliminated a business that on average generated positive earnings."[12] DBS Vickers held the view that it was an "excellent buying opportunity" for CAO's stock because:

> The trading losses are now a thing of the past. So does S$10 million [US$6 million] in trading losses justify the 30-fold loss in market capitalization?

We think not. Opportunities like this do not knock too often, to go against herd mentality with the knowledge that fundamentals support you. We are figuratively banging the table as CAO appears to be oversold. We maintain our BUY rating and S$1.89 (US$1.13) target price.[13]

A hidden problem

Standard Bank plc had sent a letter on October 15, 2004 to the directors of CAO requesting the company meet the margin calls. It was not until November 27 however, that the independent directors, the external auditors (Ernst & Young), SGX, and the shareholders were informed about the derivatives trading losses.

SGX had a real-time market surveillance system, but it only became suspicious when there were market rumors in late October 2004 that CAO might have suffered trading losses. It was finally alerted when CAO's shareholders—at an extraordinary general meeting on November 24, 2004—voted against the acquisition of a 20.6 percent stake in Singapore Petroleum Corporation (SPC), which had been announced with much fanfare in August. DBS Vickers commented that it,

> should have been a rubber stamp meeting given the 60%-owner parent company was supposedly in favour of the deal. ...
>
> The deal failing was highly unusual and we can only speculate that the ultimate parent company, the Chinese State Council, disliked something about the deal.
>
> DBS Vickers[14]

From start to finish, most of the 200 shareholders who turned up at the meeting were met with surprises at every turn. First, the usual post-meeting snacks were served before the meeting started. Then, irate investors criticised the company for polling a resolution before it was proposed or before shareholders were given a chance to ask questions. But the biggest shock came when CAO's parent company, China Aviation Oil Holding Co (CAOHC), joined dissenters and rejected a proposed deal in which CAO would pay cash for 88 million SPC shares from Satya Capital, a consortium of Indonesian businessmen.

> *The Business Times*[15]

On Sunday November 28 the two Singaporean independent directors were asked whether they could stand by for a conference call. Tan was in Australia at the time. It was only during the call that the independent directors were informed about the derivatives trading losses for the first time. They recommended that the derivatives trading losses be disclosed immediately.

On the same day, CAOHC proposed the restructuring of the company and the formation of a special task force (STF). The board appointed Madam Gu as the head of the STF, leading the restructuring and rehabilitation effort. Madam Gu, together with legal advisors from Stamford, left for Singapore first. That night, Jia and the rest of team flew from Beijing to Singapore. The next day, they started to prepare to file the bankruptcy protection application with the court.

On November 29 CAO filed an application with the Singapore high court for the suspension of trading in its shares and the restructuring of the company. It was only then that SGX was informed about the losses.[16]

The public announcement and media and market outcry

The public announcement

On November 30, 2004, the derivatives trading losses were announced to the public. Citing the reasons for the delay in disclosing the derivatives trading losses, CAO stated:

> While the company is aware of the obligations to disclose the derivative trading losses, the company's primary concern is to ensure the survivability of the company in the face of the financial crisis. The directors believe that the interest of the shareholders of the company would be better served if the company could put together at least a potential rescue plan when the trading losses are disclosed, as opposed to an immediate disclosure as and when the losses were realized without any resolution at hand for the creditor problem. Had this happened, the directors viewed that the chances of survival of the company would be greatly diminished, as the directors would not have any time to find "white knights" for the company in the confusion and turmoil.[17]

It also went on to say that Chen was relieved of his duties as CEO and managing director of the company with immediate effect, and CAO's shares were suspended from trading on SGX. The exchange appointed PricewaterhouseCoopers (PwC) as special investigative accountants to review and investigate CAO's affairs in relation to the losses incurred.* At the same time, the company began negotiations with some of its creditors to structure a settlement that would allow it more time to work out a rescue package to maintain the company's financial position.

In the announcement, CAO also reiterated CAOHC's continuing support for the restructuring and ongoing operations. In addition, it announced Temasek's expressed interest in participating in the restructuring as a

---

* According to the PwC report, after Chen informed CAOHC and the CAOHC-nominated directors of the losses on October 9, 2004, the negative MTM value of CAO's options portfolio escalated from US$367 million to US$423 million (on or about October 20, 2004), to US$443 million (on or about November 15, 2004), and then to US$567 million (on or about November 30, 2004). These figures do not include the cost of termination in respect of any remaining open positions at the relevant dates.

co-investor along with CAOHC. Temasek's participation was nonbinding and conditional.

The media and market outcry

The announcement immediately generated high media and market attention in both China and Singapore. It "had stoked anger and confusion in Singapore, a city-state that prides itself on tough corporate disclosure standards."[18] Singapore's *Business Times* newspaper described the matter as a "catastrophic failure" and asked "whether there should be a wholesale review of Singapore's financial regulations."[19]

For shareholders, this is a corporate earthquake registering, say, 9.5 on the Richter scale. This is another Barings.

David Gerald, President, Securities Investors Association of Singapore[20]

The debacle has evoked memories in Singapore of the 1995 collapse of Britain's Barings Bank, which was brought down after Singapore-based trader Nick Leeson ran up billions of dollars in losses when his market gambles went awry.

Wall Street Journal[21]

The scandal could dent Singapore's reputation as a well-regulated financial centre, raising questions about the SGX's wooing of small and medium-sized mainland Chinese companies to list in the city-state as regulators adopt a new system that puts the onus of corporate disclosure on listed companies.

Financial Times[22]

Chen gambled his company away but nobody stopped him ... Was this just accident? As Chen said, if he had been given US$500 million, he would have won the battle.

Shenzhen Daily[23]

Where there is a smoke, there is a fire—and now CAO is figuratively a burning inferno with potentially very little to salvage ... CAO used to be a market darling, but alas, someone appears to have flown CAO too close to the sun to get there SELL.

DBS Vickers[24]

The CAO case is being thoroughly investigated. Once we have the results of the current reviews and investigations, MAS will work with the other agencies to review them carefully and consider whether we need to add new rules or tighten existing ones ... However, no amount of regulation or enforcement can guarantee that companies will always comply with disclosure rules and corporate governance standards, whether in Singapore or any other financial centre.

Shane Tregillis, Assistant Managing Director (Market Conduct), MAS[25]

As part of an international financial centre, SGX is an international market place. It is not just a domestic exchange. Without compromising our listing standards, the developments at CAO should not deter efforts to build Singapore as an international venue for listings.

Hsieh Fu Hua, CEO, SGX[26]

The collapse of China Aviation Oil, the Singapore-listed subsidiary of a Chinese state company, does not just show that Beijing's international champions need to learn more about derivatives and corporate governance. It also suggests that stock exchanges outside China have been over-enthusiastic in attracting listings from the Chinese mainland.

Financial Times[27]

The answers provided gave us confidence to proceed with the placement.

Mike West, Deutsche Bank spokesman[28]

Is there a need for an independent watchdog to regularly check on corporate financial dealings?

Business Times, Singapore[29]

A massive trading bet in which the overseas arm of a Chinese state-controlled jet-fuel supplier lost at least US$550 million on oil derivatives puts a new focus on corporate governance at Chinese companies and, in particular, the risks that arise when state-owned enterprises begin operating as commercial entities.

Wall Street Journal[30]

Corporate governance is weak in China and state-controlled companies have often had particular problems controlling overseas units or those with capital market operations.

Financial Times[31]

One of the big problems, analysts say, is that China's listed state companies still haven't managed to elevate shareholder interests above political considerations. That is because listed companies often maintain unclear ties to the parent company—and to Beijing. Corporate chiefs one day can become provincial governors the next. Bosses at rival telecommunications companies might be asked to switch jobs, no matter what shareholders know or say.

Wall Street Journal[32]

It's very hard to figure out what's going on in these companies. They are a complete black box, maybe a black hole … We are not talking about penny-ante enterprises. We are talking about China's largest state enterprises, its top-ranked players. The standards of corporate disclosure should be much higher.

Fraser Howie, co-author, *Privatizing China: The Stock Markets*
and Their Role in Corporate Reform[33]

The exposure of the China Aviation Oil Corp Ltd incident makes one think of lacking the state supervision over its national property and managers. It is an urgent task on how to supervise and restrict big-sized state-run enterprise in their further deepening reform, make them take the regular road for setting up a modern enterprise system and reduce the loopholes in the running in period of the old and new systems.

People's Daily[34]

The way forward

The uncertainties remained. Could the reconstruction be made to work? What form might it take?

> There is no single model for how China handled failures of state-linked companies, with some being wound up with the consent of creditors, but forced liquidation by foreign-led investors also now a possibility.
>
> In the case of CAO, which has a near-monopoly of aviation fuel sales in China, Beijing might decide that it is in the national interest to keep the company afloat. However, if the company went into bankruptcy, pursuing claims in mainland courts would also be a viable option for foreign creditors or investors.
>
> Neil Torpey, partner, Paul Hastings, Hong Kong office[35]

> CAO has offered few details what it would do next, but we believe that the most likely scenario is pursuing Temasek and CAOHC as white-knights. A less likely scenario may be asset sales ...
>
> DBS Vickers[36]

Would the creditors and outside shareholders go along with it? What would happen next?

9 Oil on Troubled Waters

As head of the special task force (STF), Madam Gu had a three-fold mandate—to lead the restructuring and rehabilitation process, to cooperate with the investigations and to supervise CAO's day-to-day operations.

The restructuring was unprecedented for a Chinese SOE. Although there was no legal obligation for the Chinese government to support the restructuring and revival of CAO, from the outset, it had shown its support through several public announcements made by SASAC and CAOHC. However, they also made it clear that the restructuring had to be in accordance with international commercial practices. In addition, SASAC also set up a special team, led by Meng Jianming (director, Statistical Evaluation Bureau), to directly lead CAOHC and the STF and oversee the restructuring process.[1] Madam Gu and the STF also became the intermediary between China and Singapore.

As China had no previous experience in the overseas restructuring of SOEs, Jia was not sure whether all the parties needed to handle the situation would be able to be assembled and work effectively together. However, through recommendations and introductions by Stamford and Temasek, Jia's problem was solved.

The restructuring team

Stamford had initially been retained as CAOHC and CAO's legal advisor for the rescue. Because of the time pressure, Stamford had submitted the application to the court on behalf of CAO for restructuring the debt through a proposed scheme of arrangement (scheme).* When Stamford realized that there would be a potential conflict of interest if it stayed on as advisor to both the shareholder and the company, Rajah & Tann Advocates & Solicitors

---

* Under Singapore law, a scheme of arrangement is a compromise or arrangement provided for under section 210 of the Singapore Companies Act (Chapter 50) to take effect between the company and its creditors. The arrangement becomes legally binding on all of the shareholders to whom it is intended to apply if a majority in number—representing three-quarters (that is 75 percent) of the value held by all shareholders—voting in person or by proxy, votes in favor of it at the meeting convened with the permission of the court, and if the court subsequently approves it. Source: Explanatory Statement to Scheme of Arrangement between CAO and its Shareholders.

(Rajah & Tann), a major law firm in Singapore, immediately took over from Stamford as CAO's legal advisor while Stamford remained as CAOHC's advisor for the restructuring.

A few days later, although not officially part of the restructuring team, Temasek formed a small group led by Tow Heng Tan, its senior managing director in charge of investments, to help CAOHC with the restructuring.[2] In December, Temasek met directly with SASAC and formally established its relationship as a "working partner" of SASAC and said it was prepared to help "as much as possible."[3]

Deloitte & Touche Financial Advisory Services Pte Ltd (Deloitte), approached and introduced by Temasek, met CAO for the first time on November 30, 2004. The following day, Deloitte was appointed as CAO's financial advisor; its role was to come up with a restructuring plan.

Cogent Communications Pte Ltd (Cogent) was also introduced by one of CAOHC's advisors the day after the loss announcement. Cogent's mandate was mainly to deal with the media, and it was designated as the only public point of contact for the company. Based in Singapore, Cogent was a boutique investor-relations consultancy that provided advisory services to listed companies.

By the beginning of December 2004, Madam Gu already had her core team for the restructuring. It consisted of the STF members, the advisors, and some support staff.

The restructuring team faced a complex situation: strong media and market attention in both China and Singapore; legal, financial, and cultural differences; and the legal action initiated or threatened against the company by some of CAO's creditors.

Crisis management

The six-week extension

Clouds hung over CAO's office on the 31st floor of Suntec Tower in Singapore. PwC, the special investigative accountant (appointed by SGX) and the Commercial Affairs Department (CAD)* had begun their on-site investigations. At the same time, creditors—backed up by their legal and financial advisors—minority shareholders and the media were banging on the door. To make the situation worse, there was also an immediate problem for the team to tackle.

---

* CAD was formed in August 1984, within the Revenue Division of the Ministry of Finance to combat complex commercial frauds and white-collar crimes in Singapore. On January 10, 2000, CAD merged with the Commercial Crime Division of the Criminal Investigation Department and was reconstituted as a department of the Singapore Police Force, becoming the premier investigative authority on white-collar crimes in Singapore.

To react to the emergency situation and without having engaged a financial advisor, Stamford had applied to the court for only two weeks in which to present a scheme. Consequently, CAO had obtained a court order to present a scheme within 14 days and to convene a creditors meeting at which a majority in number—representing three-quarters in value—of the creditors attending was required to approve the scheme. In reality, this time-scale was neither feasible nor credible.

In addition, there was no automatic moratorium on action against the company while a scheme was being proposed. However, section 210(10) of the Companies Act provided that an application could be made to the court for an order pending against the company to be stayed.

On December 7, 2004, CAO filed an application to the court for extra time to put forward a scheme and to hold the necessary creditors meeting. Creditors that sent lawyers to the hearing included Standard Chartered Plc, Macquarie Bank Ltd., Singapore Petroleum Co., Itochu Petroleum Co. (Singapore) Pte Ltd., SK Energy Asia Pte, Glencore International AG, and View Sino International Ltd. Two parties, Glencore and SK Energy, objected to the request for the extension, asking for a shorter period.[4]

Despite the objections, after taking into consideration the scale and complexity of the matter, the court decided to grant a six-week extension (that is to January 21, 2005) for CAO to present a scheme, and a six-month extension (that is to June 10, 2005) for the creditors to consider and approve the proposed scheme.

For a number of reasons, CAO did not go back to court to seek a legal moratorium. One reason was simply that legal action had not yet started. Instead, it monitored the legal suits in relevant jurisdictions daily, for example, in Singapore and the USA, for potential class actions against the company.

Much of the first month was taken up with getting the situation under control, creditor management, closing out all open derivatives trading positions and managing the day-to-day operations.

Crystallizing the debt

As of November 30 CAO had stopped all of its oil derivatives trading activities. CAO also implemented daily reporting of open positions to crystallize its debt. As of December 8 there were no open positions in respect of futures and options oil-trading activities except for back-to-back oil option trades with three counterparties. Some of CAO's counterparties had already unilaterally terminated their trades with the company based on their contractual rights with regard to swap derivatives.*

Although there were still some trades subject to market fluctuations, CAO had informed all of its counterparties of its intention to terminate all the remaining back-to-back option trades and swap derivatives, and closely monitored the situation. By the end of December 2004, all the open positions had been closed.

---

* CAO was also involved in other derivatives trading, such as hedging and swap transactions.

Continuity of business

CAO's situation differed from that of many companies undergoing restructuring in that its core business of jet fuel procurement was fundamentally sound, and it remained the sole overseas procurement arm of CAOHC. It was therefore in everybody's interest that the company carry on with this.

On December 9 CAO set up a new wholly owned subsidiary—CAOT Pte Ltd (CAOT)—to carry on its jet fuel procurement business on an agency basis. It was to minimize the working capital requirement because of CAO's poor credit position and to provide stable income to the company from the agency commission charged to jet fuel buyers.

In addition, CAOT would also receive some financial, operational and personnel support from CAO.* The new company would benefit from the agency agreements directly with CAOHC group companies for jet fuel procurement.

On December 13 CAOT started its first tender process with CAO's former suppliers. Within a week, CAOT had successfully closed the tender process, having received offers for the entire amount of jet fuel available.[5]

Regaining trust

At the outset, the STF had formed the view that "regaining trust would be key throughout the process."[6] Accordingly, it undertook the following measures:

▷ Providing weekly updates to all key stakeholders on the latest developments and planned actions, including MAS, SGX, CAD, shareholders, CAOHC, SASAC, and the Chinese embassy.
▷ Ensuring complete information flow to key internal and external stakeholders to make sure that "facts were complete, accurate, and timely."[7]
▷ Calming the media to prevent any further escalation of the crisis.

SASAC

On December 10 SASAC briefed a press conference about the substantial losses of CAO arising from futures trading (see Exhibit 9.1 for excerpts from SASAC announcements).

---

* All support was provided via a Services Agreement and a Trust Deed signed between CAOT, CAO and CAOHC. Utilization of CAO's company premises and personnel was provided on a fee basis and financial resources were provided by CAOHC on a needs basis, which were to be held in trust.

Exhibit 9.1 Excerpts from SASAC statements

10 December 2004

Based on the information available now, the speculation of oil futures index by CAO stepped over the boundaries of authorization and violated relevant regulations. Such business seriously violated the business-decision making procedures and the operations decisions were seriously mistaken, resulting in huge losses. At present CAOHC is making full endeavour to cope with.

The losses arising from the oil futures index speculation by CAO will be handled according to the commercial principles of listed companies in Singapore. At present, CAO is looking for strategic investors and planning to restructure its debt. This is the relatively effective solutions to resolve the losses incurred by various parties and related problems.

CAO should actively cooperate with the relevant investigating parties in Singapore to assist with investigation and evidence-collection process according to the local laws and regulations.

SASAC is closely monitoring the development of the incident. After the incident is properly resolved, the responsibility of relevant persons shall be dealt with according to relevant laws. SASAC will also alert the Chinese state-owned companies under the supervision of SASAC to learn from the lessons and establish and improve the mechanisms for supervising overseas associates and for monitoring and controlling their operational risks.

28 January 2005

It is commercial activity of the company to introduce strategic investors, and to carry out the debt restructuring. As the ultimate assets holder, SASAC urges the company to consider the interests of various parties and to operate on the commercial basis. SASAC will not directly interfere with the decision making process.

30 May 2005

It is the common wish for creditors, minority shareholders and CAOHC to have CAO implement a scheme of arrangement and introduce a strategic investor, according to local law and commercial principles. As the ultimate shareholder, SASAC has always been urging CAOHC and CAO to implement well the debt restructuring work according to Singapore law and commercial principles, taking into account the interests of various stakeholders.

Based on the feedback from creditors of CAO, and with the support of CAOHC, CAO carefully considered the interests of various stakeholders including creditors, and adjusted and improved the debt restructuring scheme submitted on 24 January 2005. The revised proposal on 12 May represents sufficient sincerity and best efforts of CAO toward restructuring based on commercial principles.

As for the valuation of certain assets of CAO, some creditors have forecasted future income using historical growth trends of profits in the last couple of years, and failed to consider thoroughly the impact of some factors such as the changing jet fuel market policies in China. Thus such creditors may have different views from those of CAO on the value of existing assets of CAO. SASAC hopes that relevant creditors can evaluate the existing assets of CAO on an objective and realistic basis.

The success of debt restructuring of CAO represents the most suitable solution to best possibly minimizing the losses of various parties, effectively resolving relevant problems. SASAC hopes that creditors carefully study and analyse various favourable factors of the proposal, and seek common growth through long-term cooperation.

Source: Field research.

CAOHC

On December 14 CAOHC issued a public statement about "being a responsible parent company":

> Notwithstanding the losses suffered by CAOHC together with all other shareholders, CAOHC wishes to assure the shareholders that it will provide moral, management and financial support to CAO to ensure that CAO can resume jet fuel procurement activities as soon as possible while CAO puts together its restructuring plan.

It further went on that:

> As a commercial entity and as a Chinese state-owned enterprise responsible for a critical function in the PRC economy, CAOHC is not in a position to pledge unconditional support. As such, CAOHC would like to clarify that the support is conditional upon the following: (a) sufficient resolution of the legal and regulatory issues concerning CAO such that the restructured CAO is in a position to resume normal business operations; and (b) the acceptance of the proposed scheme under Section 210 of the Companies Act by the creditors and shareholders of CAO.[8]

Securities Investors Association (Singapore)—SIAS*

Proactively, the STF met creditors to gain their understanding and support and met with SIAS and the media to update them on the progress made and the plans instituted.

---

* SIAS was the largest organized investors lobby group in Asia, with more than 60,000 retailer investors as members.

On December 18 CAO's STF team and its advisors initiated a meeting with SIAS committee members. The purpose of the meeting was to express sympathy with the predicament of the minority shareholders and to try to better understand their concerns, and to brief SIAS on the latest developments at CAO.

Madam Gu also reconfirmed the active support of CAOHC and SASAC in coming up with an acceptable restructuring plan and helping CAO return to its core business.

According to David Gerald, president of SIAS, CAO was the first company undergoing restructuring ever to have initiated such a dialogue with SIAS. SIAS immediately called on all creditors to support the restructuring efforts and to achieve a "win–win" situation.[9]

Others

CAO was also actively involved in assisting CAD, SGX, MAS and PwC with the ongoing investigation and managing day-to-day operations. The STF briefed the SGX to gain their trust and confidence, and rebutted some of PwC's recommendations, which included, among others, placing the company under judicial management. It also managed media relations to prevent unnecessary speculative reports.

Chen had returned to China on November 30 for a "family matter," and CAOHC and the company had requested Chen to return to Singapore to cooperate with the investigation. Chen returned to Singapore to clarify the facts on December 8 while his mother was in a critical condition. He was immediately detained by the Singapore police force at Changi Airport. Chen's mother passed away while he was out on bail, and he was allowed to go back to mainland China for his mother's funeral. Subsequently, he returned to Singapore of his own accord to face the charges.

In addition, the STF met all CAO's heads of department and convened general staff meetings to explain the situation. Meanwhile, to prevent wrongful outflow of funds, the joint signatures of the head of STF and one of the two Deloitte partners were required to authorize payments.

Debt restructuring

The CAO case was unusual in that all its debt was on an unsecured basis, and there were no dominant creditors, or classification, or ranking of the creditors. The company's principal businesses—the jet fuel procurement business and its investment activities—were fundamentally sound.

A clear guiding principle established by SASAC and CAOHC at the outset was that the restructuring had to be based on international commercial practices. Even though SASAC and CAOHC had publicly announced their active support in finding a suitable restructuring plan, it was clear that they would withdraw this support if the company were put into judicial management or if shareholders proceeded with class action lawsuits.

Managing creditors' expectations

CAO's announcement on November 30, 2004 of its losses came as a surprise to all its creditors, but obviously more to some than to others. Early in August 2004, there had already been rumors in the market,[10] especially among the trading community, that CAO was having problems meeting its obligations for margin calls.

The total debt that CAO was facing was approximately US$600 million, and its 111 creditors in more than 12 countries (see Exhibit 9.2 for

Exhibit 9.2 List of major creditors of CAO

Name	Amount (US$ million)
Standard Bank London (South Africa)[a]	14.4
Macquarie Bank (Australia)[b]	2.6
Energy Risk Management	
Sumitomo Mitsui Banking	11.4
Fortis Bank of Brussels	33.1
J. Aron & Co. of Singapore	15.9
Barclays Capital	26.5
Overseas Chinese Banking Corporation (OCBC)	
SK Energy	14.3
Société Générale Asia[c]	
United Overseas Bank (UOB)	
Mitsui & Co (Japan)[d]	143.6
CAOHC	118.0
BP & its subsidiaries	
Satya Capital (a consortium of Indonesian investors)[e]	
Bank of Communication	
DBS Bank	
Other creditors	

[a] Guerrera, Francesco, Burton, John, Dickie, Mure and Leahy, Joe (2005) "Collapse causes concern about business with Beijing." *Financial Times*, January 20, 2005.
[b] Leahy, Joe and Guerrera, Francesco. "CAO looks to soften rescue plan." *Financial Times*, January 18, 2005.
[c] A group of banks led by Société Générale was owed US$152 million from a syndicated loan in 2003. Burton, John. "CAO seeks $500m debt write-offs." *Financial Times*, January 5, 2005.
[d] Prystay, Cris, Mcdermott, Darren and Santini, Laura (2004) "How a Singapore Fuel Company Lost $550 million in Oil Trading." *The Wall Street Journal*, December 3, 2004.
[e] Burton, John (2005) "CAO seeks $500m debt write-offs." *Financial Times*, January 5, 2005.

a list of major creditors) had further complicated the situation. Creditors included major international companies, such as BP, Société Générale, Barclays Bank, Itochu and Mitsui, and more than 70 small creditors spread across the globe. In addition, the different types of creditor made it inevitable that there would be very diverse views on how the restructuring plan should work.

There were essentially three large groups of creditors in terms of amount, influence, and impact: CAO's trade partners, syndicate lenders, and options creditors. The syndicate lenders, mainly Chinese banks, considered themselves as the real creditors. The trade creditors, by contrast, believed that they should be paid in full, since they were vitally important for the continuation of the business. Both groups held the view that the large number of options creditors did not deserve a cent. No formal creditors' committee was formed, as the creditors were unable to reach consensus.

With such complexity, it was a challenging task to present an acceptable scheme, even with the six-week extension. It meant that the restructuring team had to move quickly and effectively to find a solution that both the creditors and the shareholders could live with. Endless back and forth negotiations (which often characterize such situations) would not be an option.

Communication became vitally important. While calming the creditors and listening to their demands at the same time, the restructuring team also tried to get a feel for what might be an acceptable level of payout for each individual creditor. In all, CAO managed to have "eight to ten"[11] meetings with creditors a day and had taken feedback from approximately 80 percent of its creditors by value in the first six weeks.

Responding to the class action suits in the US

On January 5, 2005, some of CAO's shareholders launched a class action suit in the USA against the company for issuing false and misleading statements regarding its business and prospects.

On the one hand, the company engaged lawyers specializing in class action suits in the USA, actively seeking a legal opinion; on the other hand, on January 10 the STF met with SIAS for the second time. During the meeting, the STF expressed its strong belief that a successful restructuring plan would be a win–win situation for all concerned, and noted that it had come up with a draft framework of the plan since its first meeting with SIAS. In addition, the STF voiced its concerns about the class action suits, which—if they were to proceed—would make it difficult for CAOHC to continue to support the restructuring.

SIAS indicated that it was not opposed to legal action and would assist its members if their advice were that such an action was the best way to protect their interests. However, SIAS did not believe it was a prudent course to pursue during the restructuring process and called on all its members to put any legal action against CAO on hold until the company had completed its negotiations with creditors and investors.

The initial scheme

The key tasks of the STF were to negotiate with the creditors on the terms of the debt restructuring. The STF adopted the normal market practice of asking the creditors to assume a "haircut"* in their debts.

In meetings with the creditors, the STF prepared basic information such as preliminary estimates of the company's liquidation value, projected financials, and the proposed debt-restructuring plan. The STF discussed and obtained the views of the creditors on issues such as the value of the company, debt repayment rates, and treatment of CAOHC's shareholder loans.

Having considered the various alternatives, CAO announced on January 24, 2005 that it had filed its proposed initial scheme with the court. However, most creditors in Singapore expected that this would not be the final scheme, believing rather that it reflected the current situation and would be the basis for further negotiations.

The initial plan was a straightforward repayment scheme, containing the following principal terms, and was subject to the approval of the creditors, CAOHC and the relevant authorities in China and other relevant jurisdictions:

▷ A total payout of US$220 million, representing a repayment ratio of 41.5 percent.
▷ CAOHC and potential new investors to inject up to US$100 million cash, of which US$70 million would be paid to the creditors and the balance of US$30 million would be retained as working capital.
▷ The balance of US$120 million would be paid over a period of eight years, which was to be derived from the operations of the company and/ or dividends from the company's shareholdings in investments and/or sale of assets of the company.
▷ CAOHC would be treated the same as CAO's other unsecured creditors in the scheme with respect to its shareholder loan of US$118 million. However, as a gesture of goodwill, CAOHC would not be included in the cash distribution and the deferred debt, but would convert its debt at a discount into shares in CAO, at a price to be agreed.

The STF also issued supplementary financial information to the creditors, including a forecast of CAO's financial prospects, together with a statement

---

* "Haircut": a compromise or valuation/return that is less than optimal, especially to partially forgive a debt. Source: www.doubletongued.org

pledging that there would be no unfair treatment of creditors. As Madam Gu said:

> We believe that a successful restructuring exercise is in the interest of minority shareholders. We want to assure minority shareholders that we will continue to keep their interests in mind in the discussions regarding the equity restructuring between CAOHC and the new investors.

Meanwhile, CAO's legal advisor provided the view that "the class action suits in the US should not proceed as the US courts do not have jurisdiction over the company and the subject matter of the suit." In addition, CAO was also of the view that "the company can successfully resist the suit as currently pleaded," so the proposed scheme did not take into consideration the plaintiffs of the class action suits.

Fighting legal suits and the judicial management petition

The creditors were not happy with the proposed scheme.

On January 25 the STF and its advisors, led by Jia, met SIAS for the third time. At the meeting Jia emphasized the sincerity CAOHC had demonstrated in the scheme, the commitment it had made to the minority shareholders and the emphasis the Beijing authorities had placed on finding a solution that would be equitable to all, especially the minority shareholders. CAOHC's decision not to participate in the cash distribution and the deferred debt and instead to convert its debt to shares in the company at a discount was a further testimony to CAO's commitment to finding an acceptable solution. Any legal action such as the one currently proposed in the US did not assist the company in its restructuring efforts. Such a path, if taken by shareholders, would be obstructive to the plan to put the company back in operation.

On January 28 SASAC again announced that Temasek had expressed the intention of taking part in the restructuring process on a commercial basis, thus "providing a good start for the debt restructuring process." In addition, "as the ultimate assets holder, SASAC will not directly interfere in the decision making of the company." SASAC also stated that "the debt-restructuring process is an appropriate way or method to reduce the losses of various parties, and to provide for a solution."

Even so, some creditors were battling for preferential treatment by initiating legal action against CAO. On February 2, Sumitomo Mitsui Banking Corporation (SMBC) filed a claim against CAO for approximately US$26 million under the so-called Trust Receipt Loan Facility, and made allegations of conspiracy by Chen and CAOHC for the events leading to the losses.

The trade creditors, such as SK Energy, were particularly upset because they were expecting a much higher recovery rate. From SK Energy's own experience, SK Korea had paid its trade creditors in full during its recent restructuring exercise and it thought that the same thing should happen here. Trade partners or suppliers, especially in the oil industry, were deemed to be the most important for the continuity of the business. If they did not get paid in full, they would not continue trades with CAO.

SK Energy therefore filed an application for judicial management on March 4. Its position was that while it wanted the scheme to go ahead, it wanted the terms to be improved. As SK Energy did not believe that CAO would agree to this, it wanted the appointment of a judicial manager, who would be independent of CAO, to establish the best plan that CAO could afford.

CAO had consulted J. Aron on its two options trading restructurings in January and June 2004. J Aron's opinions had greatly influenced CAO's management. Therefore, on March 26, CAO filed claims against J. Aron seeking damages for the rescission of the two restructuring agreements as a result of various acts of misrepresentation, negligence, breach of statutory duties, and/or deceit on the part of J. Aron.

Negotiations with creditors

Following the announcement of the proposed scheme, the STF began a long period of negotiations.

Given the large number and diversity of creditors, the STF monitored the actions of the creditors to avoid additional risks, such as persuading SK Energy to withdraw its judicial management petition against CAO. Between the end of March and May 12, 2005, CAO realized that it would have to improve the terms of the scheme and garner the support of all the other creditors to fight SK Energy's judicial management petition. Achieving this would not be easy. The real questions were: What would constitute an improved scheme? When should it be announced? How should it be presented to the creditors in a way that would ensure credibility so that the company would not be pushed for further improvements?

CAO grouped the creditors into various categories to improve the effectiveness of the negotiations. Apart from the groups categorized earlier based on the nature of the operations (as physical trade creditors, options trading counterparties, and bank syndicate participants), the creditors were also classified as major or minor, based on the amount of debts owed; or as friendly, neutral or hostile, depending on their attitude towards the company.

CAO held many recurring but fruitful discussions with the creditors, including a meeting with 21 creditors and four meetings with bank syndicate members. While giving a full explanation of the background, objectives, and viewpoints of the debt restructuring exercise, the STF also listened to creditors' arguments, explanations, and requests. CAO eventually amended the initial scheme based on the feedback of most creditors and increased the repayment ratio.

The improved and final scheme

At the end of April, CAO decided to file an improved scheme and call it the "final" scheme. On May 12, 2005, CAO announced its improved and final scheme. The scheme's key elements included:

▷ A higher total payout of US$275 million, representing an average recovery rate of 54 percent.
▷ The cash injection from CAOHC and potential new investors increased to US$130 million.
▷ Two repayment options (A and B) for creditors, whereby under option A, creditors would receive a single immediate exit cash payment up to a total payout of US$45 million;* under option B, creditors would receive an initial cash distribution of US$85 million and the balance of US$145 million would be converted into deferred debts repayable over five years (from the sale proceeds of CLH and CAO's operational cash flows). Creditors who participated under option B were given the option to subscribe for up to 10 percent of equity in CAO's post-restructuring share capital.
▷ CAOHC to provide a guarantee for the repayment of deferred debts.

(See Exhibit 9.3 for fuller details of the improved final scheme.)

The same day CAOHC announced that it "had agreed in principle to the terms of the revised Scheme of Arrangement (the 'Revised Scheme')" and "As a matter of goodwill and in order to assist the company to get back on its own feet, CAOHC had agreed to the general terms of the Revised Scheme to the extent applicable to it." However, CAOHC also stated that "the present terms are already the most favorable terms CAOHC will accept, and that no revision will be considered."[12]

In addition, CAOHC also reiterated the conditions of its support in its announcement of December 14, 2004. CAOHC shared the confidence of the STF and its advisors that the revised scheme would be accepted by the requisite majority of creditors. Therefore, CAOHC stated that it would

---

* In the event that Option A was over-subscribed (i.e. creditors representing more than US$100 million of debt chose Option A), creditors would participate in Option A on a pro-rata basis to the value of their debts with any claims in excess of US$100 million being transferred to Option B. Conversely if Option A was not fully subscribed (that is creditors representing less than US$100 million of debt choose Option A), there would be a corresponding increase in the value of creditors' debts participating in Option B and any unutilized cash arising due to the under-subscription on Option A would be utilized under Option B.

Exhibit 9.3 CAO's Improved and Final Scheme

	Initial scheme (January 24, 2005)	Final scheme (May 12, 2005)
Initial cash payment US$m	100	130
Deferred debt US$m	120	145
Overall recovery value[a] US$m	220	275
Overall gross recovery %	41	54
Deferred debt repayment period (years)	8	5

[a] The recovery values under the final scheme were based on participating creditors of US$510 million.
Source: Public company announcements.

"renew its efforts to finalize the terms of the participation of strategic invest-ment in CAO and to assist in the resolution of the legal and regulatory issues concerning CAO such that the implementation of the approved scheme would not be delayed any more than necessary."

The final scheme was filed with the court on May 24, 2005.

On May 30, SASAC released its third statement regarding the revised scheme (See Exhibit 9.1, p. 118).

PwC's special investigation and CAO's response

Between November 30, 2004 and June 3, 2005, PwC carried out its special investigation. It was a time-consuming and challenging exercise, since many of the interviewees were Chinese-speaking and many of the documents were in Chinese. Based on a record comprising more than 2,000 pages of notes of interviews and several thousand primary documents and e-mails, PwC drew its conclusions and observations.

On March 29, 2005, CAO released PwC's Statement of Phase I Findings. In the initial report, PwC expressed its views on the circumstances leading to the losses without examining the issues pertaining to responsi-bilities and the causes. It concluded that the surging oil price had caused an exponential increase in the negative MTM value of CAO's option portfolio. As CAO was eventually unable to cope with its mounting margin calls, this led to the massive losses.

PwC concluded its investigation on June 3, 2005 by submitting a final report, the executive summary of which CAO released to the investing pub-lic. The final report examined the issues pertaining to responsibilities and the causes. PwC concluded that as the managing director and CEO of the company, Chen must bear the primary responsibility (see Exhibit 9.4 for excerpts from PwC report).

Exhibit 9.4 Excerpts from the PwC report

PwC concluded that as managing director and CEO of the company, Chen should bear primary responsibility for the following:

> The company commencing options trading without understanding precisely what it entailed and without ensuring that there was a proper and prior evaluation of the risks involved;

> Having committed the company to unacceptably imprudent risks in the restructurings which eventually proved financially disastrous for the company;

> Failing to report the company's MTM losses in its financial results. Chen was clearly aware that there were such MTM losses since he was involved in the January, June and September restructurings. He was informed that these MTM losses would have to be taken into account in the company's financial results by two emails sent by Peter Lim (who was the head of finance division) on 17 May 2004 and 4 October 2004. Yet he allowed announcements to be made as regards the company's financial results which did not reflect these losses; and

> Fostering a culture of secrecy. Arising from this culture of secrecy, attempts were made to conceal the losses on the options trades (which led to and resulted from the restructuring exercises which in turn led to further losses) from the board and the audit committee.

In addition, PwC concluded that the following additional factors contributed individually or collectively to the losses which CAO suffered as a result of its speculative options trading:

> A view of the oil price trend from 4Q 2003 that subsequently proved incorrect.

> A desire not to disclose losses in 2004.

> A failure to value the options portfolio in accordance with industry standards.

> A failure to appropriately recognize the correct value of the options portfolio in CAO's financial statements.

> The absence of proper and stringent risk management procedures specifically for options trading.

> Management's willingness to override risk management policies that ought to have been obeyed.

> A failure on the part of the audit committee in particular and the board in general to fulfil their duties in relation to risk management and controls applicable to CAO's speculative derivatives trading.

Source: PwC Executive Summary dated 3 June 2005.

In addition, PwC concluded that some additional factors contributed individually or collectively to the losses that CAO suffered as a result of its speculative options trading.

PwC also concluded:

> This financial debacle could only happen because of the failure at every level of CAO. If anyone at any level had independently asked more questions or delved a little deeper, or even sought to understand the position more fully, the situation might well have been averted.[13]

Despite strong requests from the media and the public to release the full PwC report, PwC, CAO, SGX, and MAS passed the buck to each other. The final released executive summary of the PwC report was only 31 pages long: a small fraction of the 600-page full report. There was widespread speculation on the real reasons behind the withholding of the full report. Some suspected that it was to protect the individual interviewees, while others speculated that it might be related to matters dealt with in Chapter 8 (the 50-day rescue of CAOHC) and Chapter 10 (on corporate governance). It was said that Chapter 8 contained evidence that the crisis management was not handled properly, while Chapter 10 contained facts related to improper governance by Chinese SOEs of their overseas subsidiaries. Furthermore, both chapters may also include evidence that CAOHC was trying to shift its responsibilities as a group on to Chen as an individual.

Following the release of the initial PwC report on March 29, 2005, the company (together with its external financial and legal advisors) reviewed the situation and took serious steps, including looking at how to improve corporate governance within the company. With PwC's investigations completed on June 3, 2005, the company intended to form a committee (which would work with the external financial and legal advisors) to study the findings and views expressed in the PwC report and make recommendations to the company on specific remedial or disciplinary actions which the company ought to take moving forward.

In addition, the company was also working with its external auditors on the audit of its financials for the year ended December 31, 2004 and would take into account the relevant findings of the report, and would make the appropriate announcements on its financial results when the audit had been completed.

The Singapore authority takes action

On June 7, 2005, the day before the scheduled creditors' meeting, a significant event occurred that cast doubt on whether the meeting would go ahead as planned.

The Singapore authorities announced that Chen (CAO's suspended CEO) and Peter Lim (head of the finance division) would be charged with certain offences under the Companies Act, the Securities and Futures Act, and the Penal Code.

Three of CAO's nonexecutive directors, including Madam Gu were also notified that they might be charged with breach of fiduciary duties and nondisclosure of price-sensitive information. Jia might also be charged with insider trading in relation to CAOHC's placement of 15 percent of its shares in CAO with Deutsche Bank.

Despite the charges against the four directors, especially Madam Gu as head of the STF, the board decided to go ahead with the creditors' meeting as planned and notify key creditors in advance of this new development.

The creditors' meeting

On June 8, 2005, the creditors' meeting was held at the Suntec Singapore International Convention & Exhibition Centre. After the proceedings were opened, Madam Gu gave an update of the situation regarding the charges, including those against her.

These events had little impact on the vote. Of the total of 92 creditors (with a debt value of US$555 million), 89* (with a debt value of US$539 million) voted for the scheme, which represented more than 97 percent in both the value and the number of the creditors present.[14]

The creditors gave their overwhelming approval to the final scheme at the creditors' meeting.

The Singapore high court formally approved the scheme on June 13, 2005.

Equity restructuring

After the success of the debt restructuring proposal, that is the creditors' overwhelming approval of the final scheme, the equity restructuring process to attract new investors and the redistribution of the shares became relatively easier.

One of the most pressing worries for the creditors and potential investors was the potential impact of the class action suits in the USA on the restructuring process. If the class action suits went ahead, the potential liability in addition to the company's existing debt would make the total amount unmanageable. Also, it would further complicate matters for the company, which was trying to obtain the necessary approval from its approximately 19,000 shareholders for the shareholders' scheme.

Although the company received legal advice that "there was no legal basis, nor jurisdiction for the class action suit,"[15] CAO's potential investors

---

* Only one creditor was against the scheme.

were seeking clear legal assurance from the company that the class action suits would have no impact on the equity side. Until November 29, 2005, when the case was dismissed by the US court, there was no certainty as to what the outcome would be.

Meanwhile, CAO had reached an out-of-court settlement with SMBC with regard to its claim.

Objectives and principles

The objectives of the equity restructuring were:

▷ to leverage on the potential strategic investors' experience and competitive advantages in the international markets and to complement CAOHC's resources and competitive strengths;
▷ to eradicate the negative impact of the options trading losses and resume growth from a higher platform;
▷ to re-establish CAO's international reputation;
▷ to create stable, long-term growth in value for shareholders.

The basic principles of the equity restructuring plan included the fact that CAOHC should retain a controlling stake of at least 50 percent.

Managing shareholders' expectations

There were a number of key issues in relation to the equity restructuring. The first centered on the valuation. In a restructuring exercise, striking a balance between making the deal satisfactory to creditors and remaining sufficiently attractive to potential investors is a common problem. Upon deciding the value of the company, the STF proposed the following equity holding structure—CAOHC, strategic investors, minority shareholders, and creditors would hold 50.7, 25, 14.3, and 10 percent respectively.

The second issue was how to handle shareholders' expectations, since, eventually, the shareholders would have to take a haircut, and the equity restructuring plan had to be approved by 75 percent by value and a majority in number of the approximately 19,000 shareholders entitled to vote, voting in person or by proxy. In addition, not every resolution proposed by the parent company would be acceptable, as there would be conflicts of interest because CAOHC was considered as an "interested person" according to the SGX listing manual.* The parent company would not be able to

---

* "Interested person" means a director, CEO or controlling shareholder of the issuer or an associate of any such director, CEO or controlling shareholder; "interested persons' transactions" means transactions between an entity at risk and an interested person. Source: SGX Listing Rules.

vote on the issuance of new shares and would therefore have to rely on the votes of the minority shareholders, which accounted for 25 percent of the company.

Gaining support from minority shareholders was critical for a successful restructuring. Apart from working with SIAS to persuade its member investors to participate in the final voting process, on January 12, 2006, the company also held an informal dialogue with SIAS members at the Singapore Power Auditorium to brief the minority investors about the equity restructuring plan and answer their questions. By the time the actual meeting took place, the shareholders were well informed about the proposals, making it easier for them to approve the equity restructuring plan.

Establishing the Corporate Governance Assessment Committee (CGAC)

Following the release of the findings of the PwC report, CAO announced the formation of a five-member CGAC on June 30, 2005. As recommended by Temasek, CAO appointed a reputable Singapore businessman, Lim Jit Poh, as chairman of the CGAC. The committee members included three Singaporeans, all experienced corporate directors and reputable business people in Singapore, together with Madam Gu, who was directly involved, and another person from CAOHC. Deloitte and Rajah & Tann, who knew the background, were advisors to the committee.

CAO established the terms of reference for CGAC to review and make recommendations to the board on the following:

▷ Changes or improvements to be made to CAO's risk-management systems and the strengthening of corporate governance within the company.
▷ CAO's board and management and staffing structure.
▷ CAO's corporate policies, protocols and systems.

From June 30, CGAC held regular meetings, examined and studied the large number of documents and records, including PwC's reports, the RMM, and the personnel manual. It also met with various parties, including the relevant regulatory authorities, auditors, independent directors, representatives of SIAS, CAOHC directors, company employees and the media.

On December 12, 2005, CGAC submitted a report with 26 recommendations to the board.

Searching for strategic investors

A critical condition for equity restructuring was procuring new investors. Concurrently, the STF had negotiations with five potential investors—Temasek, BP, Vitol, Turnmile, and Newbridge—on issues such as capital injection and shareholding structure, injection of assets, potential investors' role in CAO's rehabilitation and rebuilding process, and long-term-strategic cooperation.

CAO went through five rounds of negotiations between July and December 2005. After taking into account the reputation and strengths of the various potential investors, their potential synergy with CAO, proposals on CAO's rebuilding and their familiarity with CAO and the Chinese market, BP and Temasek (via its Aranda subsidiary) were selected as strategic investors. BP was selected because of its expertise in the oil industry and its renowned risk-management expertise. Temasek took only a small share, but this helped to rebuild Singaporean investors' confidence.

The choice of strategic investors went beyond their financial contribution. It was hoped that they would bring expertise to enable CAO to quickly rehabilitate, reconstruct, and grow to create long-term, stable, and increasing value for shareholders.

CAO subsequently signed five agreements with CAOHC, BP Investment Asia, and Aranda, including the Investment Agreement, the Subscription Agreement, the Memorandum of Understanding, the Shareholders' Agreement, and the Business Co-operation Agreement.

Under the agreements, CAOHC, BP, and Aranda together would inject US$130 million in exchange for 59.1 percent of the shares in CAO's enlarged share capital post-restructuring. CAOHC invested US$75.77 million for a 34.44 percent post-restructuring equity stake, BP and Aranda invested US$44 million and US$10.23 million for 20 and 4.65 percent stakes respectively. Together with the existing shares, CAOHC would have a majority shareholding of 50.88 percent. Existing minority shareholders' equity would be reduced to 14.47 percent (see Exhibit 9.5 for equity restructuring).

	Invested (US$ million)	Post-injection Ownership	
CAOHC (new money only)	75.77	34.44%	
BP	44.00	20.00%	
Temasek (Aranda)	10.23	4.65%	
Creditors Tranche B	22.00	10.00%	50.88%
Equity Injection	**152**	**69.09%**	
CAOHC (existing ownership)		16.44%	
Public Shareholders (existing ownership + penalty shares)		14.47%	
Total Ownership		**100.0%**	

(Left margin labels: Equity Injection; Existing)

Exhibit 9.5 **Equity restructuring**

Source: Public company announcements.

Exhibit 9.6 CAO's new board of directors

Name	Role	Year on board	Nomination or occupation	Other directorships
Lim Jit Poh	Independent chairman	2006–present	Non-executive chairman, ComfortDelGro	various
Lee Suet Fern	Independent director	2006–present	Senior director, Stamford Law Corporation	various
Liu Fuchun	Independent director	2006–present	Director & CEO, China National Cereals, Oils & Foodstuffs Corp (COFCO)	Director, COFCO
Meng Fanqui	Non-executive director	2006–present	CNAF (former CAOHC) nominee	Nil
Zhang Zhengqi[a]	Non-executive director, general manager	2007–present	CNAF (former CAOHC) nominee	Nil
Sun Li	Non-executive director, deputy chairman[b]	2007–present	President, CNAF, CNAF (former CAOHC) nominee	Nil
Zhao Shousen	Non-executive director, deputy chairman	2006 – present	CNAF (former CAOHC) nominee	Nil
Paul Reed[c]	Non-executive director	2006–present	BP nominee	Various
Michael Bennetts[d]	Non-executive director	2007–present	BP nominee	Various within BP companies

[a] Replaced Yang Chuan as the non-executive director on June 15, 2007.
[b] Replaced Zhao Shousen as the deputy chairman on April 30, 2007.
[c] Replaced Ian Springett who resigned on June 9, 2006 due to his change of role within BP.
[d] Replaced Dr. Wu Shen Kong who resigned on January 1, 2007 due to his retirement.

Source: Public company announcements.

In addition, BP was to get two seats on the newly appointed board of directors (see Exhibit 9.6 for new the board of directors).

Under the Business Co-operation Agreement, BP would provide CAO with trading expertise and other services to enhance CAO's trading and risk-management systems. BP would gain the pre-emptive right to supply the aviation fuel CAO required on terms more favorable to CAO than those obtained in the tender process, and BP would also make available various training and risk-management services.

Stock consolidation and debt-equity swap

CAO also announced the conversion of every five existing ordinary shares into one new ordinary share so that the stock price would look more reasonable once trading resumed.

On August 19, 2005, CAOHC entered into a civil penalty settlement with MAS for contravening the insider trading provisions of the Securities and Futures Act (SFA) with regard to its selling of a 15 percent stake to Deutsche Bank on October 20, 2004. CAOHC settled with MAS by paying a fine of S$8 million (US$4.8 million*) without court action.

A new provision in Section 232(5) of the SFA, which allows contravening persons to make out-of-court civil settlements with or without admission of liability, was introduced in 2004.† CAOHC's settlement with MAS became "the first case‡ in Singapore, which permitted a civil settlement for what could have been a criminal offence, which was insider trading for securities traded on the Singapore stock exchange."[16]

CAOHC, as a penalty, would swap its perpetual non-interest-bearing loan to CAO for new equity, which would then be transferred to minority shareholders. Every 1,000 shares presently held would be reduced to 200 shares after the five-to-one consolidation, and shareholders would receive an additional 70 shares from CAOHC as the penalty, ending up with 270 shares per 1,000.

In January 2006, creditors that opted for option B were offered 10 percent of shares for US$22 million of debt consideration. The shares were fully subscribed and allocated among the ten creditors subscribed for the shares, resulting in a reduction of approximately US$9.6 million in cash and US$12.4 million in deferred debt repayment under the creditors' scheme.

---

* Unless otherwise specified, the conversion rate S$1 = US$0.60 has been used.
† A new regime for controlling market misconduct, which includes the failure by a listed company to make the necessary disclosures expected by a reasonable investor in the secondary market, has been introduced, and the new Enforcement Division of the Securities and Futures Department is now empowered to take the necessary civil enforcement actions to obtain up to treble damages against people who contravene the relevant part of the SFA, which now includes market manipulation and the failure to make timely disclosures in the secondary market, where previously only insider trading was covered. The SFA has also introduced a new provision, section 232(5), which allows contravening persons to make out-of-court civil settlements with or without admission of liability. Source: Tjio Hans, Lee Suet Fern. "Developments in Securities Law and Practice," Speech at Singapore Academy of Law Conference 2006, in the Supreme Court Auditorium, 12 January 2006.
‡ On October 21, 2004, MAS took civil penalty enforcement action against three employees of the Government of Singapore Investment Corporation Pte Ltd (GIC) for breaches of insider trading involving shares of Sumitomo Mitsui Financial Group Inc., which were listed on the Tokyo, Osaka, and Nagoya Stock Exchange. However, even though this case was earlier than the CAOHC case, it was not a case for securities trades in Singapore as the SFA also covers securities traded outside Singapore in relation to a relevant act in Singapore.

Resumption of share trading

CAO formally applied to the SGX to lift the suspension on its share trading on 19 December 19, 2005, and obtained in-principle approval from SGX on January 27, 2006.

Shareholders showed overwhelming support for the equity restructuring plan at the Extraordinary General Meeting convened on March 3, 2006. All the 15 ordinary resolutions—including those relating to the equity restructuring plan and the appointment of eight new directors—were approved, along with a special resolution to amend the Articles of Association.

Conviction of individuals

CAD, Singapore's white-collar crime investigative arm, started its investigation in early December 2004. On June 9, 2005, four directors (Chen, Jia, Li and Madam Gu) and CAO's former head of finance were charged with offences under the Companies Act, the SFA, and the Penal Code (see Exhibit 9.7). These actions were concluded by March 2006.

Exhibit 9.7 Convictions of individuals

Lim (former head of finance) and Chen (ex-CEO of CAO) were charged under certain provisions of the Company Act, the SFA and the Penal Code.

▶ Lim was charged with five offences, and was sentenced to two years in prison and fined S$150,000 (US$90,000) on February 21, 2006 for making false statements to Deutsche Bank.

▶ Chen was prosecuted for a total of 15 offences and was convicted by a Singapore court on March 15, 2006 for his role in the near collapse of CAO. He pleaded guilty to six charges, including insider trading and failure to disclose financial losses, and was sentenced to four years and three months' imprisonment, as well as being fined S$335,000 (US$201,000).

The Singapore subordinate court imposed the following fines on Jia, Li and Madam Gu on March 2, 2006 under certain provisions of the Company Act and the SFA:

▶ S$150,000 (US$90,000) and S$250,000 (US$150,000) on Jia in relation to the charges under the SFA for tacitly acquiescing to CAO's non-disclosure of its losses to Singapore Exchange Securities Trading Limited (SGX-ST) and for insider trading, respectively.

▶ S$150,000 (US$90,000) on Li in relation to the charges under the SFA for tacitly acquiescing to CAO's non-disclosure of its losses to SGX-ST.

▶ S$150,000 (US$90,000) on Madam Gu in relation to the charges under the SFA for tacitly acquiescing to CAO's non-disclosure of its losses to SGX-ST.

Source: Public company announcements.

The charges against Jia in Singapore had attracted some attention because of his dual capacity as both chairman of the Singapore-listed CAO and president of CAOHC, a Chinese SOE. He also became the first head of a Chinese SOE to be charged overseas.

In addition, Jia, Li, and Madam Gu had further voluntarily undertaken not to act as a director or CEO of any publicly listed company in Singapore for one year. This thus ruled out the possibility of Madam Gu becoming CAO's next CEO during the probation period.

Despite the charges against Madam Gu, to ensure continuity, she would continue as the head of the STF in charge of the restructuring and rehabilitation of CAO as well as its day-to-day operations and management for a period of time even post-restructuring.

Completion of the restructuring

On March 28, 2006, CAO announced the completion of the 16-month restructuring process.

On March 29, CAO shares resumed trading on the main board of the SGX (see Exhibit 9.8 for share price evolution after collapse and once trading resumed). One of the conditions SGX stipulated before relisting the shares was that by May 15, 2006, at the latest, CAO had to have implemented the material recommendations made by the CGAC. On May 15, 2006, CAO announced that it had adopted all the recommendations of the CGAC based on its two announcements of February 28 and March 30, 2006 on the adoption of the CGAC's material recommendations.

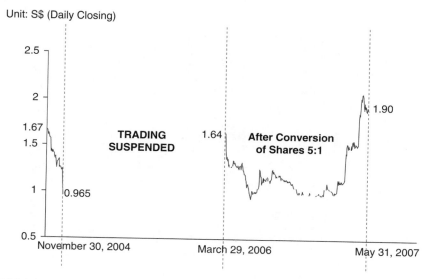

Exhibit 9.8 **Share price evolution, after collapse and trading resumed**
Source: Datastream.

Rehabilitation and rebuilding

The resumption of trading in CAO's shares on March 29, 2006 meant that CAO had been rescued from the brink of bankruptcy and was given a new lease on life. From that day onwards, the role of the STF also changed to that of implementing the decisions of the board and the senior officers' meeting (SOM), and its key task was the rehabilitation and rebuilding of the company.

Establishing a sound corporate governance and management structure

A new board was appointed on March 28, 2006. The board comprised nine members made up of four CAOHC, two BP nominees and three independent directors. An independent director was appointed chairman, while a CAOHC nominee served as deputy chairman.

With extensive business experience in both Singapore and China and the trust built up as the chairman of the CGAC, Lim Jit Poh was the natural candidate for the independent chairman, thus becoming the first foreigner to be chairman of an overseas Chinese company.

The first thing Lim Jit Poh did was to implement the CGAC's recommendations for improving CAO's corporate governance. This included establishing additional board committees, strengthening the internal audit function, setting up a whistle blowing system and improving both risk-management and internal control capabilities (refer to Exhibit 9.9 for the improved risk-management framework). A third party, to whom CAO

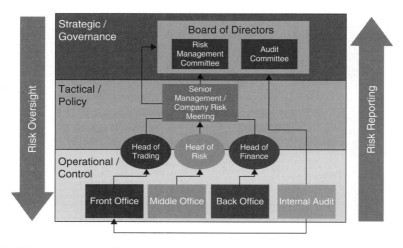

Exhibit 9.9   **Improved risk management framework**
Source: Annual report 2006.

outsourced its internal auditor function, "to give shareholders an added degree of confidence," audited the implementation process.[17] By the time CAO issued its 2006 annual report, the only recommendation yet to be implemented was the appointment of the CEO.

In the absence of a CEO, the SOM had been entrusted with the day-to-day affairs of the company post-restructuring. It revamped the internal management structure with seven functional departments, namely trading, operations, business development, risk management, finance, human resources and administration, and investor relations and adjusted the staffing, job positions and salaries.

Jet fuel procurement business back to normal

On May 25, 2006, CAO announced that it would revert to the principal model for its jet fuel procurement business from the agency basis through CAOT. CAO believed that it was the right time with access to sufficient bank facilities, having undergone scrutiny and approval by the newly established board and risk-management committee.

On June 2 CAO successfully closed its jet fuel tender for July delivery—the first to be conducted on a principal basis since the restructuring began in November 2004. Thus, the company strengthened its cooperation with end-users and suppliers, and effectively controlled risks such as market, supply source, credit, and quality. In 2006, a record volume of 4.66 million tonnes of jet fuel was procured, an increase of 53 percent over 2005.

Clearing outstanding legal cases

On November 14, 2006, CAO announced that the lawsuit against J. Aron was to be discontinued and, likewise, J. Aron would discontinue its counter-claim against CAO. CAO would accept J. Aron's claim as a creditor of CAO in the scheme dated June 8, 2005.

Review of investments

Disposal of 5 percent stake in CLH

In the scheme to repay the US$60 million debt, CAO had committed to divesting its 5 percent interest in CLH (Compania Logistica de Hidrocarburos). Accordingly, CAO announced on October 26, 2006 that it had begun this process and had appointed Deloitte as its financial advisor and Stamford, together with Deloitte Legal Spain, as its legal advisors in this regard. The divestment was in accordance with the scheme's undertaking that part of the proceeds would be used to satisfy the first installment of the deferred debt.

CAO took a systematic approach to selling the investment and conducted a highly competitive sale process. After two rounds of bidding and some intensive negotiations, on January 24, 2007, CAO announced that it had entered into a conditional share purchase agreement with Caixa De Afforros De Vigo Ourense E Pontevedra (Caixa), a private financial institution in Spain, for the sale of its 5 percent interest in CLH for €171 million (S$342 million*), which represented a gain of approximately S$183 million (US$110 million) after taxes and estimated transaction costs. The transaction was completed on April 17, 2007 (refer to Exhibit 9.10 for the post-restructuring ownership structure). The net cash proceeds from the transaction were about €150 million after the deduction of relevant transaction costs and taxes.

Reduction of stake in non-core Xinyuan

On January 29, 2007, CAO signed a share-transfer and management contract agreement with a fellow-shareholder of Xinyuan—Shenzhen Juzhengyuan Petrochemical Co., Ltd (Juzhengyuan)—under which the company's stake in Xinyuan was reduced from 80 to 39 percent. Juzhengyuan would have the majority shareholding and manage Xinyuan. The objective of this arrangement was to leverage on the strength of the local partner to turn around the loss-making business.

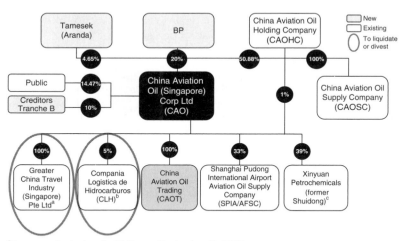

[a]Announced voluntary liquidation on September 16, 2005
[b]Announced divestment on January 24, 2007 and transaction completely on April 17, 2007
[c]Partial sale of 41% equity stake on January 29, 2007, reducing shareholding from 80% to 39% as non-core business

Exhibit 9.10   **Post-restructuring ownership structure of CAO**

Source: Public company announcements.

---

* Exchange Rate: €1 = S$1.9992, source: public company announcements.

Joint assets injection

A joint assets injection working team was formed to implement the memorandum of understanding on the joint-assets injection plan signed between CAO, CAOHC, and BP during the restructuring.

Resumption of trading in oil products

CAO proceeded with the four main areas of focus on the resumption of oil trading, including:

▷ preparing to apply for a hedging license;
▷ building a risk-management system;
▷ increasing credit facilities;
▷ building trading capabilities.

Substantial work had been done in all four areas. In preparation for the resumption of trading, the company had systematically embarked on related work under strategy, trading, operations, risk management, finance, credit management, training, IT, and corporate governance.

Rebuilding middle and back office support functions

CAO completed the various audits and financial reports for 2005 and 2006 and reviewed the Financial Management Manual.

In terms of banking facilities, CAO had credit facilities from several banks and open credit from several suppliers.

CAO revised the RMM and Traders' Guidelines, which were approved by the risk-management committee and the board before implementation.

The Human Resource Manual was reviewed. The roles, responsibilities, and duties of the various departments were formulated. Levels of authority and inter-department protocols were established. The introduction of a new performance appraisal system was also underway.

Fostering a new corporate culture and training

CAO adopted a new logo in November 2006, marking the start of a new corporate culture of "integrity, transparency and innovation," while the culture of "secrecy" of the past was eradicated. CAO had also begun training its staff and building up technical capabilities and risk-management knowledge.

Future prospects

CAO announced on February 27, 2007 that it had achieved a total revenue of S$2.9 billion (US$1.7 billion) and profit after tax of S$369 million

(US$221 million) in 2006, with improvements in its core business. It proposed a dividend of two cents per share.

The chairman of CAO, Lim Jit Poh, noted:

> The year ahead [2007] is likely to be exciting. The gas and oil industry will continue to be buoyant and volatile. We are ready to meet the challenges as our system and people are in place.[18]

Epilogue

During the two years and six months following November 30, 2004, the STF—together with its advisors—led and supported by SASAC and CAOHC, had successfully completed the first overseas restructuring and rehabilitation of a Chinese enterprise.

Since the resumption of trading in its shares on March 29, 2006, the share price was already triple the pre-suspension share price (S$0.965 or US$0.58 per share), and reached S$2.99 (US$1.79) per share (the highest price as of June 2007). The successful restructuring not only restored value for the parent company, the creditors and the minority shareholders, but also rewarded CAOHC and the new strategic investors for their newly injected equity.

Attributing responsibility

On February 7, 2007 the party committee of SASAC announced the punishment for those who should be held responsible for the debacle.

Jia, the president and interim party secretary of CAOHC and former chairman of CAO, did not perform his duties and had to bear primary responsibility for the losses. SASAC ordered Jia to resign from his posts and announced Sun Li as Jia's successor to be the head of the newly named China National Aviation Fuel Corporation (CNAF).

Chen, the former vice president of CAOHC and managing director and CEO of CAO, was held directly responsible for the massive losses. Chen was relieved from party membership and his post.

SASAC also suggested CAOHC decide on the punishment for the following and report its decision back to SASAC:

Zhang Zhicheng (former party secretary and deputy CEO of CAO) and Yang Bin (Chen's assistant).

Heads of the finance, investment, human resources department, audit, and other relevant departments of CAOHC at the time of the debacle for failing in the duties of daily supervision.

Full early repayment of outstanding debt

As there were substantial surplus sales proceeds from the sale of the stake in CLH, CAO made an early payment to its creditors on May 16, 2007 of all outstanding deferred debts, instead of the original schedule over five years (up to 2011). It saved the company US$12.7 million of interest expense on differed debt (based on the then-current LIBOR of 5.36 percent per annum).[19]

Building on the past and preparing for the future

The STF, appointed on November 28, 2004 to take over the management of the company, successfully completed its mission of the restructuring and rehabilitation of the company, and was disbanded on June 14, 2007. The STF, especially Madam Gu, were highly regarded because they had shouldered the heavy responsibilities exceptionally well under very challenging and difficult conditions.

Accordingly, the board also adjusted the management structure: the deputy head of the STF and a member of the SOM, Zhang Zhenqi, was appointed executive director and general manager of the company; Zhang Xingbo, also deputy head of the STF and a member of the SOM, was appointed deputy general manager. With the CEO position vacant, the SOM would continue to conduct the day-to-day affairs of the company.

To ensure a smooth transition, Madam Gu was appointed an advisor to the company to provide necessary advice and guidance to the company management as well as the good relations she had established with the authorities and the investing public.

10 Lessons not Learned

At the age of 67, Larry Yung Chikin (or Rong Zhijian in Mandarin), chairman of CITIC Pacific Limited (CITIC Pacific), had not thought about retiring from the company that he had founded two decades earlier, at least not in such a dismaying way. However, things changed in 2008 when an unsuccessful bet on the direction of currency moves caught the company wrong-footed amid the global credit crunch. Faced with the "great impact in society" following the Hong Kong police force's probe into the debacle, Yung was forced to resign "in the best interests of the company,"[1] ending a century-long family history in both Hong Kong and mainland China, as well as his legendary status as the "red tycoon."

Once topping the Forbes' list as the wealthiest person in China, Yung still leads his "relatively lavish lifestyle, despite the incident. He has a penchant for flashy sports cars and expensive suits," and remains "an avid racehorse owner and stalwart of the Hong Kong Jockey Club,"[2] while pursuing many other luxury hobbies. However, he faced the possibility of being held responsible for the currency debacle at CITIC Pacific, and a consequent jail term.

CITIC Pacific and the Yung family

To understand the rise and fall of Yung's family as well as CITIC Pacific, it is helpful to know a bit of the historical context. Based in Hong Kong, CITIC Pacific's businesses included special steel, power generation, aviation, infrastructure and property. It was 29 percent owned by the CITIC Group, a leading state-owned Chinese investment company. CITIC Group was established in October 1979 by Rong Yiren, Yung's late father. Rong was born into one of China's most prominent families who ran textile and flour businesses and his father, Rong Desheng, was one of China's richest men and a well-known entrepreneur in the late Qing Dynasty.

When the Chinese communist party came into power in 1949, Rong stayed in China and handed over his family fortune to the state. Thereafter he was known as the "red capitalist." This also allowed him to pursue a dual career in both business and politics. Rong played a key role in the opening of China and its economic reform. He was vice premier of China from 1993 to 1998 and helped the country to move from a centrally planned economy towards a market economy. Rong was handpicked by the then Chinese leader Deng Xiaoping to set up CITIC Group as a window for the opening up of China.

CITIC Group became a catalyst in attracting foreign investment to China. In 1986, CITIC Group acquired the Hong-Kong-listed Pacific Development and renamed it CITIC Pacific, which went on to become the first red-chip* company in Hong Kong and a Hang Seng Index constituent stock.

The eldest son of Rong, Yung was born in 1942 with the proverbial silver spoon in his mouth. However, because of his "capitalist" family background, Yung had some turbulent years during the Cultural Revolution and in 1966, he was exiled to a factory in Sichuan province. In 1978, Yung managed to move to Hong Kong. With some of the remaining family fortune that had been kept in Hong Kong, Yung, an engineer by training, set up his own electronics factory with his two cousins. Then, in 1986, he joined CITIC Hong Kong. Together with Henry Fan, the managing director of the company and a descendent of another Shanghai tycoon, Yung established CITIC Pacific in 1990. Yung's family connections to the centre of the power in China helped him to build CITIC Pacific into a sizable company through acquisitions and consolidation and made him one of China's most powerful tycoons.

The currency debacle

CITIC Pacific was dubbed by investors in Hong Kong as a "purple chip"† (a unique combination of blue chip and red chip) company. On the evening of October 20, 2008, however, the company stunned the market with the disclosure of potential losses (realized and unrealized) of HK$15.5 billion ($1.99 billion). The losses stemmed from some "unauthorized" foreign exchange trades, which had assumed the US dollar would weaken against the Australian dollar and euro, to hedge the company's substantial iron ore investments in Australia. These contracts, known as "accumulators,"‡ carried features with a limited upside but an unlimited downside. The company shares plunged by 55 percent the day after the announcement. On March 25, 2009, it posted its first annual loss (HK$12.7 billion or $1.6 billion, compared with a profit of HK$10.8 billion of the previous year).

A wrong bet beyond needs and control

The numbers disclosed by the company revealed that the exposure it had was far beyond its hedging needs—nearly five times its capital expenditure

---

* Red chip companies were mainland companies incorporated and listed in Hong Kong, with Chinese controlling shareholders.

† CITIC Pacific was a prudent blue-chip company and one of the 93 red chip companies in Hong Kong.

‡ Accumulator: nicknamed by traders as "I kill you later" due to its high-risk nature, was a leveraged derivative product that allowed investors to exit their position if the currency they were betting on strengthened, but not if it depreciated.

requirement. Its then-current estimate for its iron ore project's capital expenditure requirement was about A$1.6 billion (US$1.1 billion), and it would also need a further A$1 billion (US$0.7 billion) over the 25-year project life. At the time of the announcement, the company had already terminated some of its then-outstanding leveraged foreign exchange contracts (incurring a realized loss of HK$807.7 million (US$104.1 million). Despite that, the company still had remaining contracts amounting to A$9.4 billion (US$6.6 billion) to be marked to market at the end of the financial period.

According to Fan, the company's derivatives contracts were structured with multiple counterparts, including Citigroup, HSBC and BNP Paribas.

A role model for corporate governance?

To many, CITIC Pacific's bad news came as a surprise since it had a "fairly well-regarded management team."[3] On its website, the company claimed its commitment to excellent standards of corporate governance, which extended beyond compliance with the mandatory requirements. For example, it was one of the first companies in Hong Kong to appoint an audit committee of independent directors and to commit to fair disclosure best practices.

Yet, a week after the directors became aware of the trading losses, on September 16, 2008, the company issued a statement indicating that there was no adverse information that it should declare to the market. The company, therefore, came under sharp criticism when it emerged that it had failed to disclose the foreign exchange losses for six weeks after its directors had become aware of the trades.

What happened?

The board had taken a series of actions during that six-week time: (1) a special board meeting was held to discuss the issue; (2) the audit committee was authorized to begin an independent investigation; and (3) it sought assistance of its parent company in Beijing. In addition, it also invited PwC to study ways to improve its internal control.

The investigation by the audit committee concluded that "there was no reason to believe fraud or other illegal activities were involved."[4] That said, none of the directors (executive or independent) had suggested that appropriate disclosure be made to the market.

On October 22, 2008, the Hong Kong Securities and Futures Commission (SFC) announced that it had started an investigation of all of the company's 17 directors for failing to reveal suspected irregularities in its foreign exchange trading. No further details were given and the investigation did not commence until January 1, 2009.[5]

Most of the directors, including Yung's son, were long-serving members of the board and directors of other CITIC group companies. If it were to be proved that the statement had contained misleading information, the company and the directors could be prosecuted:* the maximum penalty could be a fine of HK$10 million ($1.3 million) and a 10-year jail term.

A sign of improvement?

On October 20, 2008, CITIC Pacific announced two resignations. One was its group finance director because of his failure to follow the company's hedging policy, obtain prior approval from the chairman and for conducting transactions that were beyond his authority limits. The other was its group finance controller due to his failure to act as a check and balance in oversight, and, in particular, his failure to bring to the chairman's attention unusual hedging transactions. As head of the finance department, Yung's 37-year-old daughter, Frances Yung's role in the incident, remained unclear. She avoided the sack, but was demoted and received a pay cut.

Yet, neither the currency trades, nor the losses, had any effect on Yung as the chairman of the company. At the company's 2008 annual results briefing on March 25, 2009, Yung said that he had no intention of resigning. It was only after April 3, 2009, when the Hong Kong police force raided CITIC Pacific's company premises, that Yung was forced to step down. The Commercial Crime Bureau of the Hong Kong police force formally launched an investigation into CITIC Pacific's currency debacle. The investigation was focused not on the losses, but on the six-week delay in disclosing these to the public. On October 20, 2008, trading in the shares of CITIC Pacific was suspended.

The state bailout

To ensure the company's survival, the CITIC Group agreed to extend a $1.5 billion standby loan facility and indicated its willingness and ability to support CITIC Pacific. This was followed by other actions, including an equity injection and the take-over of the majority of the loss-making foreign exchange contracts—positions that could face significant further declines.

As a result, CITIC Group's shareholding in CITIC Pacific increased from 29 to 57.6 percent, while Yung's own ownership was diluted from 19 to 11.5 percent. CITIC Pacific shareholders welcomed the arrangement and voted 99.9 percent in favor of the proposal. On February 17, 2009, Moody's Investors Service (Moody's) acknowledged such strong support by upgrading CITIC Pacific's rating from Ba2 to Ba1.

The backing from CITIC Group, wholly-owned by the Chinese government, stabilized CITIC Pacific's financial situation, restored creditors'

---

* According to David Webb, a shareholder activist in Hong Kong and a former independent director of the Hong Kong Stock Exchange.

confidence and sustained the operations of CITIC Pacific's main businesses. "Without these benefits, the standalone rating of CITIC Pacific rating is Ba3," said a Moody's analyst.[6]

In early May 2009, Yung sold 60 million CITIC Pacific shares for HK$732 million (US$94.4 million) at a deep discount, further reducing his shareholding in the company from 11.5 to 9.9 percent. Morgan Stanley arranged the sale. The order book was closed within an hour and was more than five times oversubscribed with strong interest from new investors including mutual funds, hedge funds and private wealth management clients. Yung's move drew a generally positive market reaction as "it will help reduce the personal image of Mr. Yung in the firm and give investors hope that its parent will do something good for its Hong Kong unit."[7]

Pause for Reflection

Memories are short, and lessons have not been learned. Following the CAO incident in 2004, CITIC Pacific became another casualty—another Chinese SOE venturing abroad that incurred substantial losses due to "speculative" derivatives trades. Clearly, CITIC Pacific was not an isolated case of betting wrongly on the Australian dollar. There were many other Chinese companies in the same boat: news reports at the time claimed that about 28 Chinese SOEs were involved in derivative trades and that most of them were facing losses.

China had never been comfortable with the complex nature of derivatives. It was only relatively recently that China created a domestic derivatives market, with extreme caution and strict oversight. In the international derivatives markets, however, due to some high-profile trading scandals in the recent years, Chinese regulatory authorities had strictly limited the participation of mainland Chinese companies. However, the overseas subsidiaries of mainland Chinese SOEs, including those in Hong Kong and Singapore, such as CAO and CITIC Pacific, were often off the radar screen.

CAO and CITIC Pacific were the direct beneficiaries of the China growth story and their close links with their Chinese parent. Both cases illustrate the importance of sticking to what you know. As it is dangerous to get into a business where you do not understand the inherent risks, it is important for Chinese companies to acquire new skills and be better equipped when entering the international arena. The real questions are how and at what cost?

Learning is essential for Chinese companies venturing overseas to enable them to establish the systems to acquire the competencies in order to compete in the global arena. Although successful and international in their own right, the debacles at CAO and CITIC Pacific also exposed the inherent problems of some Chinese companies.

1: CEO and chairman dual role is a major source of potential conflict of interests

Consider the CAO case. Often, an overseas assignment for a senior Chinese executive can be a stepping-stone to future career advancement, especially in the political dimension. Consequently, it is common for top executives of overseas Chinese companies to hold dual roles in their parent companies. CAO and CAOHC were no exception. The downside risk, as the Chinese saying goes—"Out of sight, out of mind"—can be much bigger. While it is not clear how Chen actually performed his duties as the EVP responsible for CAOHC's overseas investments during his tenure, it is likely that political motivation lay behind certain of his decisions.

A similar rationale applies to Jia's hands-off approach performing his duties as chairman of the Singapore entity. On the one hand, Chen's business acumen and proven track record had been a reassurance, but on the other hand, Chen's "boldness" and "smartness" perhaps became Jia's major concern. Thus, despite Jia and his predecessors having mainly managed CAO at the "macro" level, they had also placed their "ears and eyes" in the Singapore entity to "counterbalance" Chen. In this case, these "ears and eyes" not only reported to Jia or CAOHC directly, but also had equal authority with Chen on certain management issues. During Chen's absence, for instance, Zhang (the party secretary sent by the parent company) signed the first margin call that CAO paid on its speculative derivatives trading in the form of letter of credit. In retrospect, if Zhang had not approved the payment in relation to the speculative derivative trading, the CAO incident might have been avoided.

To make things even more complicated, CAOHC was also CAO's major customer. This fact may be one of the underlying motivations for Chen to "manage upward," hence the sponsorship of EMBA courses for CAOHC employees, who were not directly involved in CAO, not to mention the setting-up of a travel agency solely to meet its domestic customers' international travel needs.

2: Understand how the Chinese management system and board work, and their decision-making process

Management systems in China have their own unique characteristics. In the CAO case, many decisions were made by the Chinese parent instead of the board. According to CAOHC's internal management policy for its overseas subsidiaries, all reports and materials had to be submitted, reviewed and revised before they were submitted to the board. Furthermore, certain CAO reports were submitted to CAOHC directly, who in turn, gave instructions to the CAO management, bypassing the CAO board.

In addition, the majority of members of the CAO board were nominated by the Chinese parent. The board did not consider it was necessary to set up a nomination committee. Consequently, new directors were appointed by board resolutions, which gave the majority shareholder much more control over appointments, and there was no formal system for assessing the performance of the board.

Further, the Chinese directors were inexperienced—they had had no previous directorships with any publicly listed companies in Singapore. Language was an issue, and formal training was, at the time, not specifically required by the SGX. The directors, therefore, had to rely on the Chinese translation of the IPO prospectus, reviewed and approved by relevant Chinese authorities. Chen had arranged certain training sessions, before and during the IPO processes, to inform the Chinese directors of their duties. However, this was far from sufficient, as the training obligations were ultimately delegated to Chen.

Further, the fact that the CAOHC-nominated directors generally shared Chen's view was not uncommon. In general, the Chinese directors (especially the ones from the same parent company) would have agreed among themselves beforehand on key subject matters to be discussed at the board meetings. Under such circumstances, the role of independent directors becomes ultra-important.

In addition, when dealing with executives at Chinese SOEs or their subsidiaries, it should be borne in mind that management decisions are often group decisions. The course of action followed by CAO and its Chinese parent after they realized that the company had suffered from the massive losses is a perfect illustration. So too was CITIC Pacific's delay of its announcement to the public.

Mini-Case: CNOOC

CNOOC was the listed arm of the China National Offshore Oil Corporation (the parent)—the third-largest state-owned oil company in China. It went public in Hong Kong in 2001, and was 70 percent owned by its parent company. David Webb, an influential shareholder activist in Hong Kong, had campaigned to defend the rights of minority shareholders over several governance issues. These issues ranged from connected-party transactions, through a change of noncompete agreement by the parent, doubts over the independence of financial advisors, to retaining disqualified independent directors.

The CNOOC-related campaigns were great examples set by shareholder activists safeguarding minority shareholders' rights. These were often issues that the minority shareholders were either naïve about or simply ignored. Sometimes they were just too complicated for the minority shareholders to understand, especially when they were dealing with majority shareholders that were Chinese SOEs.

Repeated related-party transactions with parent company

According to Webb, "CNOOC has a history of seeking minority shareholders' approval for proposals against their interests."[1] Since 2002, CNOOC had repeatedly broken the Listing Rules of the Hong Kong stock exchange by failing to seek prior approval to place cash deposits of RMB6,600 million with CNOOC Finance, an unlisted subsidiary of its parent.[2] Webb said: What is at stake here is a worrying trend among the mainland government-controlled groups to set up in-house finance vehicles for the pooling and control of group cash, mixing the assets of listed companies with those of their parents and siblings and ensuring that the purse-strings are controlled by the parent.[3]

Webb had campaigned for voting against the arrangement twice. At both occasions, CNOOC chose the night before a holiday break to seek sharehold-ers' approval when minority shareholders were less likely to gather enough votes against its proposals.

The first attempt was in 2004. At that time, CNOOC denied that it had done anything wrong. However, a subsequent investigation by the Stock Exchange of Hong Kong Limited (the Exchange) confirmed that the shareholders were right, and on October 6, 2005, the Exchange censured CNOOC for failing to seek shareholders' approval for the prior transactions. Richard Williams, head of listing division of the Exchange, commented:

The Exchange views the failure to disclose and obtain prior independent share-holder approval of connected party transactions very seriously. The case is another example of the granting of financial assistance by a listed issuer to a connected party over a lengthy period of time without proper approval. Such conduct prejudices the interests of independent shareholders in that they are not being given information on a timely basis or invited to approve the transac-tions before they are implemented.[4]

However, the censure came too late. The attempt failed due to the tight meeting notice period resulting in a low voter turnout and the failure to mobilize enough shareholders to go along with the against vote. Therefore, CNOOC got its three-year approval, which expired in 2007, when CNOOC again sought minority shareholders' approval for the arrangements.

The second attempt was on March 30, 2007, when 52.2 percent of CNOOC's inde-pendent shareholders voted against it. Following a similar case in late 2006, when CNOOC's sister company, China Oilfield Services Ltd., had asked its shareholders to approve transactions of the same nature with CNOOC Finance, the sharehold-ers campaigned against the proposal and it defeated by 62.92 percent of votes.

Change of noncompete undertaking by the parent

CNOOC had a noncompete undertaking with its parent, as set out in its IPO prospectus. The undertaking assured that the parent would not engage in oil exploration and production, and any deals worth doing would be done by CNOOC. However, CNOOC's parent proposed an amendment to the undertak-ing to exclude deals onshore or outside of China. The shareholders lobbied against the proposal, and in a meeting on New Year's Eve, shareholders voted it down by 59.08 percent of votes. Nine days later, on the evening of January 9, 2006, CNOOC announced a deal in Nigeria, and its stock gained 3.7 percent the following day. Webb believes that the Nigerian deal might well have gone to the parent if the vote had gone the other way.

The independent financial advisor

ICEA Capital Limited, a subsidiary of Industrial and Commercial Bank of China (ICBC), which was listed in CNOOC's annual report as one of its principal bank-ers, acted as an independent financial advisor and issued a fairness opinion. In similar situations, ICEA also issued fairness opinions to PetroChina Co. Ltd. on September 22, 2005 and to China Petroleum & Chemical Corp (Sinopec) on April 21, 2006. This not only caused concerns over conflict of interests, but also cast doubts on whether a subsidiary of a principal banker should be allowed to act as an independent financial advisor to a company.

The disqualified independent directors

On Webb-site.com, Webb also advised shareholders to vote against the re-election of CNOOC's independent directors because they had done a poor job of advising independent shareholders by telling them to vote in favor of pro-posals that were not in their best interests

3: Independent directors are key to a functional and effective board

Both the CAO and CITIC Pacific case raise the question whether independent directors actually performed their duties. In the CAO case, for example, the two Singaporean directors were both recommended, if not imposed, by DBS Vickers—CAO's issuing manager. According to people who were familiar with the situation, CAO was not given the flexibility to look for other candidates at the time. Lee could be a qualified independent director and chairman of the audit committee as he had all the technical qualifications. However, one could question his real "independence," since he had been a senior partner of the CAO's former external auditors and tax advisors. Besides, Lee also held directorships in various other companies. One might question how much time he could actually dedicate to the company. Tan's case was different as he was newly retired and took on the directorship in CAO as a personal interest. Despite being a former finance director at Singapore Airline, Tan had no formal accounting qualifications. He spoke some Mandarin, but was not fluent. The only Chinese independent director, Dr. Yan, despite having had much international exposure, was a pure academic.

In general, finding qualified independent directors remains a challenging task for most boards of overseas listed Chinese companies. The pool of qualified or experienced independent directors in China/Asia is limited. Not to mention that, often, directors have been appointed based on connections or reputations. Those who are qualified are often in high demand and, if overworked, risk not being able to dedicate enough attention to the companies they serve.

4: The pros and cons of being a Chinese company—two sides of the same coin

The nature of Chinese companies gave CAO and CITIC Pacific the advantage of benefitting directly from the rapid growth of Chinese economy. CAO, for example, achieved de facto monopoly status as the importer of jet fuel into China, supported by CAOHC. While CITIC Pacific was able to acquire certain strategic assets mainly due to its close connection to the state.

It is debatable, however, whether the fact that CAO was a Chinese company had any bearing on its problems. Certainly, a SOE mentality and management style existed, where ownership and management were not separate. Management philosophy and company culture were still pretty much Chinese even though the company claimed that it had formed its culture based on the fusion of East and West. However, somehow there was also the possibility that Chen had placed too much emphasis on "Chinese Wisdom," perhaps to the exclusion of CAO's international workforce (who made up about 90 percent of the payroll).

Besides, corporate governance was still weak in China. CAO was publicly listed on the SGX, while its Chinese parent was one of the top Chinese SOEs. The issues it had to deal with, such as connected-party transactions or asymmetry of information flow, were not unusual.

5: Be careful who you are dealing with

When dealing with their Chinese counterparts, Western companies need to watch out whom they are dealing with—the parent or the subsidiary.

Consider the CAO case. At different occasions, CAO representatives told their counterparts that the options trading or the share placement was on behalf of CAOHC, and no executive members from CAOHC ever denied it when they received delegates from these counterparts. Instead, they assured the delegates that CAOHC would help resolve the CAO issue.

Deutsche Bank, for example, did not further verify the validity of Chen and Lim's representations with CAOHC in Beijing. In addition, it did not question why the sale proceeds, which were supposedly to be used for CAOHC's purchase of vessels and for investment purposes, did not even go into CAOHC's account but, rather, straight into CAO's. Of this money, 96 percent was paid to four counterparties to meet margin calls.

6: Be aware of the implicit/explicit implications for Chinese companies becoming listed companies overseas

Once a Chinese company is listed overseas, it exposes itself to public scrutiny and regulatory requirements in both China and the host country. What are the implicit/explicit implications then?

Transparency

Both SGX and the Hong Kong Stock Exchange required full, frank and timely disclosure of information to investors. This was quite different to the way SOEs operated in China, where transparency was still inadequate. Therefore, equal/complete information flow to both the majority shareholder and minority shareholders became vitally important.

Market expectations/investor relations

The value of a listed company depends not only on its performance but also on market expectations. This may have indirectly triggered the subsequent events that led to CAO and CITIC Pacific trying not to let their share price slide by hiding losses.

CAO also hired a former DBS Vickers security analyst to build and manage investor relations to boost its share prices. This raises the question on the role of security analysts. On the one hand, security analyst coverage can enhance the monitoring of corporate governance by reducing information asymmetries and making stock prices more transparent. On the other hand, the views of analysts may be biased and the "independence" of security analysts is questionable.

Risk management and corporate governance

Much of the "rigorous" risk management and corporate governance at CAO and CITIC Pacific was in form rather than substance. Both claimed to be modeled on what was recognized as the best practice. However, the real question was whether these risk-management systems were properly set up, executed or continuously improved.

Regulatory environment

The role of different regulatory bodies was also controversial, if not conflicting. Consider the CAO case.

First, the fact that relevant Chinese regulatory authorities approved oil derivative trading as part of CAO's businesses was a major factor leading to the debacle.

Second, under the terms and conditions of the Approved Oil Trader (later GTP) status, CAO was obliged to meet certain minimum requirements as set by the Singaporean government to maintain its GTP status and to enjoy tax advantages. Such requirements, as well as the endorsement from CAO's parent company and its board, were major factors in driving CAO to its massive losses.

Third, the SGX was both marketer and regulator. Despite it claimed that there was a Chinese Wall between the two departments, the question was were there any conflicts of interests?

Hong Kong's regulatory independence

One aspect to note from the CITIC Pacific case is Hong Kong's regulatory independence, as there had been doubts on how the Hong Kong government would handle the issue, due to the close links between the company and the governments of both mainland China and Hong Kong.

> How Hong Kong handles the matter has important implications for the principles of "one country, two systems" and the high level of autonomy that the central leadership pledged.[5]

Plus, Hong Kong was literally a society strongly influenced by local tycoons. According to *The Wall Street Journal*, the Hong Kong Stock Exchange had recently backed down from a plan to tighten restrictions on the trading of shares by company insiders after local tycoons objected.

The Chinese government had tried to clear the doubts. Shortly after the Hong Kong police force raided CITIC Pacific's office, Chinese Premier Wen Jiabao said, in an interview, that the issue should be addressed in accordance with the laws and financial supervision regulations of Hong Kong, and no interference from the mainland or other parties would be allowed. Wen also stressed the importance for the company's management and its supervision to draw lessons from the incident after the investigation was done and all the facts were clarified.

Mini-Case: Netease—the "Fantasy Westward Journey"

> The new management team knows that the earnings misstatement was a very big problem. Another mistake like that could be catastrophic for the company.
>
> Denny Lee, Chief Financial Officer, Netease

Netease.com Inc. (Netease) was one of the Chinese dot-com fantasies on NASDAQ. However, an incident of revenue misstatement had made Netease's westward journey a bit rocky and almost eliminated a 30-year-old Chinese entrepreneur rising to the top of the list of China's richest. In 2001, Netease, a leading Chinese internet technology company listed on NASDAQ, looked destined for the dot-com graveyard.

Netease began the year of 2001 with the departure of its CFO due to health-related reasons,[6] followed by an internal investigation starting in May, into possible incorrect reporting. The investigation included a review of its audited financial statements for the fiscal year 2000, and led to the resignation in the following month of the company's CEO and COO.

William Lei Ding, founder and chief architect* of the company and chairman of the board of directors, was back at the helm as acting CEO and COO. In July, pending the result of the internal investigation led by the board through its audit committee, the company was facing a possible delisting due to its failure to file its annual report with NASDAQ and the Securities and Exchange Commission (SEC).

---

* Chief architect: A non-managerial position in which Ding gives advice to the board regarding the company's strategic direction and product development.

What had happened?

In April 2001, a potential purchaser of Netease identified a large amount of past-due accounts receivable balances and questioned Netease's revenue-recognition practices. As a result, the Netease board authorized its audit committee, together with the company's outside counsel and independent auditors, to conduct an internal investigation to determine whether Netease's financial statements were prepared in accordance with the US Generally Accepted Accounting Principles (GAAP).*

By August 31, 2001, the audit committee had completed its internal investigation It concluded that Netease inflated its revenue by US$4.3 million or 109 percent (for five consecutive fiscal quarters) due to widespread circumvention of internal accounting controls in connection with hundreds of contracts and at least fifty customers.[7] In light of these findings, Netease restated its fiscal year 2000 financial statements and corrected, before public dissemination, its financial results for the quarter ended March 31, 2001.

---

* GAAP generally permits revenue recognition for an advertising arrangement if a contract was executed, the advertising service was performed and the collection of the associated account receivable is probable.

7: The role of the intermediaries needs to be further examined

Of the three banks that CAO approached, Deutsche Bank was the only one that went ahead. Within just one week, Deutsche Bank completed the secondary placement compromised mainly with institutional investors and the shares were fully subscribed within a short four hours. This raises several questions.

First, what was Deutsche Bank's motivation? In our view, it was probably mainly driven by two factors: (a) the commission received from the placement; and (b) the bank's desire to establish/strengthen its presence in the region.

Second, on what basis did Deutsche Bank conduct its due diligence prior to the placement of shares? SGX did not require a prospectus to be issued for the placement of existing shares. Therefore, Deutsche Bank conducted its due diligence purely based on the financial information—and the representations and warranties—provided by Chen and Lim, CAO's head of finance. Both acted on behalf of CAOHC. On paper, the due diligence was done according to procedures.

Last, but not least, did Deutsche Bank ever question, or seek to verify, the legitimacy of Chen and Lim's claim that they were acting on behalf of CAOHC, or even deal with CAOHC directly? During the entire due diligence process, Chen and Lim presented themselves as the representatives of CAOHC. In Chen's case, it probably made a certain sense, as he was then the EVP of CAOHC in charge of its international business. However, Lim was only the head of finance of CAO. In addition, how was it possible that

Deutsche Bank could actually tell Chen and Lim that the purposes of the proceeds of the placement were actually not important?

Deutsche Bank's case was perhaps not unusual. For varieties of reasons, the due diligence processes for overseas listed Chinese companies can be a challenging exercise both from the process and timing perspective. The role of intermediaries need to be further strengthened.

In both cases, however, it is perhaps safe to assume that international financial institutions (for instance, the counterparts of CAO) or CITIC Pacific's derivatives transactions had also provided the same services to many other Chinese companies that have the same needs. The extent of losses from oil and currency derivative trading among Chinese companies had also attracted scrutiny from Chinese regulators and the local media. Some Chinese publications had depicted Western investment banks as predators that hoodwinked unsuspecting Chinese executives. Investment bankers argued, however, that Chinese companies tended to prefer less expensive structures to the safer alternative—buying options.

In an extreme case, Goldman Sachs got into a dispute with a small power company in southern China—Shenzhen Nanshan Power Station Co. (Shenzhen Nanshan) over its losses on oil-related derivatives. Shenzhen Nanshan refused to pay for the losses of tens of millions of dollars incurred on oil-related derivatives, claiming that these transactions with Goldman Sachs were "unauthorized." As with the CAO case, Goldman Sachs' commodities arm in Singapore, J. Aron & Co., (J. Aron) had acted as the counterpart for a number of derivatives contracts by Chinese companies that hedged their oil exposures and had run up substantial losses recently, such as Air China and China Eastern Airlines.

An article from a Chinese online publication depicted that Goldman Sachs as "running a derivatives casino." It concluded that Chinese enterprises, only "beginners" in the international financial markets, were doomed to "pay expensive fees to learn the ropes."

> The designer of derivatives in Goldman Sachs is perhaps a casino master. In the gamble of oil prices, it seems that one Chinese firm hit the tables at Vegas and left without his shirt.[8]

It might be an exaggeration to say investment banks are running derivatives casinos. Yet, in reality, the banks did play several conflicting roles as both trading counterparts and professional advisors. In the CAO case, for example, J. Aron did act as both counterpart and professional advisor to CAO and suggested extensions of the company's trades to bet on the downfall of the oil prices.

In addition, investment banks had created complex structured products that few financial officers could fully comprehend. There had also been doubts about whether investment banks had made the nature of risks clear to financial officers or executives: by not protecting the downside risks, for instance, CITIC Pacific faced only limited upside but unlimited downside risks. In any case, the investment banks gained both ways.

Ironically, almost all the high-profile debacles were due to "unauthorized" trades. This inevitably raised questions on what constitutes properly authorized trades and what should be the proper procedures to go through. Part of the explanation could be that investment banks had granted hidden national credit to their Chinese counterparts. The Shenzhen Nanshan case should serve as an alert to investment banks that they may also get themselves into trouble.

There is another point worth noting here, as we discovered during our field research. In the CAO case, PwC was appointed by the SGX as the special investigative accountant. However, PwC also recommended that CAO be placed under judicial management because PwC wanted to become the judicial manager of the company. This highlights the importance of examining the role of intermediaries, as they often hold or seek conflicting roles.

8: It is more than business

When dealing with your Chinese partners, it is important to understand that there are often considerations beyond the purely financial.

In the CAO case, nonfinancial considerations were vital, especially for a successful restructuring in such a complex situation. There are a few key factors for success to highlight here:

▷ Although SASAC and CAOHC showed their support, but they also laid out the principles for the restructuring: (1) it had to be based on international commercial practices; (2) the support was not unconditional. Creditors, therefore, should have realistic expectations when dealing with such a situation.

▷ In most restructuring cases, minority shareholders are often the group at great disadvantage. Taking into consideration the need to find an equitable solution for all concerned, including minority shareholders, was a key to the success. The case showed that dialogues with SIAS prepared the ground for gaining support from a large number of minority shareholders, thus leading to a successful debt and equity restructuring later on.

▷ It was in the interests of the Chinese state that CAOHC retained a majority shareholding in CAO. Ultimately, CAO was a company majority-owned by a Chinese SOE and was strategically important to both other major state-owned companies and China as a country.

▷ It was also important that CAO gained support from friendly creditors in fighting against the imposition of a judicial management petition. This made it possible to retain control of the company and continue with the business.

▷ The criteria for choosing strategic investors went beyond purely financial considerations. The criteria were based on what would be the best for the company in the long run. This required not only strong financial backing, but also the knowhow on risk management and corporate governance that they could bring into the company.

The role of Stamford and Temasek remained controversial and cannot be overlooked. Both Stamford and Temasek knew about the situation well in advance of the investing public but they were still willing to help SASAC and CAOHC to solve the problem. It is hard to say whether or not political factors due to their close link to the Singapore government played a part. Not to mention that, in recent years, Temasek had been actively seeking investment opportunities in the region, including China.

Temasek became SASAC's "working partner" and advisor. Stamford remained as CAOHC's advisor. Together, they suggested restructuring as the third option and explained to the crisis management team the basic concept and how it would work. They also helped Madam Gu find advisors, and the independent chairman.

In addition, the fact that Temasek expressed an interest in participating in the restructuring as a co-investor along with CAOHC (even if it was non-binding and conditional) had a calming effect and helped restore investor confidence in Singapore. Temasek was selected as one of the strategic investors for the same reason.

Mini-Case: China Life

The China life Insurance Company Limited (China Life) was formed in June 2003 by cherry-picking the healthiest assets from its state-owned predecessor, China Life Insurance (Group) Co (CLIC) prior to its listing. China Life went public on December 17, 2003 and became the largest IPO of the year by raising US$3.5 billion. CLIC remained as China Life's controlling shareholder with a 72 percent stake.

In March 2004, a group of US investors filed a class-action suit against China Life and certain officers and directors, alleging the company had failed to disclose an audit report that uncovered accounting irregularities worth about RMB5.4 billion (US$652 million) up to 2002 at its state-owned predecessor firm. The audit report was announced by the Chinese National Audit Office on February 4, 2004: during a routine audit it discovered that CLIC had made investments that were not permitted by the nation's insurance laws and used agents who were legally unqualified, while some CLIC branches had misstated expenses and income leading to underpayment of taxes.

China life was probably the first Chinese SOE listed in the US market to encounter this type of lawsuit. Given the dual-listing nature of the company in the USA and Hong Kong, both the US Securities and Exchange Commission and the Hong Kong Securities and Futures Commission made informal* inquiries into the matter. Shares of the company plummeted roughly 36 percent during the approximate 8-month class period—from the class period high of US$34.75 per share on the NYSE and HK$6.55 on the HKSE to US$21.76 on the NYSE and HK$4.25 on the HKSE on April 29, 2004.

---

* There are two types of investigations conducted by the SEC—informal and formal. An informal investigation is conducted on a voluntary basis and with the co-operation of the company being investigated. Informal SEC inquiries don't always lead to allegations of wrongdoing.

The case was dismissed by a US court on September 3, 2008, and on October 14, 2008, plaintiffs filed a notice stating their intention to appeal. On January 8, 2008, the appeal failed to advance as a New York federal appeals court granted a motion of voluntary dismissal of appeal, which was granted by the Second Circuit Court on the same day, thus, making the summary judgment decision granted on September 3, 2008 (New York time) by the New York Southern District Court final. The appeal was therefore dismissed with prejudice.

9: Communication in a transparent manner is essential

Consider the CAO case. When CAOHC engaged with Stamford and Temasek, it was transparent about its problem. Having learned from the lessons administered during the initial phase of crisis management, the Special Task Force led by Madam Gu was transparent with all major stakeholders involved in the restructuring—for instance, various Singaporean authorities, creditors, minority shareholders and the media—on the actions it had taken and its plans for next steps. This not only helped CAO management control the situation and regain trust but also contributed to restoring investor confidence later on.

Since the debacle had attracted much attention in both Singapore and China, communication became the key to a successful restructuring:

▷ A single public contact point was established—Cogent as the investor relations advisor.

▷ Complete information flow to all major stakeholders was ensured.

▷ Madam Gu had the incredible ability to work with people from diverse backgrounds, and personally built good working relationships in Singapore, and gained trust.

▷ Madam Gu had the ability to communicate with key stakeholders in both Singapore and China, including the Chinese parent, SASAC and the working team. She also had the ability to see the big picture and make decisions—and communicate them.

Mini-Case: Gome: the Fall of China's Sam Walton

On November 24, 2008 Huang Guangyu, chairman of Gome Electrical Appliance Holdings Ltd (Gome*), was detained by the police for allegedly manipulating shares of a listed company controlled by his brother, Huang Junqin. On the same day, the company shares were suspended from trading on the Hong Kong

---

* The leading retailer of household appliances in China, the brand name "Gome" was first adopted in 1993.

Stock Exchange. On November 28, 2008, the China Securities Regulatory Commission (CSRC) confirmed that a probe into Huang was mainly because of his alleged irregularities in asset restructuring and swaps in two listed companies. CSRC had forwarded the case to Beijing police and Xinhua (the state news agency) reported that the case was under direct charge of the ministry of public securities.

Known as the "price butcher" or "China's Sam Walton," Huang, at the age of 39, was ranked as the country's richest man on October 7, 2008 by *Hurun Report** with an estimated asset of RMB43 billion (US$6.3 billion). On 23 December 2008, Huang was suspended from his post as chairman and controlling shareholder of the company. Huang's wife, Du Juan, quit her post as director on the same day and was also detained in early January 2009. Huang and his wife owned approximately 35 percent of the company shares. After nearly six months in detention, in April 2009, news report said that Hung had attempted suicide but he was discovered in time and recovered.

Back in July 2006, Huang and his brother were already investigated by the police for illegally receiving RMB1.3 billion in loans from a Beijing branch of the Bank of China more than a decade earlier. Huang was later released and cleared of all charges. However, he remained on the list of suspects of the police. According to the *Economic Observer*, Huang was suspected of seven crimes, ranging from bribery, tax evasion, money laundering, manipulation of share prices and asset transfer through an underground banking system.

Not long ago before Huang was arrested, several rich list celebrities had run foul of the law, typically over financial misconduct. Zhou Zhengyi, the eleventh-richest person in China in 2002 and the boss of Nongkai Group, was sentenced to 16 years in jail in 2007 for bribery, embezzlement and tax fraud. Zhang Rongkun, the sixteenth-richest in 2005, and the owner of Fuxi Investment, was sentenced to 19 years in June 2008 for his role in a billion-dollar pension fund scandal in Shanghai. Huang was not the first, nor would he be the last.

The fall of a self-made billionaire not only broke a classic Chinese rags-to-riches tale but also revealed loopholes that China had ignored while concentrating on its economic growth. Huang's detention also inspired people to call for a healthier market environment for business owners to compete in.

Gome was registered in Bermuda and listed on the Hong Kong Stock Exchange; CSRC said that it would also offer assistance to the Hong Kong regulators where necessary. In connection to Huang's case, Zhou Yafei, group CFO, was also being investigated and was removed from his post. In the weeks following Huang's detention, Gome took strides to distance itself from its founder. Gome's CEO, Chen Xiao, replaced Huang as chairman, and the company's shares were suspended from trading. As of late December, the company was reportedly mulling over the sale of a strategic stake to overseas buyers. Even though the company remained unconnected to the probe, there would be some negative impact on the company's finances.

---

* A leading luxury publishing and events group, comprising a magazine and active events business targeted at China's high net worth individuals, established in 1999 by Rupert Hoogewerf, the "godfather" of the China Rich List.

10: Innocence, ignorance and indecisiveness were the key factors which led to the massive losses

Although the logic behind CAOHC's intention to rescue the company was initially good, by doing so, CAOHC had hidden material information, which may have affected the share price, from the whole investment community and therefore had breached the law. Furthermore, top executives at both CAO and CAOHC, including Chen and Jia were inexperienced in derivatives trading and did not have much idea of the nature of the transactions and how big the losses could be. This was evident from the fact that the company did not stop the losses immediately, but waited to find a rescue solution. Having said that, it may be arguable when would have been the best time to materialize the losses. Still, for nearly two months, neither CAOHC nor CAO had been able to decide how to go about dealing with the losses. Hence, they had piled up from the initially estimated US$180 million to US$550 million, from a manageable level to a massive amount, not to mention the costs (in both time and money) of the restructuring. To be fair, as the majority owner of publicly listed company in Singapore, CAOHC perhaps had taken a too big role for itself and too many responsibilities.

At the time of the CAO case, Chinese companies were still inexperienced in derivatives trading and dealing with the investment community. Therefore, it was perhaps understandable that innocence, ignorance and indecisiveness had partially contributed to the massive losses. In the CITIC Pacific case, however, one suspects that the state interference and rescue model was intentionally copied, which led to the six-week delay in announcing the news to the public. What had been learned from the CAO case, though, was the need to be swift and efficient in closing positions and materializing losses.

What was more worrying was that clearly, many Chinese companies had also taken on exposures that were beyond their control. Of those Chinese companies that had expanded in Australia, few had been equipped to handle, nor had the experience of managing, currency risks or risks associated with derivatives trades. Not to mention that few had anticipated the global credit crunch that had brought down many more sophisticated players in the world of derivatives. According to a veteran Hong Kong banker,

> Financial officers at new, fast growing Asian companies often don't want to spend the cash on buying unlimited downside protection, which can often be done by buying a "put" option. What is common… is a straight-up form of speculation, whereby a financial officer simply bets on the direction of a form of currency or commodity through a derivative, or zero-cost options that provide unlimited protection above a certain price but also unlimited losses below another price. "If there is a theme there, it's that very few treasurers who haven't been through a proper cycle understand what a proper hedge is…"[9]

It was difficult to judge whether financial officers failed to understand the derivative contracts that they were entering into, or whether they were, knowingly, speculating in an effort to maximize their profits. One would have imagined that if financial officers buy products, they probably understand the risks. It does seem clear, however, that those "unconventional" derivative contracts were certainly beyond what CITIC Pacific needed for hedging purposes, and few executives predicted how quickly the bets could go wrong, how much money they stood to lose, and how poorly defended they were against such a downfall. Tom James, a UK-based energy risk-management consultant, commented:

> Even if you understand the product, you've got to make certain that you have the solid risk-management structure: the people, the system and most importantly the reporting.[10]

Perhaps it is time to examine what qualifications and skill sets that financial officers should possess. The increasing sophistication and complexity of newly innovated structured banking products posed new challenges for experienced financial officers, and so to a company's risk-management structure, reporting and corporate governance.

11: The leadership style of the key players, in particular Chen and Jia as CEO and chairman, respectively

Chen* was perceived at CAOHC as "the smart and bold." The fact that he had turned the Singapore business around was a great proof. However, this, perhaps to certain extent, had also caused some discontent or jealousy within CAOHC. Even though Chen did not have much formal business education, he was born with business acumen and was quite strong in languages. It was possible that Chen got the job initially mainly because of his language capabilities. Still, it was his strong entrepreneurial spirit, drive and ambition, and his strong relationship-building and influencing skills, which formed the basis for CAO and Chen's personal success. For instance, Chen created the "transfer account" approach to leverage on the creditworthiness of other domestic Chinese companies; created a level playing field for competing with international oil companies by convincing CAOHC to adopt an open-tender process; lobbied CAOHC to issue two management directives, thus gaining de facto monopoly status; secured competitive trading financing facilities; and lobbied to apply international industry standards for jet fuel.

At CAO, Chen kept a flat management structure that all division heads reporting to him directly. Some perceived this as too dominant and thus fostering a culture of "secrecy." Even the office layout—which meant that all employees had to pass his office to get to their desk—would have caused discomfort to some people. Nonetheless, Chen never gained the wholehearted

---

* Chen was released from jail in January 2009. He was appointed as the deputy general manager of China Gezhouba Group Corporation (CGGC) International Co., Ltd. in June 2010. CGGC was founded in 1970 and constructed the whole Gezhouba Hydroelectric Project.

trust of the parent company, as Jia had placed his "eyes and ears" at CAO to counterbalance Chen. Some of the "eyes and ears" were not even qualified either because of their language weaknesses or the lack of certain skills, especially financial skills, and were sent back. Again, this was perceived as Chen being too arrogant to manage.

Chen's outgoing personality made the problem even worse, especially all the publicity and visibility that he had received over the years in Singapore and mainland China. Chen gave his mobile number to journalists. He was perceived as, and admired for, maintaining a "modest lifestyle" in Singapore even though he was the "king of the working class." (Incidentally, most of Chen's income did not go to his personal pocket but to CAOHC.) He was voted as one of the 40 New Asian Leaders by the World Economic Forum in 2003 and was a regular speaker at international forums; published a book as well as a number of articles in both Chinese and overseas newspapers and magazines.

Jia,* on the other hand, already knew that Chen was "smart and bold" and not an easy one to manage when he became the president of CAOHC. However, he had to place trust in him, since Chen had a superb track record of turning the company around, or perhaps he had no better candidate than Chen. It was a delicate balance. On one hand, it seemed that he had perhaps placed a bit too much "trust" in Chen, including delegating many of his responsibilities as chairman of the company. On the other hand, Jia had also shown his "distrust" by placing his "ears and eyes" around Chen. Still, as long as things were going well, this would have not been a problem.

Jia did not realize the extent of the problem when Chen first told him that CAO was incurring massive losses due to derivatives trading. Jia asked Li to follow up on the matter. Both Jia and Li were still on holiday, and so neither of them took immediate action. However, Jia assured Chen when Chen called him that he would do his best to help CAO resolve the issue. Still, instead of taking immediate actions to fix the problem, Jia carried on enjoying his vacation as well as other prearranged business trips.

12: Chinese companies may have shouldered a lot more responsibilities than they should have

The CAO case was a beautifully handled restructuring. The debt and equity restructuring was completed in a short period of 16 months, and the rebuilding process was completed within 30 months of the losses being announced. The share price at one point tripled in price after the trading resumed.

In hindsight, perhaps CAO/CAOHC shouldered a lot more responsibilities than they should have. For example:

▷ Restructuring as a going concern, e.g. CAO changed its business model by setting up CAOT to carry on the jet fuel procurement business on an

---

* Jia became vice president of China Aviation Supplies Holding Company in March 2008.

agency basis, then reverting back to the principal basis once the situation was stabilized.
▷ The aim of the restructuring was to find a commercial solution rather than a political one, though political support was vital for the successful restructuring.
▷ Proactive dialogue with SIAS to gain support, which also later laid the ground for the equity restructuring and became a template for restructuring companies in Singapore.
▷ It was key to retain control of the company—fighting against the imposition of judicial management.
▷ The choice of strategic investors also helped to restore investor confidence and improve risk management and corporate governance.
▷ Restructuring, the continuity of the businesses and the strengthening of corporate governance proceeded in parallel.
▷ Appointed a reputable Singaporean businessman as the independent chairman, which not only helped restore investor confidence but also brought management knowhow and strengthened corporate governance.
▷ Most of the CGAC members also became independent directors or senior officers of the company. This ensured that the recommendations made by the CGAC were practical and implemented.

It was a surprise to all that the STF initiated the dialogue with SIAS to protect minority shareholders—no companies undergoing restructuring in Singapore had done it before. "Being a responsible company" has a bit of a different meaning in the Chinese context.

13: Develop your human capital

Consider the CAO case. Under usual circumstances, the board should consider the following key criteria, in terms of personality, experience and professional competences when appointing a head of the STF:

▷ proven experience in crisis management;
▷ familiarity with the Singapore regulatory and legal environments and customs;
▷ strong network in CAOHC and SASAC;
▷ the personal competences to manage extremely difficult stakeholder relations between creditors, shareholders, the media and regulatory bodies in both Singapore and China;
▷ experience in CAO's core business areas—the Chinese aviation oil industry and oil-related investments;
▷ strong finance/banking/language capabilities;
▷ ability to recruit, motivate, manage and lead people from diverse background;
▷ willingness and ability to act decisively;
▷ ability to understanding the big picture and set priorities.

On the surface, Madam Gu may have not appeared as a suitable candidate as the head of the STF for the restructuring. For instance, she had no prior overseas experience, nor had she any prior experience in dealing with the Singaporean authorities. Plus, her language skills may not have been very good. Worse, during the restructuring process, she was personally charged with certain offences under Singapore's Companies Act. It took tremendous courage to carry on her duties as the head of the STF under this pressure.

However, Madam Gu* had kept an open mind and was aware that things would work differently in Singapore and so prepared herself to manage this. Coincidentally, or luckily, her personality fitted the Western style well. In addition, she was an excellent people person and good at grasping the big picture of a complex situation. Most importantly, the fact that she had an established network at CAOHC and SASAC, as well as the way Chinese companies work also helped in the circumstances.

The magazine *China Entrepreneur* recently released a report entitled "Globalization Index of Chinese Enterprises and Top 50 Chinese Multinational Corporations." It highlighted the key leadership qualifications needed for Chinese managers going global. Top of the list was "A global vision and mind"; second was "Cross-cultural management and communicative capacity"; tied for third were "A profound understanding of the strategic goal of the enterprise" and "The ability to integrate international resources." (Source: *China Entrepreneur magazine.*)

---

* Madam Gu later joined Temasek and became the Chief Representative of its Beijing office.

Last but Not Least

Much has been said about China as an emerging economy. The reality is that the China story has sold itself, and enthusiastic investors in their zeal to tap into China's growth have overbought. Many have come to China in search of opportunities; in fact, there has been too much money for too few opportunities. While some have overcome their fear of the unknown and met with initial successes, others have run into trouble. Concerns about transparency, corporate governance, and accounting practices are not new, but perhaps they have taken on special meaning when applied to China. Or, could it be that investors simply do not apply the same rigorous evaluation of their ventures in China as they do to their investments elsewhere?

How long can this situation last really? Is it only a matter of time before the investment environment becomes increasingly selective? Only the fittest will survive, and there is no doubt that Chinese companies and professionals are eager to acquire best practices to sustain investor interest. But there is a long way to go and investors may have to bear the cost of rapid economic growth and the yet-to-improve corporate governance standards. So, what's the best way to do business in and with China? Following are some of our suggestions:

The merit of "The Chinese Contract"

> The Chinese contract ... embodied a principle which went far beyond the making of lasting commercial deals. It was about the importance of compromise as a prerequisite of progress. Both sides have to concede for both to win. It was about the need for trust and a belief in the future. Writ large, it was about sacrifice, the willingness to forgo some present good to ward off future evil, or, more positively, it was about investment—spending now in order to gain later.
>
> Charles Handy[1]

We can't give you a surefire formula for success, but the essence of the "Chinese Contract" as Charles Handy described it almost two decades ago, remains. Compromise is a fact of business life and is not merely a way to gain access into Chinese minds, but also a way to win their hearts. Genuine respect is the ultimate currency and be sure you make your best investment in it. It will take you a long way.

Adjust your mindset and perspective

To enter and compete in the global marketplace, Chinese companies will have to face many different problems, such as financial, legal and cultural differences in the international market versus their domestic market. In short, the "rules of the game" are different. The same principle applies to Western companies entering the Chinese market or working with Chinese companies internationally.

We have often heard of instances where "culture differences" are blamed if things do not go as well as planned. The questions really are: Do we understand the differences? Have we attempted to? In the CAO case, when Madam Gu came under the spotlight after the announcement of the losses, she was aware that things would be different in Singapore and had prepared herself accordingly. She also determined to understand and work with the differences.

> Western world people are continually bombarded by a filtered and unduly negative version of Chinese reality by their news media.[2]

In general, with few exceptions, and perhaps apart from the China growth story, Western media tends to focus on the negative stories about China, whether its corruption, human rights violations, food and toy security, or Tibet issues. Indeed, these stories are not all untrue. Like any country in the world, China has its problems and it is not an easy place to do business. Yet, it has been making progress at a much faster pace than most of us realize. In fact, most people who complain about it have never set foot in China. You must go and see the changes in China with your own eyes. But, you must go with an open mind and leave your biases and preconceived notions behind. You must be willing to acknowledge that there are differences, and you must be ready to understand and work with those differences. It is only in this way that you can be part of China's growth and part of its progress.

Do the right thing

It is really just a matter of doing the right thing. But what is the right thing? The answer depends on the context. Chinese companies have learned it the hard way. As the CAO case illustrates, state bailout is perfectly legitimate in China, but the process must be handled with care and take into account the local norms. Chinese companies must continuously raise their transparency levels to international standards.

Face-saving was, and still is extremely important in China. For Chinese executives, it comes even before reason and the law. It is the complete opposite in the Western world—the law comes first and face comes last. Despite good intentions, the outcomes can be devastating, sometimes with people ending up in jail, as was the case with CAO.

Build up a proven track record

It's important to build a proven track record to boost investor trust and confidence in your company. In order to do this, you must set the highest standards for your company. This will help you avoid potential "issues" that can easily escalate into "crises." Apply the same high standards both at home and internationally, so that you don't fall into the trap of doing the right thing in one place but not in another. Over time, you can manage your investors' expectations and build their confidence in you. But, a few words of caution: Don't overpromise. Make sure that you can deliver on your promises every time.

Communicate, actively and proactively

Traditional Chinese culture and values promote doing the right thing, but doing it quietly. It is not the same tale in the financial world of capital markets, where most investors have already developed their own perceptions of Chinese companies, and these perceptions are often inaccurate or negative. Therefore, it is important to make sure that others know that you are doing the right thing. And, it's particularly important to make sure that there are no surprises, especially bad news shocks.

Beware that "China issues" can turn into "crisis"

The CNOOC case exemplified certain "China issues" and the importance of stakeholder management, including shareholder activists, which most Chinese companies have never encountered. The risks of ignoring such groups are enormous.

Corporate governance issues such as accounting irregularities, weak risk management, and internal control are not unusual in China. The cases in this book were used to demonstrate the importance of overseas listed Chinese companies aligning themselves with international standards and building a track record for doing so. Those Chinese companies which can demonstrate such a track record, will have a distinct advantage over their peers that fail to do so.

Conversely, for some Chinese companies trading in North America, "issues" can turn into "crisis." Thus, have not only become the prime targets of short sellers, but also received increased scrutiny from regulators due mainly to their lack of transparency and possible accounting frauds. For example, Muddy Waters Research (Muddy Waters), founded by the 35-year-old Calson Block, has gained much prominence since its first research report in June 2010, despite assertions of market manipulations. Muddy Waters claims that it "sees through the appearances to a Chinese company's true worth"[3] and Block short-sells the stocks ahead of these reports.

Although some companies disputed Muddy Waters' claim, the value destruction is almost devastating. According to Bloomberg, the five companies* that Muddy Waters has publicly reported on had lost almost US$4.4 billion in market value from the last trading day before the publication of the reports through June 3, 2011.[4]

Likewise, Western companies need to handle the relationship with their Chinese counterparts with extreme care. China business has become an integral part of many and has added increasing value to their own company worth. For example, investors believe that Yahoo!'s most valuable asset is its 40 percent stake in Alibaba.[5] Without exception, the stock price of all three companies, Google, Danone and Yahoo!, plummeted during their disputes with Chinese government or partners.

Don't walk in the dark

Yet, some Western companies also contributed to the problems. On July 5, 2009, four of Rio Tinto's executives in China were detained by the Chinese government and were accused of taking bribes and stealing commercial secrets. They were formally charged on August 12, 2009, went on trial in Shanghai on March 22, 2010 and, following the trial, were sentenced to jail terms of between 7 and 14 years, along with heavy fines.

> The Rio Tinto saga demonstrates that walking in the dark may be costly to one's reputation, costly to one's future interests, and could put employees in Chinese jails for a long time.[6]
>
> Stephen Smith, the Australian foreign minister[7]

For Rio Tinto, the costs of the saga were probably much lower than CAO. Rio Tinto dismissed the four employees after the court hearings and carried on its businesses with its Chinese partners. Still, instead of walking in the dark, foreign businesses in China should not only learn about the Chinese customs, but also laws and regulations. Likewise, Chinese companies should do the same in countries where they operate.

A new imperative

Over the past thirty years, the Chinese economy has experienced remarkable growth, as have the numbers, toughness, and wealth of Chinese entrepreneurs. Not only have they learned hard skills, but they have also grown in confidence or even arrogance in some cases. Try to understand where your Chinese partners have come from.

---

* The five companies are: Orient Paper Inc., RINO International Corp., China Media Express Holdings, Duoyuan Global Water Inc. and Sino-Forest Corporation.

Though the wealth created by the Chinese entrepreneurs seems remarkable, it may also be controversial in some cases, since things are never black or white. Be careful not to become a moral policeman, but make sure you work on a solid legal basis during the cooperation process.

When working with Chinese entrepreneurs with strong characters, you also need to be strong—gain their respect and trust, the rest will follow.

Successful partnerships should be based on equality and mutual interests, leveraging on the strengths and striving for the win–win. Danone obviously had only focused on its own interests instead of those of its partner. Had Danone thought and acted differently, the partnership might have played out differently.

Develop a sense of continuity and direction for the future

The CAO case was a typical case illustrating that companies/executives should deal with their present problems, or problems inherited from the past, with a clear sense of continuity and with a direction for the future in mind. It shows the logic of "building on the past and preparing for the future." There had been never a radical change—rather a smooth transition was made. For instance:

▷ Chen remained as the head of the initial crisis management team when CAOHC was first informed about the losses.
▷ When Jia, Madam Gu and Li were charged, Madam Gu remained as the head of the STF throughout the whole restructuring and rehabilitation period; Jia stayed as the chairman and headed the restructuring from the parent company in Beijing.
▷ Madam Gu was a member of the CGAC, with Deloitte and Rajah & Tann—who were both involved in the restructuring—as advisors.
▷ When the STF was disbanded once its mission of restructuring and rehabilitating the company had been accomplished, Madam Gu remained as an advisor to the board and management.

Such sense of continuity and direction for future should be based on having learning as your strategic objectives and build up resources and capabilities. Ultimately, no matter whether it is Western companies doing business in or with China, or Chinese companies venturing overseas, it is the ones who learn fastest and best who win the race.

In December 2010, Morgan Stanley cleared the way to sell its 34.4 percent stake in China International Capital Corporation (CICC), ending a 15-year joint venture partnership that created the first Sino-foreign investment bank in China. Morgan Stanley invested US$35 million in CICC in 1995 and the 34.3 percent stake was valued at around US$1 billion and expected to record a US$700 million pre-tax gain once the sale closed at the end of 2010. Morgan Stanley helped establish the first Chinese investment bank and lay the groundwork for the opening of the Chinese capital market to foreign players. Despite huge financial gains, however, Morgan Stanley ceded management control to its Chinese partner in 2000 and has had no real influence ever since on the business. Another typical example of a foreign partner underestimating its Chinese partner's and employees' ability to learn fast, as well as failing to build up true expertise in the domestic Chinese market.

A few words of wisdom

When it comes to your company's goals in China, we have a few words of wisdom that may seem counter-intuitive or unpopular these days:

First, define your niche. Attempting to conquer the 1.3-billion Chinese market isn't going to get you anywhere. You need to do your homework, think about what you want to achieve in the long run, and focus on the most relevant and important elements to help you achieve your objectives. In other words, you need to define and focus on your niche.

Second, start small. "Small opportunities are often the beginning of great enterprises." Focus on processes and execution, rather than outcomes.

Last, let us borrow the words of Alibaba's CEO Ma Yun: "If you want to do business in China, send the people who are best at serving your customers, and not the investors."[8] The same applies to Chinese companies expanding overseas.

Notes

Prologue

1. Battelle, John (2005, 2006) *The Search: How Google and Its Rivals Rewrote the Rules of Business and Transformed Our Culture*. Nicholas Brealey.
2. OECD (2006) "Business China." *OECD Observer* No. 255, May 2006.
3. McGregor, James (2005). *One Billion Customers: Lessons from the Front Lines of Doing Business in China*. A Wall Street Journal Book published by Free Press.
4. McGregor, James (2006). "No More Chinese Whispers." http://www.danwei.org/business_and_finance/no_more_chinese_whispers_by_ja.php (accessed August 30, 2011).
5. Wuttke, Joerg (2010) "China is beginning to frustrate foreign business." *Financial Times*, April 7, 2010, http://www.ft.com/cms/s/0/e67d9a9c-4273-11df-8c60-00144feabdc0.html (accessed August 30, 2011).
6. Elaine Kurtenback, "Danone Dispute Heats Up as JV chairman Resigns." *Shanghai Daily*, June 8, 2007, http://en.ce.cn/Business/Enterprise/200706/08/t20070608_11651588.shtml (accessed August 30, 2011).
7. "Multinational companies dominate list of commercial bribery cases: an indictment of the hidden rules of the Chinese market?" Xinhua News Agency, August 3, 2009 (In Chinese) http://news.xinhuanet.com/fortune/2009-08/03/content_11815532.htm (original published on China Youth Daily).
8. Park, Seung Ho and Wilfried R. Vanhonacker (2007) "The Challenge for Multinational Corporations in China: Think Local, Act Global." *MIT Sloan Management Review*, July 1, 2007.
9. Rogers, Jim (2007) *A Bull in China— Investing Profitably in the World's Greatest Market*, p. 11. John Wiley & Sons.

Chapter 1

1. Google Corporate Blog. http://googleblog.blogspot.com/2006/02/testimony-internet-in-china.html (accessed August 30, 2011).
2. Rifkind, Hugo (2009). "Google: going cold turkey." *The Times*, June 12, 2009. http://technology.timesonline.co.uk/tol/news/tech_and_web/article6480401.ece (accessed 20 June 2009).

3. Google company website.
4. Battelle, John (2005, 2006) *The Search: How Google and Its Rivals Rewrote the Rules of Business and Transformed Our Culture*. Nicholas Brealey.
5. Battelle, John (2005, 2006) *The Search: How Google and Its Rivals Rewrote the Rules of Business and Transformed Our Culture*. Nicholas Brealey.
6. Battelle, John (2005, 2006) *The Search: How Google and Its Rivals Rewrote the Rules of Business and Transformed Our Culture*. Nicholas Brealey.
7. Google Company Blog, http://googleblog.blogspot.com/2006/02/testimony-internet-in-china.html (accessed August 30, 2011).
8. Battelle, John (2005, 2006) *The Search: How Google and Its Rivals Rewrote the Rules of Business and Transformed Our Culture*. Nicholas Brealey.
9. Cowley, Stacey (2006) "Google CEO on censoring: 'We did an evil scale'," IDG News Service, 27 January 2006, http://www.infoworld.com/article/06/01/27/74874_HNgoogleceocensoring_1.html (accessed August 30, 2011).
10. Google Corporate Blog. http://googleblog.blogspot.com/2010/06/update-on-china.html (accessed August 30, 2011).
11. Analysys International (2011) http://english.analysys.com.cn/article.php?aid=108692 (accessed August 20, 2011).
12. Baidu company website (financial report).
13. Analysys International (2011) http://english.analysys.com.cn/article.php?aid=108692 (accessed August 20, 2011).
14. http://www.reuters.com/article/idUSSGE6680F920100709 (accessed August 30, 2011).
15. Zittrain, Jonathan and Benjamin Edelman (2002) "Localized Google Search Result Exclusions." http://cyber.law.harvard.edu/filtering/google/ (accessed August 30, 2011).
16. Analyst Report dated February 25, 2010 by Morningstar Equity Research.
17. Helman, Christopher (2010) "Microsoft's Ballmer Calls Out Google Over China Stance," *Forbes*, http://blogs.forbes.com/energysource/2010/01/22/microsoft-ballmer-google-china-stance/ (accessed August 30, 2011).
18. Google Company Website. http://googleblog.blogspot.com/2010/01/new-approach-to-china.html (accessed August 30, 2011).
19. Yifan, Ding (2010) "Google's exit a deliberate plot," *China Daily*, updated 25 March 2010, http://www.chinadaily.com.cn/opinion/2010-03/25/content_9638825.htm (accessed August 30, 2011).
20. Worthen, Ben (2010) "Soviet-Born Brin Has Shaped Google's Stand on China," *The Wall Street Journal*, March 12, 2010, http://online.wsj.com/article/SB10001424052748703447104575118092158730502.html (accessed August 30, 2011).

21. Worthen, Ben (2010) "Soviet-Born Brin Has Shaped Google's Stand on China," *The Wall Street Journal*, March 12, 2010, http://online.wsj.com/article/SB10001424052748703447104575118092158730502.html (accessed August 30, 2011).

22. Johnson, Bobbie and Tania Branigan (2010) "Web censorship in China? Not a problem, says Bill Gates," *The Guardian*, January 25, 2010, http://www.guardian.co.uk/technology/2010/jan/25/bill-gates-web-censorship-china (accessed August 30, 2011).

23. Yixuan, Zhang (2011) "Google, what do you want?," *China Daily*, June 10, 2011, http://www.chinadaily.com.cn/opinion/2011-06/10/content_12674156.htm (accessed August 30, 2011).

24. Barboza, David (2011) "Microsoft to Partner With China's Leading Search Engine," *The New York Times*, July 4, 2011, http://www.nytimes.com/2011/07/05/technology/05microsoft.html?_r=1&emc=eta1 (accessed 20 August 2011).

Chapter 2

1. Interview with Franck Riboud, April 2008, "2007 marks the beginning of a new venture," http://www.danone.com/images/pdf/dan_discfr_en.pdf (accessed August 30, 2011).

2. Danone company press release May 2009 http://www.danone.com/en/press-releases/cp-mai-2009.html (accessed August 30, 2011).

3. Danone 2006 annual report.

4. Edmondson, Amy C., Bertrand Moingeon, Vincent Dessain, and Ane Damgaard Jensen (2007) *Global Knowledge Management at Danone*. Harvard Business Review Publications.

5. Gwyther Matthew (2006) "The MT Interview: Franck Riboud." August 1, 2006, http://www.managementtoday.co.uk/news/575823/MT-Interview-Franck-Riboud/?DCMP=ILC-SEARCH (accessed August 30, 2011).

6. Choi, Mina (2008) *CIB* April 2008 Print Edition, "Face-to-Face: Pierre E.Cohade." http://www.cibmagazine.com.cn/Features/Face_To_Face.asp?id=363&pierre_e.cohade.html. (accessed August 30, 2011).

7. Jianqiang, Liu (2007) "Love or Hate Danone." *China Entrepreneur*, April 5, 2007, http://www.cnemag.com/en/magazine_view.asp?a_id=26&m_id=9 (accessed January 20, 2008).

8. "Danone Loses Skirmish in China." December 10, 2007, *New York Times*, http://www.nytimes.com/2007/12/10/business/worldbusiness/10iht-danone.4.8675288.html (accessed August 30, 2011).

9. Authors' field research.

10. He, Runxin and Ying Zhuang (2007) "Wahaha—Atypical Commercial Dispute." *Caijing Magazine*, 185, May 14, 2007.

11. Authors' field research.

Chapter 3

1. Wahaha company website.
2. Wahaha company website.
3. "Wahaha's New Fairy Tale." (In Chinese) http://www.people.com.cn/GB/jinji/33/172/20020827/808874.html 27 August 2002, (accessed January 20, 2008).
4. Wahaha company website.
5. Wahaha company website.
6. Wahaha company website.
7. He, Runxin and Ying Zhuang (2007) "Wahaha—Atypical Commercial Dispute." *Caijing Magazine*, 185, May 14, 2007.
8. Luo Jianxin (2008) "Zong Qinghou and Wahaha— An In-depth Analysis of A Known Chinese enterprise." *China Machine Press*, 2008.5.

Chapter 4

1. Areddy, James T. (2009) "Danone Pulls Out of Disputed China Venture." *The Wall Street Journal*, October 1, 2009. http://online.wsj.com/article/SB125428911997751859.html (accessed August 30, 2011).
2. Wahaha company website.
3. He, Runxin and Ying Zhuang (2007) "Wahaha—Atypical Commercial Dispute." *Caijing Magazine*, 185, May 14, 2007.
4. "The Truth behind the Wahaha Dispute with Danone." (In Chinese) *Sina Finance*, April 13, 2007, http://finance.sina.com.cn/chanjing/b/20070413/10043499496.shtml (accessed 15 January 2008).
5. Areddy, James T. and Deborah Ball (2007) "Danone's China Strategy Is Set Back: Dispute with Venture Partner Highlights the Risks of Not Going It Alone." *Wall Street Journal*, June 15, 2007.
6. "Danone Responds to Our Article." *China Economic Review*, September 2007, http://www.chinaeconomicreview.com/en/node/24241 (accessed August 30, 2011).
7. "The Truth Behind the Wahaha Dispute with Danone." (In Chinese) *Sina Finance*, April 13, 2007, http://finance.sina.com.cn/chanjing/b/20070413/10043499496.shtml (accessed 12 January 2008).
8. "Danone Responds to Our Article." *China Economic Review*, September 2007, http://www.chinaeconomicreview.com/en/node/24241 (accessed August 30, 2011).
9. Dueck, Cameron and Tom Miller (2007) "Danone and Wahaha Vie for the Last Laugh." *South China Morning Post*, June 11, 2007.
10. "Danone Responds to Our Article." *China Economic Review*, September 2007, http://www.chinaeconomicreview.com/en/node/24241 (accessed August 30, 2011).

11. "Danone Responds to Our Article." *China Economic Review*, September 2007, http://www.chinaeconomicreview.com/en/node/24241 (accessed August 30, 2011) and authors' field research.
12. Deutsche Bank report dated June 25, 2007.
13. "Danone Responds to Our Article." *China Economic Review*, September 2007, http://www.chinaeconomicreview.com/en/node/24241 (accessed August 30, 2011).
14. Transcript of Interim 2007 Groupe Danone Earnings Conference Call on July 30, 2007.
15. "Danone Responds to Our Article." *China Economic Review*, September 2007, http://www.chinaeconomicreview.com/en/node/24241 (accessed August 30, 2011).
16. "Danone Responds to Our Article." *China Economic Review*, September 2007, http://www.chinaeconomicreview.com/en/node/24241 (accessed August 30, 2011).
17. Transcript of Interim 2007 Groupe Danone Earnings Conference Call on July 30, 2007.
18. "Danone Responds to Our Article." *China Economic Review*, September 2007, http://www.chinaeconomicreview.com/en/node/24241 (accessed August 30, 2011) and authors' field research.
19. Transcript of Interim 2007 Groupe Danone Earnings Conference Call on July 30, 2007.
20. "Wahaha President Accuses Danone of Setting Up Disputed Units." *Forbes*, June 27, 2007, http://www.forbes.com/feeds/afx/2007/06/27/afx3861908.html (accessed August 30, 2011).
21. He, Runxin and Ying Zhuang (2007) "Wahaha Victim of Low-ball Buyout by Danone." *Caijing Magazine*, 185, May 14, 2007.
22. He, Runxin and Ying Zhuang (2007) "Wahaha—Atypical Commercial Dispute." *Caijing Magazine*, 185, May 14, 2007.
23. Hua, Chen and Xu Yiping (2007) "Wahaha Protected National Brand, Jian Libao Announced Support." *Oriental Morning Post*, April 4, 2007.
24. Sina.com, April 3, 2007, http://finance.sina.com.cn/g/20070403/09403467234.shtml (accessed January 15, 2008).
25. Danone Press Release, April 10, 2007.
26. Danone Press Release, May 9, 2007.
27. "Wahaha President Accuses Danone of Setting Up Disputed Units." *Forbes*, June 27, 2007, http://www.forbes.com/feeds/afx/2007/06/27/afx3861908.html (accessed August 30, 2011).
28. Areddy, James T. and Deborah Ball (2007) "Danone's China Strategy Is Set Back: Dispute with Venture Partner Highlights the Risks of Not Going It Alone." *Wall Street Journal*, June 15, 2007.
29. He, Runxin and Ying Zhuang (2007) "Wahaha—Atypical Commercial Dispute." *Caijing Magazine*, 185, May 14, 2007.
30. He, Runxin and Ying Zhuang (2007) "Wahaha—Atypical Commercial Dispute." *Caijing Magazine*, 185, May 14, 2007.

31. "Wahaha Staff Boycott Danone Takeover Attempt." *Shanghai Daily*, April 15, 2007; Wai-yin Kwok, Vivian. "Danone's Chinese Food Fight Gets Messier." *Forbes*, June 14, 2007.
32. Wai-yin Kwok, Vivian. "Danone's Chinese Food Fight Gets Messier." *Forbes*, June 14, 2007.
33. Areddy, James T. (2007) "Trademark Ruling Favors Wahaha." *Wall Street Journal*, December 11, 2007.
34. Kurtenback, Elaine (2007) "Danone Dispute Heats Up as JV chairman Resigns." Shanghai Daily, June 8, 2007, http://www.shanghaidaily.com/sp/article/2007/200706/20070608/article_318848.htm (accessed January 31, 2008).
35. Kurtenback, Elaine (2007) "Danone Dispute Heats Up as JV chairman Resigns." Shanghai Daily, June 8, 2007, http://www.shanghaidaily.com/sp/article/2007/200706/20070608/article_318848.htm (accessed January 31, 2008).
36. Danone Press Release, December 18, 2007.
37. Group Danone company announcement, December 21, 2007, http://media.corporate-ir.net/media_files/irol/95/95168/press/Wahaha_211207_UK.pdf (accessed August 30, 2011).
38. Barboza, David (2007) "Truce Reached in Fight over Chinese Beverage Company." *New York Times*, December 22, 2007.
39. Société Générale report, November 26, 2007.
40. Société Générale report, November 26, 2007.
41. "Wahaha rejects Danone's new corporation plan, says negotiation hard to go on." http://news.xinhuanet.com/english/2008-03/10/content_7751872.htm (accessed August 30, 2011).
42. "Danone behind tax probe, Zong claims." http://english.zjol.com.cn/05english/system/2008/04/18/009434265.shtml (accessed August 30, 2011).
43. "Wahaha bidding to buy out Danone." http://www.china.org.cn/business/2008-07/18/content_16031367.htm (accessed August 30, 2011).
44. Wahaha and Danone company websites.
45. Zhao Hejuan. "Danone Says Arbitration Win not to Affect Wahaha Settlement." *Caijing Magazine*, http://english.caijing.com.cn/2009-11-09/110307863.html (accessed August 30, 2011).

Chapter 5

1. "Zong Qinghou Tax Storm," *Caijing Magazine*, 14 April 2008.
2. Wang Jiafen (2008) *Fresh. My 15 years with Bright Dairy.* China: CITIC Press.
3. Jianqiang, Liu. "Love or Hate Danone." (In Chinese) *China Entrepreneur*, April 5, 2007, http://www.cnemag.com/en/magazine_view.asp?a_id=26&m_id=9 (accessed January 20, 2008).

4. Wang Jiafen (2008) *Fresh. My 15 years with Bright Dairy.*
5. Wang Jiafen (2008) *Fresh. My 15 years with Bright Dairy.*
6. Wang Jiafen (2008) *Fresh. My 15 years with Bright Dairy.* p. 140.
7. Wai-yin Kwok, Vivian (2007) "Danone Sells Out Of Bright Dairy." Forbes.com, October 16, 2007, http://www.forbes.com/2007/10/16/danone-bright-dairy-markets-equity-cx_vk_1016markets02.html (accessed August 30, 2011).
8. Wang Jiafen (2008) *Fresh. My 15 years with Bright Dairy.*
9. Wang Jiafen (2008) *Fresh. My 15 years with Bright Dairy.*
10. Wei, Ding (2007) "Finding Qin." *China Entrepreneur*, April 5, 2007, volume 7/2007.

Chapter 6

Pause for Reflection

1. MacLeod, Calum (2007) "Best Buy, Home Depot find China market a tough sell." *USA Today.* February 23, 2011. http://www.usatoday.com/money/industries/retail/2011-02-23-bestbuy23_ST_N.htm (accessed August 30, 2011).
2. Leander, Tom (2007) "John Noble, Best Buy International." *CFO Asia*, March 22, 2007. http://www.cfo.com/article.cfm/8869962/c_2984273/?f=archives (accessed August 30, 2011).
3. Andrew Hill, "Why do so many get it so wrong in China?" *Financial Times*, March 7, 2011. http://www.ft.com/cms/s/0/f293577c-4907-11e0-af8c-00144feab49a.html#ixzz1I5kO4hnR (accessed August 30, 2011).
4. Hamel, Gary, Yves L. Doz, and C.K. Prahalad,. "Collaborate with Your Competitors and Win." *Harvard Business Review*, January–February 1989.
5. "Zong Qinghou: The Truth." (In Chinese) July 20, 2007, http://biz.zjol.com.cn/05biz/system/2007/07/20/008626310_04.shtml (accessed June 23, 2008).
6. Prahalad, C.K. and Gary Hamel. "The Core Competence of the Corporation," *Harvard Business Review*, May–June 1990.
7. Hamel, Gary, Yves L.Doz, and C.K. Prahalad, "Collaborate with Your Competitors and Win." *Harvard Business Review*, January–February 1989.
8. McGregor, James (2005). *One Billion Customers: Lessons from the Front Lines of Doing Business in China.* A Wall Street Journal Book published by Free Press.
9. Dueck, Cameron and Tom Miller (2007) "Danone and Wahaha Vie for the Last Laugh." *South China Morning Post*, June 11, 2007.
10. Yahoo! press release.

11. Hamel, Gary, Yves L. Doz, and C.K. Prahalad,. "Collaborate with Your Competitors and Win." *Harvard Business Review*, January–February 1989.
12. "Wahaha-Danone Brand Name Feud Highlights Pitfalls of China Business Ventures." International Herald Tribune, June 27, 2007, http://thestar.com.my/news/story.asp?file=/2007/6/28/apworld/20070628113413&sec=apworld (accessed August 30, 2011).
13. Jianqiang, Liu. "Love or Hate Danone." (In Chinese) *China Entrepreneur*, April 5, 2007, http://www.cnemag.com/en/magazine_view.asp?a_id=26&m_id=9 (accessed January 19, 2008).

Chapter 7

1. Berkshire Hathaway Inc. 2002 Annual Report.
2. Scholtes, Saskia and Richard Beales (2007) "Risks of derivatives 'not fully evaluated.'" *Financial Times*, March 26, 2007.
3. http://ir.zaobao.com/caosco/caosco_devt.html (In Chinese) (accessed April 13, 2007).
4. http://ir.zaobao.com/caosco/caosco_devt.html (In Chinese) (accessed April 13, 2007), confirmed during field research.
5. Li Yin. "'King of Jet Fuel' Chen Jiulin and CAO: who created who?" *Southern Metropolis Daily*, March 19, 2006.
6. IPO Prospectus dated November 26, 2001.
7. IMD field research.
8. Public Company Reports.
9. Kim Eng Securities Report dated November 30, 2001.
10. 2001 and 2002 Annual Report.
11. Field research.
12. PwC Executive Summary dated June 3, 2006, and DBS Vickers Report dated October 1, 2002.
13. 2002 Annual Report.
14. 2002 Annual Report.
15. Field research.
16. "China Aviation Oil IPO eight times taken up." *The Straits Times*, December 6, 2001.
17. DBS Vickers Report dated December 27, 2001.
18. 2001 Annual Report.
19. Public Company Announcements.
20. Public Company Announcements.
21. Public Company Announcements.
22. DBS Vickers Analyst Report dated October 21, 2003.
23. "China Aviation Oil (Singapore) Corporation Ltd Celebrates its 10th Anniversary." *The Business Times*, May 26, 2003.
24. 2003 Annual Report.
25. 2002, 2003 Annual Report.

26. Public company announcement.
27. DBS Vickers Analyst Report dated October 20, 2003.
28. DBS Vickers Analyst Report dated October 20, 2003.
29. DBS Vickers Analyst Report dated October 21, 2003.
30. Public company announcements.
31. 2002 Annual Report.
32. "Cover Story: How to Clean Up." *The Edge Singapore*, June 13, 2005.
33. Public company announcements.
34. DBS Vickers Analyst Report dated August 19, 2006.
35. Public company announcement.
36. Public company announcement.
37. "Chen Jiulin: China's Nick Leeson." *Shenzhen Daily*, December 13, 2004.
38. Public Company Announcement.
39. Field research.
40. Various media reports.
41. Mcdermott, Darren and Bruce Stanley in Hong Kong and Cris Prystay in Singapore (2004) "Big Oil-Trade Loss Puts Focus on China." *The Wall Street Journal*, December 2, 2004.
42. Chen, Jiulin (2004) *Leveraging on China, Going Global*. Candid Creation Publishing.
43. "NUS Business School Alumnus Hailed as New Asian Leader by World Economic Forum," Press Release, National University of Singapore, October 22, 2003.
44. IPO Prospectus dated November 26, 2001.
45. 2002 Annual Report.
46. 2001 Annual Report.
47. 2002 Annual Report.
48. DBS Vickers Analyst Report dated October 21, 2003.
49. DBS Vickers Analyst Report dated July 2, 2002.
50. DBS Vickers Analyst Report dated October 21, 2003; Public Company Announcement.
51. DBS Vickers Analyst Report dated October 21, 2003.
52. PwC Executive Summary dated June 3, 2006.
53. Public company announcement.
54. 2002 Annual Report.
55. 2003 Annual Report.
56. PwC Executive Summary dated June 3, 2006.
57. Quoted in the SGX Q1 FY2005 Press Release dated October 8, 2004.
58. FT staff and John Burton in Singapore (2004) "China seeks to contain Aviation Oil scandal." *Financial Times*, December 1, 2004.
59. SGX 2004 Annual Report.
60. SGX-ST Listing Rules Practice Note 2.1 Equity Securities Listing Procedure.
61. SGX 2004 Annual Report.
62. IPO Prospectus dated November 21, 2001.
63. PwC Executive Summary dated June 3, 2006.

64. PwC Executive Summary dated June 3, 2005.
65. Field research.
66. PwC Executive Summary dated June 3, 2005.
67. Field research.
68. Field research.
69. Agency France Presse, July 18, 2006, http://www.uofaweb.ualberta.ca/chinainstitute (accessed March 29, 2007).
70. Field Research.
71. 2001 Annual Report.
72. Field research.

Chapter 8

1. IMD field research.
2. "Deutsche Bank completes equity placement for China Aviation Oil. http://www.newswit.com/enews/2004-10-22/0854-deutsche-bank-completes-equity-placement-for/ October 22, 2004 (accessed May 24, 2007).
3. Burton, John, Mure Dickie and Joseph Leahy. "Model of Corporate Governance." *Financial Times*, December 2, 2004.
4. Public company announcements.
5. Chen Jiulin's affidavit to the court on March 8, 2006.
6. DAC NOS. 23240/2005 TO 23254/2005 PP V Chen Jiulin Representation.
7. Author field research.
8. Author field research.
9. Cheng Lingfeng. "Deciphering the Restructuring of CAO." *China Entrepreneur Magazine*, April 5, 2006.
10. Author interview.
11. DBS Vickers report dated November 17, 2004.
12. DBS Vickers report dated November 17, 2004.
13. DBS Vickers report dated November 17, 2004.
14. DBS Vickers report dated November 24, 2004.
15. "CAO parent blocks SPC deal in shock move." *The Business Times*, November 25, 2004.
16. Field research.
17. CAO public company announcement, http://phx.corporate-ir.net/External.File?item=UGFyZW50SUQ9NzYzNXxDaGlsZElEPS0xfFR5cGU9Mw==&t=1 (accessed August 30, 2010).
18. Dow Jones Newswires. "Accountants Sift Books at Stricken China Aviation Oil." *Wall Street Journal*, December 2, 2004.
19. Dow Jones Newswires. "Accountants Sift Books at Stricken China Aviation Oil." *Wall Street Journal*, December 2, 2004.
20. FT staff and John Burton in Singapore. (2004) "China Seeks to contain Aviation Oil Scandal." *Financial Times*, December 1, 2004.

21. Dow Jones Newswires. "Accountants Sift Books at Stricken China Aviation Oil." *Wall Street Journal*, December 2, 2004.
22. Burton, John (2004) "Singapore Tries to Limit $550m Trading Scandal." *Financial Times*, December 2, 2004.
23. "Chen Jiulin: China's Nick Leeson." *Shenzhen Daily*, December 13, 2004.
24. DBS Vickers Report dated December 1, 2004.
25. Quoted in MAS press release dated December 16, 2004.
26. Quoted in SGX press release dated December 16, 2004.
27. "China's Champions." *Financial Times*, December 3, 2004.
28. Quoted in "China Aviation Oil Losses Serve as "Reminder" of Risks in China." *Bloomberg*, December 9, 2004.
29. Dow Jones Newswires. "Accountants Sift Books at Stricken China Aviation Oil." *Wall Street Journal*, December 2, 2004.
30. McDermott, Darren and Bruce Stanley in Hong Kong and Cris Prystay in Singapore. "Big Oil-Trade Loss Puts Focus on China." *Wall Street Journal*, December 2, 2004.
31. Burton, John, Mure Dickie and Joseph Leahy. "'Model of Corporate Governance' Fights for Survival." *Financial Times*, December 2, 2004.
32. Quoted in Wonacott, Peter (2004) "Overseas-Listing Boom in China Has Downside." *Wall Street Journal*, December 3, 2004.
33. Wonacott, Peter (2004) "Overseas-Listing Boom in China Has Downside." *Wall Street Journal*, December 3, 2004.
34. "Dissolve Mystery of China Aviation Oil Incident." *People's Daily Online*, December 10, 2004.
35. Quoted in Burton, John, Mure Dickie and Joseph Leahy. "'Model of Corporate Governance' Fights for Survival." *Financial Times*, December 2, 2004.
36. DBS Vickers Report dated December 1, 2004.

Chapter 9

1. Lingfeng, Cheng (2006) "Deciphering the Restructuring of CAO." *China Enterpreneur Magazine*, April 5, 2006.
2. Lingfeng, Cheng (2006) "Deciphering the Restructuring of CAO." *China Enterpreneur Magazine*, April 5, 2006.
3. Lingfeng, Cheng (2006) "Deciphering the Restructuring of CAO." *China Enterpreneur Magazine*, April 5, 2006.
4. "China Aviation Unit Broke Rules, Gets More Time for Debt Plan." *Bloomberg*, December 10, 2004.
5. Public company announcement.
6. Author interviews.
7. Author interviews.
8. Public company announcement.
9. SIAS Press Release on December 18, 2004.

10. Author Interviews.
11. Author Interviews.
12. CAO public company announcement, May 12, 2005, http://media.corporate-ir.net/media_files/irol/16/164043/CAOHCStatementon CAOImprovedScheme120505.pdf (accessed August 30, 2011).
13. PwC Executive Summary dated June 3, 2005.
14. Public company announcements.
15. Public company announcements.
16. Author interviews.
17. 2006 Annual Report.
18. 2006 Annual Report.
19. Field research.

Chapter 10

1. Company public announcement.
2. "Citic Pac's charmed tycoon runs out of luck," Reuters, April 8, 2009, http://www.reuters.com/article/reutersEdge/idUSTRE5373M820090408?pageNumber=1&virtualBrandChannel=0 (accessed August 30, 2011).
3. Lee, Yvonne and Laura Santini (2008) "Citic Pacific May Face Big Hit on Currency Wagers Gone Bad," *The Wall Street Journal*, October 21, 2008, http://online.wsj.com/article/SB122450500213849835.html (accessed August 30, 2011).
4. Company announcement dated October 20, 2008.
5. Company announcement dated January 2, 2009.
6. "TEXT-Moody's upgrades CITIC Pacific to Ba1; outlook negative," Reuters, February 17, 2009, http://uk.reuters.com/article/2009/02/17/idUKWLA758120090217 (accessed August 30, 2011).
7. Liu, Lilian (2009) "CITIC Pacific falls 2.4% after Yung's sale of 60 mln shares," *China Daily*, May 7, 2009, http://www.chinadaily.com.cn/hkedition/2009-05/07/content_7751134.htm (accessed August 30, 2011).

Pause For Reflection

1. www.webb-site.com.
2. Wing-Gar Cheng (Bloomberg News) (2007) "CNOOC shareholders bar fund shifts." *International Herald Tribune*, April 2, 2007.
3. www.webb-site.com.
4. http://webb-site.com/articles/CNOOCloans.asp (accessed August 30, 2011).
5. Chung, Olivia (2008) "Citic Pacific stress tests HK," *Asian Times*, October 31, 2008, http://www.atimes.com/atimes/China_Business/JJ31Cb01.html (accessed August 30, 2011).

6. Public Company Announcement dated January 3, 2001.
7. SEC Complaint, http://www.sec.gov/litigation/complaints/comp 19578.pdf (accessed September 6, 2011).
8. CSC Staff. Is Goldman Sachs Running a Derivative Casino?," *China Stakes*, November 25, 2008, http://www.chinastakes.com/Article.aspx?id =855 (accessed August 30, 2011).
9. "TEXT-Moody's upgrades CITIC Pacific to Ba1; outlook nega-tive," Reuters, February 17, 2009, http://uk.reuters.com/article/ 2009/02/17/idUKWLA758120090217 (accessed August 30, 2011).
10. Flaherty, Michael (2008) "Bad currency bets pile up for Asia firms," Reuters, October 30, 2008, http://business.inquirer.net/money/ breakingnews/view/20081030-169281/Bad-currency-bets-pile-up-for-Asia-firms (accessed August 30, 2011).

Last But Not Least

1. Handy, Charles (1995) *The Empty Raincoat: Making Sense of the Future.* Arrow Books.
2. "Looking past Western media bias against China," http://www.china. org.cn/international/opinion/2008-02/28/content_11021569.htm (accessed August 30, 2011).
3. http://www.muddywatersresearch.com (accessed August 31, 2011).
4. Dune Lawrence and Nikolaj Gammeltoft. "Short Seller Block Takes On Paulson, Greenberg in China." Bloomberg, June 6, 2011, http://www. bloomberg.com/news/2011-06-06/muddy-waters-block-takes-down-giants-paulson-greenberg-with-china-shorts.html (accessed August 31, 2011).
5. Cherniak, Cyndee Todgham (2010) "Lesson Learned From Rio Tinto Convictions: Doing Business in China Is Like Walking In The Dark," http://www.tradelawyersblog.com/blog/article/lesson-learned-from-rio-tinto-convictions-doing-business-in-china-is-like-walking-in-the-dark/ (accessed August 30, 2011).
6. A recent capital injection of US$1.6 billion to Alibaba for a stake of under 5 percent by a private-equity-led group gives Yahoo!'s stake in Alibaba a value of US$12.5 billion on a fully diluted basis, comparing with Yahoo!'s market value of US$16 billion (net of cash). *Financial Times*, September 26, 2011. http://www.ftchinese.com/story/001040885/en, and October 2, 2011, http://www.ft.com/cms/s/2/2fb8b2e8-ed07-11e0-be97-00144feab49a.html#axzz1bQn7kooS (accessed October 21, 2011).
7. Hongyi, Wang and Tang Zhihao. "Sino-Aussie ties strong despite Rio Tinto case," *China Daily*, May 19, 2010, http://www.chinadaily.com.cn/ world/2010-05/19/content_9865773.htm (accessed August 30, 2011).
8. Hesseldahl, Arik (2011) "Alibaba Group CEO Jack Ma on the Alipay Affair, Yahoo and Treating Employees Well," June 1, 2011, http:// allthingsd.com/20110601/alibaba-group-ceo-jack-ma-live-at-d9/ (accessed August 30, 2011).

Index

Readers can look up company acronyms used in subheadings in main headings. Chinese names are indexed with surname preceding first names unless westernized in which case the name is inverted, for example, "Fan, Henry." Names beginning "Mc" are filed as "Mac."